European Identities in Discourse

Bloomsbury Advances in Critical Discourse Studies

Series Editors: Michal Krzyżanowski, David Machin and John Richardson

Bloomsbury Advances in Critical Discourse Studies is a series that looks
at exciting, cutting edge work in critical discourse studies, in terms of its
multidisciplinarity of method, theory, and topic of analysis. The series explores
how critical discourse studies engages with the social, political and ideological
landscape of the modern world, and how these contexts are reflected, (re)
produced and mediated through language and other modes of communication.

Titles published in the series:

European Identities in Discourse

A Transnational Citizens' Perspective

Franco Zappettini

BLOOMSBURY ACADEMIC

LONDON • NEW YORK • OXFORD • NEW DELHI • SYDNEY

BLOOMSBURY ACADEMIC
Bloomsbury Publishing Plc
50 Bedford Square, London, WC1B 3DP, UK
1385 Broadway, New York, NY 10018, USA

BLOOMSBURY, BLOOMSBURY ACADEMIC and the Diana logo are trademarks of
Bloomsbury Publishing Plc

First published in Great Britain 2019
Reprinted 2019

Cover design: Toby Way

A catalogue record for this book is available from the British Library.

Library of Congress Cataloging-in-Publication Data
Names: Zappettini, Franco, author.
Title: European identities in discourse : a transnational citizens' perspective / Franco Zappettini.
Description: New York, NY: Bloomsbury Academic, [2019] | Series: Bloomsbury advances in
critical discourse studies | Includes bibliographical references and index.
Identifiers: LCCN 2018050780 (print) | LCCN 2018054616 (ebook) | ISBN 9781350042971
(epub) | ISBN 9781350042995 (epdf) | ISBN 9781350042988 (hardback)
Subjects: LCSH: Discourse analysis–Europe. | Transnationalism–Europe. | Ethnicity–Europe. |
National characteristics, European. | Nationalism–Europe. | Europe–Ethnic relations.
Classification: LCC P302.15.E85 (ebook) | LCC P302.15.E85 Z37 2019 (print) |
DDC 306.44094–dc23
LC record available at https://lccn.loc.gov/2018050780

ISBN: HB: 978-1-3500-4298-8
ePDF: 978-1-3500-4299-5
eBook: 978-1-3500-4297-1

Series: Bloomsbury Advances in Critical Discourse Studies

Typeset by Deanta Global Publishing Services, Chennai, India
Printed and bound in Great Britain

To find out more about our authors and books visit www.bloomsbury.com and sign
up for our newsletters.

Contents

List of Illustrations

Figures

Tables

Acknowledgements

This monograph is based on an empirical study conducted with members of a transnational non-governmental organization called European Alternatives. I would like to thank the directors of European Alternatives Nicolo Milanese and Lorenzo Marsili for initially granting me access to the organization and all members of European Alternatives for their availability to participate in this study. Their contributions were essential and their views to me represented much more than data. I am also grateful to Ruxandra Comănaru for moderating the Romanian focus group.

I acknowledge that some of the data and ideas presented and discussed in this research have been disseminated in sole or joint publications (McEntee-Atalianis and Zappettini 2014, Zappettini 2014, Zappettini and Comănaru 2014, Zappettini 2016, Zappettini 2017). These sources have been appropriately referenced throughout the book.

Abbreviations

CDA   Critical Discourse Analysis

CDS   Critical Discourse Studies

DHA   Discourse Historical Approach (to CDA)

EA   European Alternatives

EPS   European Public Sphere

EU   European Union

NGO   Non-Governmental Organization

TEN   Trans Europa Networks

1

Introduction

1.1 The case for investigating the emergence of 'new' European identities

From mainly representing a philosophical concern, identity has increasingly been interpreted as a multifaceted social and discursive construct dependent on historic, economic, political and cultural contingencies. While for a long time ethnic and national identities have represented established referents of groupness, in recent years an increasing interest in the exploration of identity construction has emerged in many social disciplines in the wake of major societal changes throughout the period of 'late' or 'post' modernity (Lash 1990, Giddens 1991, Beck, Giddens and Lash 1994, Bauman 2000, MacLuhan, Gordon and Nevitt 2005). Processes of globalization[1] and de-industrialization, the commodification of lifestyles, the merging of public and private spheres, the rise of the 'network society' and the decline of 'grand' narratives[2] (cf., inter alia, Habermas 1987, Lyotard and Benjamin 1989, Castells 1996b) have all had a profound impact on the negotiation of collective and individual identities by making them more uncertain and 'fractured' (Hall 1996)[3] and, at the same time, more dynamic and open to new arrangements.

In particular, social processes related to, for example, increasing cross-border interaction, virtual mobility and the 'glocalization'[4] of practices have been reflected in a 'spatial turn' in the social sciences (Soja 1989, Urry 2003, Warf and Santa 2009) whereby scholars have focused on the impact that the deterritorialization of cultural practices has had on the reconfiguration of social spaces, on the consequent (re)definition of community (Appadurai 1995) as well as on the development of a new 'politics of space' (Rumford 2008).

In this context, one of the most active areas of research on identities has focused on the impact of transnational flows and practices on the way we make sense of who we are in the social world (Vertovec 2001, Levitt and Schiller 2004,

Vertovec 2007, Beck 2008, Rembold and Carrier 2011). Transnational processes have had a major impact on geopolitical orders, as well as on established notions of affiliations, belongings and imaginaries of communities, challenging, in particular, social identities constructed around nationhood (Featherstone 1990, Basch 1994, Albert 2001, Sassen 2002) and encouraging more self-reflexive and cosmopolitan views of the world and society (Beck 1994, Beck 2006, Held 2010).[5] If we follow Robertson's (1992) argument that globalization is about individual awareness of the processes of global interdependence just as it is about the processes themselves, then globalization prompts us to (re)position ourselves in relation to the 'oneness of the world' and, likewise, to create new meanings of the relations with the communities to which we understand ourselves belonging (Rumford 2008).

Moreover, such individual perspectives are crucially being brought into and are reflected in the political arena where they are creating new loci of debate about the politics of belonging and solidarity (Castles and Davidson 2000, Westwood and Phizacklea 2000, Yuval-Davis 2006, Bauböck and Faist 2010). The politics of identity in modern democracies has thus been confronted with new antinomies and tensions between the particularism and universalism of identity and space (Wodak 2010, Pries 2013), the quest for world and local societal orders (Robertson 1992) and the paradox of recognizing inclusion through the regulation of exclusionary boundaries (Connolly 1991).

In the European context, the changes of 'late' modernity have taken on further connotations in relation to the integration project of the EU which has been predicated on post-national[6] narratives and which has manifested itself in economic, social and political fields typified, for example, by the removal of borders and the emergence of supranational forms of governance. While transnationalism has received much attention in migration and cultural studies (especially in relation to diasporas) the impact of transnationalism on European identities has often been explained with the theory of the Europeanization of society (see p. 29) which assumes that social integration and the development of a European *demos*[7] and a common European identity will occur as a functional by-product of the convergence of legal, economic and political systems. From such perspectives nationhood has often been assumed a relatively stable key component of European identity that can be recontextualized and accommodated with other loyalties (Herrmann, Risse-Kappen and Brewer 2004, Risse 2010). For most scholars in the field of European politics, however, the question remains whether a European *demos* has been consolidating at a transnational level (Cederman 2001, Eriksen and Fossum 2002, Cerutti 2003), especially in the wake of the global financial crisis and the resurgence of populism which has clearly shown the limitations of neoliberal policies driving the integration process and the weakness of the European social project (Delanty 2014, Calhoun 2017).

From these perspectives, and building on Featherstone (2003), Delanty and Rumford (2005) have argued that the process of identification with Europe as a transnational referent has to account for wider dynamics than economic integration and has to be explained/analysed through the processes of cultural and territorial reorganization of communities depending on shifts in 'cognition, discourse, and identity' (Delanty and Rumford 2005, p. 7) of cross-national networks. According to Delanty and Rumford (2005) the analysis of the 'Europeanization' of society is therefore best approached from social constructivist and reflexive perspectives and in the wider context of globalization, where practices of late modernity can also be understood within the historical context of transition from national to post-national – and arguably cosmopolitan – forms of conceiving the organization of political communities and social orders (cf. Delanty 1995, Linklater 1998, Held 1999, Habermas 2001, Habermas 2003, Beck 2008, Delanty 2013). Furthermore, as Delanty and Rumford (2005) point out, in a global context, no one single institutional or civic actor is exclusively capable of controlling the process of identification with European referents and, therefore, while normative aspects must be taken into account in the construction of Europe(anness), a wider variety of actors has also to be acknowledged. In this vein, an emerging European identity is best interpreted as a dynamic interplay between structural and agentive forces made up of institutions, citizens and global actors, 'reflexive' processes and cosmopolitan imaginaries. In an investigation of the recent transformation of European identities Krzyżanowski (2010) concludes by claiming that, at a discursive level,

> identities are increasingly moving away from top-down and often highly-ideological and normative projects and are becoming strongly diversified along context- and actor-specific lines. (p. 201)

One key insight of Krzyżanowski's research is that, in the complexity of late modernity and the diversification of Europe, identities emerge discursively as a combination of the individual, the social, the agentive and the structural dimensions of society and are therefore equally driven by 'individual experiences [and] collective visions' (2010) with no preordained arrangement. From a similar stance, Checkel and Katzenstein (2009) argue that

> European identity construction is occurring at the multiple intersections of
> elite projects and social processes; at both supranational and national-regional
> levels; within EU institutions but also outside them, in daily practice and lived
> experience. (p. 226)

Acknowledging that the development of Europeanness occurs at multiple sites
thus offers many possible standpoints for its examination. Delanty (2013), for
example, suggests that

> rather than look for identity as an underlying structure of meaning or a holistic
> system or a cultural system, it is best evidenced in specific sites of communication.
> In the case of European identity one such place to look for it is in debates about
> Europe. (p. 265)

This study builds on the aforementioned insights, attempting an investigation
of Europeanness from bottom-up[8] and transnational perspectives. Although
a large body of research exists that has investigated European identities from
several angles, the transnational/cosmopolitan and bottom-up perspectives
remain overlooked by mainstream research in CDS as it will be further argued. It
is therefore the aim of this book to contribute to the advancement of knowledge
on the discursive construction of European identities by offering insights from
the specificity of these standpoints.

The data for this study is derived from focus groups and individual interviews
conducted with members of a NGO called EA that characterizes itself as a
'transnational' association of citizens. EA's main aim is the promotion of citizens'
democratic participation in the debate on 'European' issues with a view to exert
influence on European policy-making and thus to 'build a Europe of justice,
democracy, and solidarity'[9] from bottom-up. One of the original themes of EA's
'mission statement' is the proposition that

> in an increasingly closer Europe understood as a space of exchange, rather than
> in geographic or ethnic terms ... the nation-state is no longer the appropriate
> political form in which to define democratic decision-making and active
> citizenship[10]

and consequently political decisions concerning European citizens must be taken
transnationally rather than (inter)nationally.[11] The salience of investigating this
particular organization lies therefore in the fact that, unlike the general public, EA
constitutes a community of citizens with a distinct investment in 'Europeanness'
while, at the same time, their discourses are likely to offer ideological and social
perspectives on European issues that are different from the institutional ones.

1.2 Book aims and objectives

The main aim of this study is to contribute to the existing body of CDS literature on the interaction between language and society in particular by taking forward the work of a group of CDA scholars that have focused on the transformation of discourses of Europe, most notably Ruth Wodak (Wodak 2003, 2004, 2007, 2010) and Michał Krzyżanowski (Krzyżanowski and Oberhuber 2007, Triandafyllidou, Wodak and Krzyżanowski 2009, Krzyżanowski 2010). This aim is articulated in three objectives: the first is to investigate how transnational perspectives shape the imagination of the European community in relation to local and global 'places' and 'others'; the second objective is to illuminate how Europeanness is (re)produced at a bottom-up level by providing insights into the relation between linguistic devices, social practices/structures and political agency; thirdly this study attempts to formulate a critique of the transformation of nationhood and new forms of European democracy within and limited by the specificity of the data analysed.

The original contribution of this study lies in the specific bottom-up and transnational standpoints it takes in examining processes of identity formation in discourse. Rather than focusing on top-down discourses of European identity, an area which has been extensively researched in many academic fields, this study therefore explores how identities are formed in the discourses of members of a transnational citizens' initiative,[12] thus bringing to the fore the dynamic context of (new) social movements and non-governmental sector, as highlighted by much recent social research (for a review of the literature in this field; cf. Benford and Snow 2000, Checkel 2001, Tarrow 2001, Mercer 2002).

The reason for adopting these angles emerged in relation to the desire to fill two specific gaps found in the literature on European identity (as discussed further in the next chapter). The first gap relates to the underrepresentation of 'active' citizens (i.e. citizens engaged in the debate on Europe) and their role as social actors in the transformation of Europe. This study, thus, intends to make up for this lack of research, taking up Krzyżanowski's (2010) call for research on discourse and Europeanness to turn to 'social action as the main force driving the dynamics of contemporary identities' (p. 201). Second, this monograph intends to contribute to the development of a theoretical approach to the study of European identity that departs from 'national' paradigms or 'methodological nationalism' (Wimmer and Schiller Glick 2002) – that is treating the development of Europeanness as largely predicated on the reproduction of national elements. While this study does not intend to dismiss the national component altogether, it aims to offer a post-national interpretation of Europeanness that departs from such established interpretative models subscribing to Wodak and Weiss's (2005) view that 'the discursive relationship "identity-legitimisation-representation" [is] to be understood beyond the nation-state' (p. 132).

To address the gaps in the literature discussed above, this study seeks to answer three main research questions:

- How are national, European and transnational identities (re)produced, challenged and transformed in the discourse of members of EA?
- How do multiple identities interplay in the discourses of members?
- Through which linguistic strategies and devices do members realize their (European) identities?

1.3 Structure of the book

The DHA to CDA elaborated by Ruth Wodak and her colleagues within the Vienna School of Discourse Analysis (Wodak 2009) underpins the design of this research. The DHA thus informs theoretical and analytical frameworks as well as the overarching structure of this book. While a more comprehensive discussion of the DHA will be provided in Sections 4.1 and 4.2, I will succinctly outline some principles of the DHA here, detailing how the appropriation of the DHA has informed the structure and the content of this study. In particular I will outline the relation between theory and data and the definition of context proposed by Wodak (2009).

The relation between data and theory is illustrated in Figure 1.1. This model sees empirical research as a circular process in which key concepts and assumptions are drawn from 'grand' and 'middle-range'[13] theoretical perspectives to analyse texts, assist (but not determine) the interpretation and critically feed back into the theory, helping to formulate a social critique. Furthermore as expounded in the DHA manifesto

> the theory as well as the methodology is eclectic; that is theories and methods are integrated which are helpful in understanding and explaining the object under investigation … the approach is abductive: a constant movement back and forth between theory and empirical data is necessary. (Wodak 2009, p. 69)

The structure of this study has also been informed by the DHA's multilevel approach to text on macro, meso and micro dimensions of contextualization

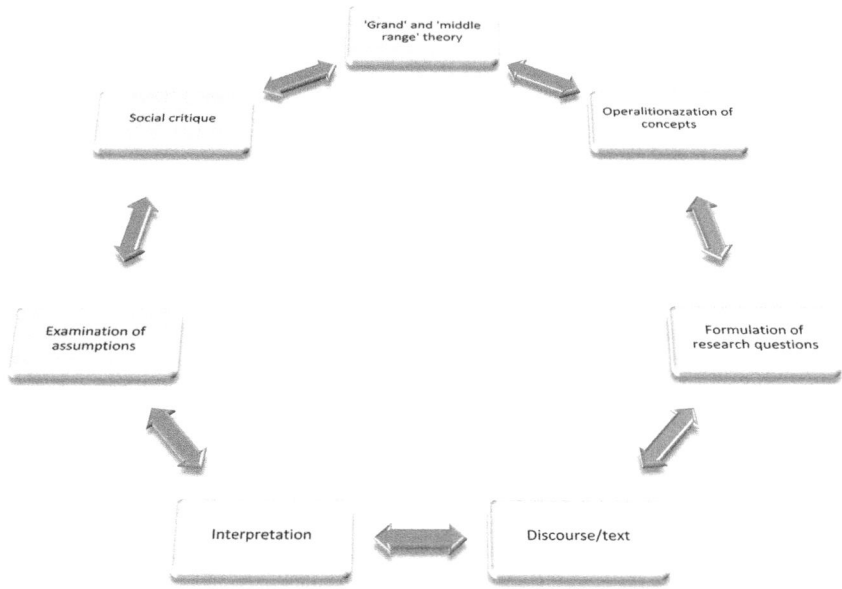

Figure 1.1 An adaptation of the DHA approach to theory and data as discussed in Wodak (2009).

which are seen as distinct but interrelated levels of theory and analysis (see Section 4.3 for details).

I will therefore briefly discuss the notion of context and explain how it has been applied to this study. The DHA builds on the key principle that discourses represent 'texts in context' as they are socially produced and consumed in relation to specific socio-historical conditions. As every text is embedded in a specific context, an appropriate contextualization is therefore essential to interpret texts and to derive meanings. Notably, DHA advocates for an approach to the contextualization of texts that includes social, historical and political dimensions. DHA is concerned with

> integrat[ing] systematically all available background information in the analysis and interpretation of the many layers of a written or spoken text. (Fairclough and Wodak 1997, p. 364)

in order to relate 'micro and macro levels with each other, text and context, structure and discourse, insider and outsider perspectives' (Wodak 2008, no page).

Specifically, in the DHA, the historical dimension refers to both the inclusion of 'as much available information as possible on the historical background ... in which discursive "events" are embedded' (Wodak et al. 2009, pp. 8–9) and to the study of changes occurring to discourses diachronically. In the DHA, contextualization is typically operated on distinct but interrelated micro, meso and macro levels and applied to both theoretical and analytical dimensions as represented in Figure 1.2. Such a model is largely based on Wodak's (2009) concept of context which operates on four levels (with the first one being only descriptive). These levels take into account

a. the immediate, language or text internal co-text;
b. the intertextual and interdiscursive relationship between utterances, texts, genres and discourses;
c. the extra-linguistic social/sociological variables and institutional frames of a specific 'context of situation'; and
d. the broader sociopolitical and historical contexts, within which the discursive practices are embedded (Wodak 2009, p. 67).

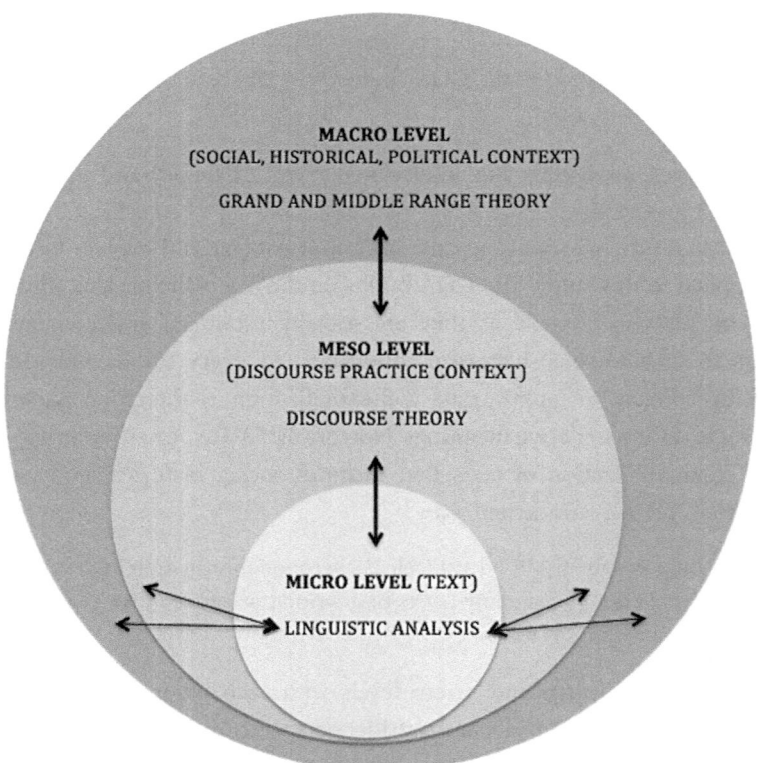

Figure 1.2 Distinct levels of contextualization and analysis adopted in this study. Diagram adapted from Wodak (2009) and Koller (2012).

In this monograph the multilevel approach to text has therefore been applied: (a) to the theoretical contextualization which embeds data into discourse theory and grounds the latter in middle-range and 'grand sociological theory'; and (b) in the linguistic analysis through the recognition of different levels at which discourses are treated (Krzyżanowski 2010, p. 78). Furthermore contextualization has been used for triangulation purposes as 'discursive phenomena are approached from a variety of methodological and theoretical perspectives taken from various disciplines' (Wodak et al. 2009, p. 9).

Following the aforementioned considerations, the structure of this book has been configured as follows:

Chapter 1 makes the case for investigating the emergence of 'new' European identities from transnational and bottom-up perspectives. In keeping with the DHA, it is recognized that the construction of Europeanness must be examined in the context of macro-social, cultural, political and economic transformations as well as in its local instantiations. To do so, this study taps into (pro)European political activism as a 'field of action' drawing, in particular, on the discourses of members of a NGO called EA whose salience as a European actor in the EPS is discussed in two ways. First, an overview is given of the wider social context in which transnational/ European civil societies and other civic initiatives have (trans)formed in recent years. Second, the specific background of EA, its activities and my involvement with the organization are discussed, thus contextualizing the object of this study into the wider frame of the debate on European issues from civic positions.

Chapter 3 is extensively dedicated to the exploration of a number of relevant key concepts for this study at 'grand' and 'middle-range' level. The construction of the 'toolbox' is achieved by building on a review of the literature on identity and discourse from sociolinguistic and critical perspectives. The review is then taken to a more specific 'European' level by interpreting Europe as an increasingly salient sociopolitical construct at the juncture of historical processes of transformation of national structures. The impact of global phenomena, such as transnationalism, on processes of social identification, belonging and the (re)'imagination' of communities is discussed with specific attention to its European implications for civic engagement, cultural citizenship and solidarity. Equal attention is paid to the role of networks in the construction of transnational political communities. Through the literature review, the EPS is identified as an interesting point of entry for examining the emergence of new discourses of European identities.

Chapter 4 discusses in detail the methodology adopted in this study. This includes an account of the nature and range of data collected via focus groups and individual interviews, as well as providing details on how data was collected and explaining the rationale for choosing these methods. DHA, the analytical framework adopted in this study, is also discussed thoroughly in this chapter, followed by a few reflections on its limitations.

Chapter 5 presents and discusses the findings, providing several examples of the analysis to support the interpretations. The presentation is organized around a taxonomy of strategies, topoi and linguistic realizations, with the major insights consolidated and summarized in the final section of the chapter.

Finally, Chapter 6 concludes the book highlighting the contribution of this study, reflecting on its limitations and introducing ideas for future research.

1.4 Sociopolitical contextualization: The European civil society

The *civil society* can be defined as 'a community of citizens linked by common interests and collective activity' (Oxford dictionary 2009). For Heidbreder (2012) two dominant but distinct academic conceptualizations of the civil society (in terms of its functions and features) are distinguishable in the EU-ropean context.[14] On the one hand, civil society can primarily be interpreted in a governance-related approach and refer to the inclusion of organized groups of interests in policy-making procedures (e.g. lobbies, interest groups and pressure groups). On the other hand, civil society can represent a wider sphere of social interaction constitutive of the public sphere (see Section 3.5.1) that, in a deliberative democracy, represents the counterpart to the institutions and to 'structured politics' (Teets 2008).

For a long time, the role of a European civil society has relied on the procedural inputs of Brussels-based, professionally organized groups into highly institutionalized policy-making processes (Heidbreder 2012). However, for the last two decades, the emergence of a European civil society has increasingly been seen as a response or a 'cure' to the democratic deficit of the EU set up and as an essential feature of the EU as a deliberative democracy (Rumford 2003, Steffek, Kissling and Nanz 2008, Lang 2013).

As the 'permissive consensus' granted by citizens to the EU institutions has been waning (Hooghe and Marks 2009), the EU's discourse has increasingly focused on an interpretation of civil society as participatory democracy 'by the people' rather than participatory governance 'for the people' (Scharpf 1999). This conceptual and discursive shift became a prominent item on the EU's political agenda in the new millennium as clearly marked by documents such as the White Paper on European Governance (Commission 2001). It was in particular in the debate about the 'future of Europe' generated by the 2001 European Convention, that citizenship rights and civil society (hitherto representing two separate concepts) emerged as facets of the same discourse (Smismans 2009) fostering the emergence of civil actors in addition to the more traditional Brussels-based NGOs and interest groups and spawning a series of civic initiatives aimed at the bottom-up construction of Europe.

Although some have critically seen forms of civic participation 'activated from above' as ways to integrate grassroots activities in Brussels' 'routine practices' (Pleines 2006), there is a large consensus that such initiatives have, in fact, contributed to enlarging the discursive arenas in which European political actors interact (see, for example, Risse 2010) and that, ultimately, they may contribute to the emergence of a truly transnational EPS. In particular, in recent years, much attention has been paid by academics and the media to the increasingly important role played by social movements in EU politics (Fossum and Trenz 2006, Kriesi, Tresch and Jochum 2007, Koopmans and Statham 2010, Ruzza 2011). While, in some cases, the political mobilization of grassroots movements has seen the anti-European or Eurosceptic movements consolidating into an 'un-civil society' (Ruzza 2009), a large number of pro-European civic organizations have also developed which, while not necessarily aligned with the EU institutions, have entered into a 'dialogue with Brussels' to shape the future of Europe from bottom-up. The next section will shed more light on the character of EA, an organization emerged as one of these civic initiatives which, as introduced earlier, represents the object of this study.

1.5 Background on the organization

EA describes itself as 'a civil society organisation devoted to exploring the potential for transnational politics and culture'[15] and its main aim is the promotion of citizens' democratic participation in the debate on 'European' issues with a view to exert influence on European policy-making and thus to 'build a Europe of justice, democracy, and solidarity' (European Alternatives website) from the bottom-up. EA is structured as a network of activists across Europe grouped under one transnational umbrella called TEN. TEN started from an initial base in London and further expanded in France, Italy and Romania with a total of five offices (London, Paris, Rome, Bologna and Cluj) and ten employees (see Marsili and Milanese 2018 for a full account of the development of EA). In addition to this structured set up, TEN has relied on a growing number of volunteers/members that have organized themselves in local groups and have regular meetings at local branches.[16] To date there are local groups based in: Brussels, Amsterdam, Berlin, Prague, Lublin, Bratislava, Belgrade, Sofia, Cardiff, Istanbul and Valencia. EA's activities are themed around specific topics such as migration, civil rights, media pluralism, social justice, unemployment issues, and they are typically organized as: on and offline campaigns; workshops; debates; publications and public forums. TEN has also been actively promoting the European Citizens' Initiative and various activities under the Active Citizenship Programme.[17] Furthermore, TEN organizes the 'Trans Europa Festival', a yearly festival of culture, arts and politics, taking place simultaneously in several different cities all over Europe. This event, aimed at showcasing EA's activities and raising citizenship awareness was awarded the Prize 'Translating EU values into action' in 2011 by the European Economic and Social Committee. An overview of EA's activities by 'field of action' and 'genre'[18] of text produced is presented in Figure 1.3.

A way to understand EA's 'field of action' is to see their activities originating from the political debate on the democratic future of Europe that followed the failed European Constitution in 2004–5. In the aftermath of the French and Dutch rejections of the Draft Constitution – which had prompted the EU Heads of Government to call for a 'period of reflection'[19] on the future of Europe – the Commission launched the so-called PLAN D for Democracy, Dialogue and Debate.

The plan sought to address 'the need to listen to citizens' expectations by fostering a debate between the EU institutions and citizens'[20] and wider participation of

Figure 1.3 An overview of EA's activities by 'field of action' and 'genre' of texts produced.

the civil society on European issues. Recognizing the 'widening gulf between the [EU] and the people it serves'[21] and aiming to close the 'communication gap', citizens' organizations and other stakeholders were encouraged to set up forums of debate to improve civic education, connecting citizens with each other and with the institutions. At the same time, such initiatives were regarded by the Commission as a way to reconnect the EU project with its demos and thus to legitimize the EU itself and its institutional goals. EA originated in 2006 from the initiative of a few activists who took advantage of this 'open channel' with the EU and received a few grants available under the Plan D scheme.[22]

EA is thus closely engaged in a symbolic (in a Bakhtinian sense) and practical dialogue with EU institutions and the EPS and, in many respects, EA's activities can be located both at the sites of 'production' and 'reception' (Dijk 1985) of discourses of Europe. While, to some extent, EA's discourses could be expected to reproduce institutional 'voices', one of the original themes of the organization's 'mission statement' is the proposition that political decisions concerning European citizens must be taken transnationally rather than (inter)nationally.

In this sense, therefore, the self-characterization of EA as a transnational actor clearly relates to an idea of the European project that differs substantially from mainstream institutional visions – that is Europe as a 'Union of States' and national interests. The notion of 'dialogue with institutions' that EA stands for is rather informed by a critical approach to the 'system' (also found, for example, in the organization's agenda for re-establishing a 'balance' between 'powerful' and 'disempowered'). The use of the word 'alternatives' in the organization's literature consulted can therefore be interpreted as the search for democratic alternatives to the current system of governance and also alternative visions in the 'imagination' of European society.[23]

In this respect the discourses of EA can be considered 'alternative' in at least two ways: in Fairclough's (2003) sense of nonconformist to the dominant 'order of discourse' and in being part of that global civil society that Delanty and Rumford (2005) see distinct from the 'EU-as-polity normative vision' (p. 169). The salience of investigating this particular organization lies therefore in the fact that, unlike the general public, EA constitutes a community of citizens with a distinct investment in 'Europe' while, at the same time, their discourses are likely to offer ideological and social perspectives on European issues that are different from the institutional ones.

Exploring Identities in Discourse: Conceptual Tools

2.1 A 'late modern' approach to identities

Philosophical concerns with knowing who or what we are have long existed in the history of human thought. While throughout the classical and medieval eras identity remained an unquestionable 'given' for most individuals, it is only with the emergence of the Enlightenment that the notion of identity was primarily treated from a humanistic point of view and interpreted in relation to the Cartesian 'thinking self' (Chimisso 2003). Since the Enlightenment emphasized rationality and human agency, identity came to be regarded as a project of 'self-determination' (Benwell and Stokoe 2006) and for many centuries it constituted the dominant view in the 'Western' world. Such a view gradually came to be questioned with the development of psychology in the late nineteenth and early twentieth century. Although the 'self' remained the focus of psychological disciplines, the latter highlighted the importance of socialization in processes of identity formation, therefore redefining identity as an intersubjective rather than a simply subjective accomplishment. Many theoretical perspectives have thus developed in social psychology that have essentially regarded the 'self' as a socially mediated process (Mead, Herbert and David 1982). One strand of social psychology has, for example, conceptualized social identities primarily from behavioural perspectives. In this area, one of the best known theories has suggested that social identities derive from the process of 'in' and 'out' group categorization and that one individual's membership in one particular category can determine his or her perceptions of other individuals and groups (Tajfel and Turner 1979).

From a different angle, the structuralist school of thought (cf. Barthes and Lavers 1972, Levi-Strauss 1979, Lacan and Miller 1988, Althusser and Matheron 2003) emphasized the role of social structures (differently interpreted as practices, norms, institutions instantiated, inter alia, in cultural and semiotic representations) in intersubjective dynamics and the social anchoring of one's self. Consequently, 'subjects' came to be seen by structuralists as formed vis-à-vis specific historical, cultural and social structures with, for example, 'social class' identities typically understood in relation to the Marxist 'class struggle'. Meanwhile the work of philosophers of language such as Wittgenstein (1953) was significantly influential in promoting the innovative view that language is an active constructor and not only a 'mirror', or a passive descriptor, of reality. The so-called 'linguistic turn' in social sciences that followed Wittengstein's work was instrumental in a change of ontological perspectives on 'reality' which came to be regarded as socially constructed (Berger and Luckmann 1984). Social constructivism has clearly underscored how, since meanings and knowledge are embedded in processes of socialization and institutionalization mediated by language (Vygotskii 1962, Piaget 1970, Searle 1997), the definition of 'social categories' and 'social groups' is not predetermined but emerges from social interaction and it is ultimately predicated 'on dynamic normative and epistemic interpretations of the material world' (Adler 2005, p. 92).

While to different degrees social constructivism sees the (re)production of values, symbols and practices occurring in discourses as instrumental in maintaining or transforming social structures, such a strict correlation has been challenged by poststructuralists (cf., inter alia, Derrida 1976, Kristeva and Moi 1986, Deleuze and Boundas 1993) for whom structures alone cannot account for social phenomena.[1] Building on the intersubjective nature of reality asserted by social constructivism, the poststructuralist current has primarily interpreted identities as social constructs too, emphasizing how they are produced in relation to systems of knowledge shaped by specific historical, political and economic conditions.

The works of Michel Foucault and Pierre Bourdieu have been highly influential in this sense. For Foucault (1984) individuals are constrained to make sense of the world and to position themselves in the world as subjects by what is 'thinkable' or 'sayable' in a society. As for Foucault the 'normalization' of societies relies on systems of knowledge which are produced by discourses and by the use of power, the self is ultimately a product of discipline and produced under specific historical circumstances. For Foucault understanding 'discourses of the self' (that is identification processes) must therefore occur through the systems of knowledge that have produced them and through the power traceable in discourse. Bourdieu (1991) regards identity as the deterministic processes of reception and reproduction of social structures enacted through *habitus* (i.e.

the internalization of the social order). For Bourdieu culture represents a major system of identity reproduction which embodies social-historical conditions of its production (for example Bourdieu sees national languages emerging from the process of standardization and reproduced through the education system as the predominance of one dialect over another).

Overall, poststructuralist thinking tends to dismiss identities as grounded in an 'ontological truth' (Connolly 1991), stressing instead the situatedness of subjects and foregrounding the dynamics of power at play in the definition of individual and collective identities. Moreover, poststructuralism tends to dismiss the objectivity of sciences appealing to the 'inescapability' of language in any analysis of phenomena. Thus poststructuralist views treat discursive acts as linguistic instantiations of rational intentions and, in most cases, strategically oriented towards the 'fixing' of meanings. In this light, identities constitute strategic and positional concepts (Hall 1996) whose meaning is constantly negotiated through 'difference'[2] (Derrida 1976) and which can only partially or temporarily be 'closed'[3] (Laclau and Mouffe 2001). As Hall (1996, pp. 3–4) contends,

> Identities are never unified ... [but] increasingly fragmented and fractured; never singular but multiply constructed across different, often intersecting and antagonistic discourses, practices and positions. They are subject to a radical historicisation, and are constantly in the process of change and transformation. Identities are thus points of temporary attachment to the subject positions which discursive practices construct for us.

Despite the difference of foci between social constructivism and poststructuralism, both schools of thought have interpreted identities beyond something that exists 'out there'. Instead, they have contributed to shifting the focus of research on identity from treating the latter as a reified essential *product* to identification as the 'unfinished' *process* of (re)production of meanings of 'who we are'. Because it is social and historical contingencies that allow certain identities to be filled with certain meanings it is really the '*hows*' and '*whys*' that should concern us in the study of identities (Mole 2007).

Our understanding of identities has been further influenced by social changes that have occurred over the last few decades and often referred to as 'high', 'late' or 'post' modernity (Habermas 1987, Lash 1990, Giddens 1991). Such a period has been characterized by various phenomena including the globalization and de-industrialization of society, the commodification of lifestyles, the merging of public and private spheres and 'the erosion of fixed forms and clear boundaries [of groups]' (Brubaker 2003, p. 554). As a result, the individual production of identities through their anchoring in specific social locations has become increasingly complex, differentiated and elusive, resulting in 'fractured' (Hall 1992, 1997) 'liquid' (Bauman 2004) and hybridized (Bhabha 1994) forms and processes of identification.

Beck, Giddens and Lash (1994) characterize the general context in which these processes take place – as well as the understanding of the interplay between their causes and implications – as 'reflexive modernity'. For Beck, Giddens and Lash (1994) 'late modern' individuals (including scientists) are reflexive (i.e. conscious) actors capable of perceiving themselves in-between the duality of structural and agentive dimensions when questioning their identities. For Giddens (1991), although 'late modern' subjects are not the same free agents imagined by the Enlightenment philosophers, they are not entirely determined by structures as they can actively create structural conditions for themselves.[4] Therefore while identities may have become more ephemeral, new possibilities for identity redefinition have also opened up through what Giddens (1991) calls 'reflexive' projects of the self. However, as the self still relies on a system for structuring social activities and to derive an 'ontological security' (that is a sense of continuity in one's own life narrative), reflexive projects of the self exist in such duality: on the one hand, they rely on a renewed postmodern narrative of agency and, on the other, as Delanty and Rumford (2005) put it, on 'the belief in the self-transformative capacity of modern societies to shape themselves in the projection of their imaginary' (p. 19).

On the back of the premises discussed above, this study treats identities as primarily social constructs produced and negotiated intersubjectively in discourse and emerging at the intersection of personal experiences, macro-social contexts and the modern politics of belonging (see, for example, Yuval-Davis 2011). In this sense, this study does not dichotomize the social and individual dimensions of identity assuming that 'collective identity cannot exist over and above individuals just like individuality … cannot exist over and above society' (Triandafyllidou and Wodak 2003, p. 211). Instead, it is assumed that integrating social and individual dimensions constitutes a vantage point for the interpretation of identities as it allows for 'equal recognition of the identity-forging potential of both individual experiences and concerns, and of collective visions and ideologies' (Krzyżanowski 2010, p. 201).

Overall, in this study, identities are approached holistically as a set of processes (re)producing and transforming 'one's sense of who one is, of one's social location, and how (given the first two) one is prepared to act' (Brubaker and Cooper 2000,

p. 17). Such self-understanding or 'situated subjectivity' (Brubaker and Cooper 2000) is understood in this study in its dual interplay with the transformation of social orders, in line with Giddens' (1991) structuration theory. Processes of identification are thus treated in this study as the combination of two facets. On the one hand, identities are understood as 'self-reflexive projects' having an 'ontological depth' (Connolly 1991) insomuch as they provide individuals with a security through 'narrative continuity' (Giddens 1991). On the other hand, rather than unifying 'truths' (Connolly 1991) processes of identification are interpreted as contingent on historical, political and cultural discourses, as these are capable of interpellating or 'hailing' (Hall 1997) social actors to invest in and negotiate existing identities or claim new ones. Therefore as pointed out by Triandafyllidou and Wodak (2003) 'identity is about attributing meaning' a process which is not intrinsic to words but which is socially negotiated and 'implies a degree of reflexivity' (p. 206).

2.2 Investigating identities through language

As language represents one of the main ways in which we interact as social beings, it clearly constitutes a major tool for making sense of 'reality' (cf. Searle 1997, Burr 2003). Before the development of social sciences however the relation between language and identity was typically treated in essentialist and deterministic terms, for example regarding languages as 'natural' expressions of a 'common character' shared by all members of a group (*ethno*) (Joseph 2004). Even with the establishment of the disciplines of linguistics, scholars following in the steps of Ferdinand de Saussure (de Saussure et al. 1986) were concerned with the study of 'langue' (the language system) rather than 'parole' (the social use of language). Since the development of sociolinguistics as a distinct discipline in the 1960s and the 1970s, different perspectives have been brought into the understanding of the interplay between language and identity, in particular, treating language use as the effect of social stratification. Following the seminal work of Labov (1966) variationist sociolinguistics has mainly been concerned with describing linguistic distribution and language variations in relation to a wide range of variables (including geographical and class variables as well as gender and professional status) treating identities as relatively stable entities (at least as predetermined categories of investigation).

In contrast to variationists, another theoretical framework, interactional sociolinguistics – studies the relation between social structure and linguistic structure (cf. Gumperz 1971, 1982), who was instrumental in developing this approach. Interactional sociolinguistics holds that meanings are created in communication and that they are dependent on sociocultural contexts for their interpretation. In investigating the role of (micro) communication in the production of social identities, Gumperz (1982) argues that parameters like gender, ethnicity and class cannot be taken for granted 'but are communicatively produced' (p. 1). In this vein, while early variationists tend to see identities as relatively stable entities, interactional sociolinguists have pointed to a more fluid and dynamic understanding of identity. In line with social constructivist perspectives it is now a widespread view in sociolinguistics to consider the relation between language and identity as mutually constitutive: language contributes to constructing one's social identity and one's social identity influences one's own linguistic choices (Meyerhoff 2006). Much research has sought to underscore this view from different standpoints, with studies focusing, for example, on code-switching (Auer 1984, Myers-Scotton 1998) speech styles, repertoires and codes (Le Page and Tabouret-Keller 1985, Rampton 1995) revealing the diversity and fluidity of performing identity. In general most recent sociolinguistic frameworks have stressed that identity is a process that 'yields constellations of identities instead of individual, monolithic constructs' (De Fina, Schiffrin and Bamberg 2006, p. 2) and that, while such 'repertoires of identities' (Kroskrity 1993, p. 222) are generated and enacted in discourse, the salience of individual identities is often context-dependent (see, for example, Zimmerman 1998, Benwell and Stokoe 2006) making identities 'resources used in talk' (Antaki and Widdicombe 1998, p. 1) by social actors. Similarly, Bucholtz and Hall (2005) see linguistic interaction as the micro context in which the construction and negotiation of identity – that is 'the social positioning of self and other' (Bucholtz and Hall 2005, p. 586) – occur. Bucholtz and Hall (2005) thus emphasize the *relationality* of identities; that is 'identities are never autonomous or independent but always acquire social meaning in relation to other available identity positions and other social actors' (p. 598).

2.3 Critical approaches: Discourse and identity in CDA

A different approach to the study of language and society has been taken by a group of scholars often recognized as Critical Linguists or the CDA school (inter alia M. Billig, A. Blackledge, N. Fairclough, G. Kress, M. Krzyżanowski, M. Reisigl, T. van Dijk, R. Wodak). Grounded in a common philosophical background (the Critical theory of the Frankfurt School) rather than a strictly defined methodology,[5] CDA constitutes an approach to the analysis of language and society that subscribes to the poststructuralist thinking that language is not a simple mirror of reality, but also has an active role in the construction of objects, subjects and social phenomena (Fairclough and Wodak 1997). CDA assumes that the creation of social reality resides in the intersubjective interpretation and negotiation of meanings mediated by discourse (cf., inter alia, Derrida 1976, Foucault 1980, Berger and Luckmann 1984, Bourdieu et al. 1993, Laclau and Mouffe 2001) and that there is 'a dialectical relationship between a particular discursive event and the situation(s), institution(s) and social structure(s), which frame it' (Fairclough and Wodak 1997, p. 258). In other words, CDA sees discourses reflecting the specific social-historical and political contexts in which they are produced and reproduced while, at the same time, it recognizes that discourses are capable of shaping social structures, for example, by constructing, transforming, deconstructing them or by maintaining their status quo. In this sense, in CDA the term 'discourse' is often referred to as 'language in use' (Fairclough 2003, p. 3) or 'text in context' (Wodak and Weiss 2005, p. 127) to emphasize the social significance carried by any text[6] or indeed any semiotic practice (Hodge and Kress 1988) and to highlight that, while broader discourses may not be entirely 'graspable' through individual texts, the latter always carry semiotic 'traces' of the discourse they constitute and for which they are produced and consumed (Fairclough 2001, Fairclough 2003). The linguistic analysis in CDA is therefore aimed at establishing a 'discourse ontology' or 'the "reality" that is entertained or meta-represented by the speaker' (Chilton 2004, p. 54). In this sense, texts represent convenient 'entry points' and major foci for the analysis of social phenomena which must be 'read in connection with knowledge of the world [to make sense]' (Wodak 2008 no page). Moreover, CDA views texts and discourses related intertextually and interdiscursively. This means that, although discourses can be framed as semantically coherent units, they are also interpreted as permeable systems in which topics, meanings and discursive practices can be recontextualized (i.e. reformulated and transformed) by moving across genres and fields (Wodak and Meyer 2009).

Fairclough (2003) distinguishes between the term 'discourse' (that he uses to refer to the generic relation between language and social structure) and a more specific (thematic) use of discourse – for example the 'discourse of globalisation', the 'discourse of new Labour' and so on. Furthermore he refers to discourses in the plural not only to signify the heterogeneity of topics available for analysis but also to describe different ideological visions of the same topic (hence 'discourses of globalisation') on the assumption that 'different discourses are different ways of representing aspects of the world" (2003, p. 215). Similarly, Paul Gee (1990) differentiates between 'small d' discourses and 'big D' Discourses. For Gee, a 'discourse' is part of a 'Discourse', the latter always being more than just language, as it is constituted by 'ways of being in the world ... certain behaviors (ways of talking, valuing, thinking)' (p. 142) which constitute a sort of 'identity kit' enabling individual to validate their membership to the group (e.g. 'being' an American, a woman, a worker, etc.).

CDA has widely dealt with issues of identity from different theoretical and empirical stances, exploring, inter alia, the construction of gender, ethnic, national, institutional and religious identities in organizational, political, educational and media discourses. In keeping with a poststructuralist grounding that takes into account historical, political and ideological views of the social world and that explicitly deals with power structures, CDA sees identity realized at the micro-discursive level and, at the same time, as an expression of wider discourses carrying specific ideological implications. Critical Linguists have thus paid much attention to the identification process by focusing on the dialectical tension between social structures and individual or collective agency, often choosing a 'constructivist structuralism' approach (Chouliaraki and Fairclough 1999) more in line with Giddens' structuration theory (see footnote 4) and only partially embracing Foucault's account of identities as the structural (re)production of dominant discourses which suggest little or no room for agency of individual 'subjects'. In other words, CDA has highlighted how identification dynamics operate in-between structural and agentive dimensions and through discourses in which actors choose their social location while constrained to make sense of the world by positioning or 'subjecting' themselves to the power of existing discourses. From this stance, CDA scholars have highlighted how the definition of identity is inextricably concerned with relations of power and issues of agency; this has resulted in political discourse and identity politics being the focus of much work in CDA (Kendall 2007).

Broadly speaking, this body of work regards identities as discursive constructs by which groups and their interests are defined and their social position in relation to other groups is claimed, challenged and negotiated (van Dijk 1997) so that the construction of identities effectively can be interpreted as the construction of meanings and relationships (Gergen 2001). From this perspective, the 'critical analysis of discourse' therefore has been concerned with how individuals categorize themselves and others by laying claim over identities as socially shared resources and by constructing meanings sometimes bringing into being new 'categories', new ways of being – that is new discourses.

Hence, one major area of interest for Critical Linguists has been the exploration of issues of identity from the perspective of group categorization, social exclusion and legitimization processes with particular reference to public discourses, the media and institutional contexts (see, for example, Chouliaraki and Fairclough 1999, Grad and Rojo 2008, Galasinska and Krzyżanowski 2009, Wodak et al. 2009, Krzyżanowski 2010). Similarly, 'identity' has been analysed in relation to the ideological function of language in producing, sustaining and transforming social inequalities by Wodak (1997) and by Van Dijk (1995, 1997) in the context of racist and anti-Semitic discourses. Van Dijk acknowledges the role of cognition as a mediator between discourse and society, and the role of discourses as semiotic mediation between situations, representations and structures. In this light, he sees discourses as shared forms of knowledge (in a Foucauldian sense), stored in a social 'semantic' memory, that have concrete expressions in texts or utterances through syntactic structures and other linguistic devices such as, for instance, tropes and metaphors.

Focusing on the relation between identity politics and discourse from a 'post-Marxist' perspective, Laclau (1994) has examined the emergence and transformation of political identities in contemporary society. Building on Derrida, Laclau (1994) sees the articulation of discursive practices (i.e. their specific social usage) capable of establishing, challenging and dismantling relations among discursive elements. A discourse, therefore, is interpreted as the temporary fixation of meaning(s) around 'privileged' signs or, put differently, around 'nodal points'. 'Nodal points' can thus constitute sites of discursive and social struggle in which social reality is constructed through attempts to partially fix meanings and concepts in a discursive field and to relate them to institutionalized structures (such as, for example, the concept of nation and the functions of the state).[7] Consequently, Laclau's view is that the definition of identities requires the examination of 'floating signifiers' constructed around the nodal point, that is, for example, meanings associated with in the signifier 'Europe' in their lexical, semantic and discursive web of relations.

The construction of national, linguistic and cultural identities represents another area where CDA has been actively engaged and it will be dealt with in the next section.

2.3.1 The discursive construction of national identities

Over the last few centuries 'national' referents have provided individuals with a major source of group identification and belonging (Smith 1991, Alter 1994, Hobsbawm 1997, Gellner 2006, Guibernau 2007, Hobsbawm 2010). While Smith (1991) defines a nation drawing on 'ethnosymbolic', cultural, historical and political components suggesting that emotional investment in these elements lies at the basis of community solidarity and fellowship, Gellner (2006) regards nations as a modern construct born out of industrialization and the need to organize society in structured systems. From similar premises, Anderson (2006) interprets nations primarily as social constructs embedded in the historic context of a shift from a religious-based order of the world to one founded on 'enlightened' notions of reason and progress. Anderson sees this shift coinciding with the development of technology and capitalism and, for example, he suggests that the invention of the printing press was crucial in the spread of 'national' languages which, in turn, was key in processes of national unification. For Anderson, therefore the aforementioned historic conditions and the political agendas of newly born nation states accelerated, sustained and crystallized the cultural reproduction of national communities and the organization of political life (for instance, in the notion of citizenship) developing 'nationhood' into naturalized referents for one's group identity. Thus Anderson (2006) famously argued that large communities such as nations exist as 'imaginary' entities primarily in the mind of their members who will never get to know their fellow nationals but who will nevertheless feel the communion of belonging to a group. This view has been further corroborated by other scholars who have explained how the imagined component of 'we-ness' in national identities is constantly (re)produced, negotiated and instantiated in tangible symbols, practices, discourses of 'nation', of collective belonging and shared spaces via the definition of 'in' and 'out' groups (cf. Said 1979, Billig 1995, Hall 1997). In particular, narratives of nation states – articulated through discourses of perceived spatial and social homogeneity of the 'in-group' and its differentiation from 'out-group' – have instrumentally informed the politics of belonging that, in modern democracies, has regulated the attribution of citizenship rights (Dieckhoff 2004).

From a perspective similar to Anderson's, Stuart Hall (1996) interprets national identity primarily as constructed within, not outside, representations in discourse and for the purpose of positioning 'subjects' politically. For Hall (1996)

> National identity is a discourse – a way of constructing meanings which influences and organises both our actions and our conception of ourselves ....

> National cultures construct identities by producing meanings about 'the nation' with which we can identify. (p. 613)

For example one comes to understand one's own 'English identity' 'because of the way "Englishness" has come to be represented, as a set of meanings, by English national culture' (Hall 1992, p. 292). Consequently, the process of 'imagining' oneself as a member of a community is realized discursively in 'shared representations of a collective self' (Checkel and Katzenstein 2009, p. 4) and achieved, inter alia, via the articulation of discourses of belonging, otherness, cultural and political values. Drawing on the many insights of constructive perspectives of nation, CDA has also argued that national identities are ultimately a construct of discourse reproducing narratives of 'national culture' and 'imagined communities'. Billig (1995), for example, sees the 'banal nationalism' of everyday interaction (embodied, for example, by the mundane, yet powerful, use of symbols and artefacts such as a flag in a public office) instrumental in the reproduction of national affiliations. Similarly, Billig (1995) highlights how national categorization is also effectively achieved in everyday discourses through rhetoric and linguistic devices functionally aimed at constructing 'in' and 'out' groups, for example through positive representations/ evaluations of 'us' and the negative representations/evaluations of 'them'.

One of the most notable works on the discursive construction of national identities in CDA is provided by Wodak et al. (2009).[8] Using the DHA, Wodak et al. highlight the historic dimension of discourses of nationhood and the role of sociopolitical contexts in their transformation and recontextualization. Focusing on the specific case of Austrian national identity and analysing public and semi-private discourses, the authors illustrate how the Austrian national community is discursively constructed in reference to (internal) sameness and (external) differences along a temporal dimension that highlights the narrative continuity of a 'shared past' and a 'common destiny'. Wodak et al. (2009) insightfully correlate the use of micro linguistic elements (such as synecdoche, metonymies and metaphors) with general macro-propositions of discourses (such as the debate on Austria's accession to the EU). Such a correlation is carried out via the epistemic function of discursive strategies, such as constructive/ destructive strategies as well as strategies of perpetration, of justification and of transformation.[9] In the case of Austrian identity, Wodak et al. (2009) argue that although the majority of discourses draw on typical topics to construct internal sameness and differences with other national groups (e.g. the 'national character'), discourses are not 'distinctive and unified' (p. 198) but dependent on the context and the 'social macro-function involved' (Wodak et al. (2009)) resulting in 'highly diverse, ambivalent, context-determined discursive identity constructs' (p. 188). In other words for Wodak et al,

> There is no such thing as one national identity in an essentialist sense, but rather ... different identities are discursively constructed according to context, that is, to the degree of public exposure of a given utterance, the setting, the topic addressed, and so on. (Wodak et al. (2009), pp. 186–7)

At the same time, Wodak et al. (2009) highlight the 'circularity' of national discourses suggesting that national identities are constructed and reproduced through the recontextualization of institutional discourses in everyday discourses by 'ordinary' citizens as 'habitus' (see pp. 16–17).

2.4 European identity: 'National' discourses in transformation?

As discussed so far, the 'imagination' of national communities and their discursive reproduction has permeated the construction of nation states for over four centuries, representing one of the most powerful ways in which individuals have made sense of their locations, their social relations and their sense of belonging. This is not to say that the idea of Europe did not exist before the development of nationhood in a modern sense. Indeed Europe as a geographical term has been used as far back as Greek historian Herodotus and, as a cultural term, since Charle Magne (cf. Smith 1997, Pagden 2002). Moreover, the concept of Europeanness has been passionately debated at least since the Enlightenment (Chimisso 2003) and, in many cases, it has played an active role in the discursive constructions of national identities albeit instrumentally appropriated by and recontextualized in the political agendas of nation states in the making (Malmborg and Strath 2002).

It is, however, in the last sixty years, with the emergence of the EU, that the idea of Europeanness has increasingly become relevant and debated in public discourses. Although the EU cannot be assumed to be the only embodiment/ referent of European identities, institutional discourses have contributed the production of a normative vision of 'the kind of identity Europe ought to have' (Delanty 1995, pp. 2–3), a view also shared by Laffan (2004) (summarized in Herrmann, Risse-Kappen and Brewer 2004, p. 255) for whom the EU institutions have achieved 'identity hegemony in terms of increasingly defining what it means to belong to Europe'.[10] Much literature has thus suggested that, in modern discourses, the idea of Europe reclaimed by the EU institutions in relation to the project of economic and political integration (Malmborg and Strath 2002) has increasingly been associated with the civic and political dimensions of the EU (Jansen 1999, Bruter 2005, Millar and Wilson 2007, Castiglione 2009) and, at the same time, it has cascaded in many different social fields as an 'empty signifier' (Eder 2009).

In the last decades, therefore, there has been a surge of academic interest in the notion of Europe and the 'European community' as sociopolitical constructs primarily in relation to an increased politicization of identities, legitimization processes of the EU institutions, as well as sociocultural flows and historical perspectives (Diez 1999, Rosamond 1999, Kohli 2000, Shore 2000, Cowles, Caporaso and Risse-Kappen 2001, Paasi 2001, Ifversen 2002, Balibar 2004, Eriksen and Fossum 2004, Herrmann, Risse-Kappen and Brewer 2004, Wodak 2004, Robyn 2005, Wodak and Weiss 2005, Fligstein 2007, Mole 2007, Oberhuber 2007, Cerutti and Lucarelli 2008, Fligstein 2008, Checkel and Katzenstein 2009, Eder 2009, Galasinska and Krzyżanowski 2009, Recchi and Favell 2009, Ilie 2010, Krzyżanowski 2010, Stråth 2010, Walsh, Wilson and O'Connor 2010, DeBardeleben 2011, Friedman and Thiel 2012).

The fuzzy and contested aspects of Europeanness that emerge from the aforementioned literature are not possible to discuss in depth in this publication. By and large, however, the literature analysed raises a compelling argument for framing the analysis of European identity in relation to two distinct perspectives that are relevant to this study. Drawing on Checkel and Katzenstein (2009) I will thus discuss specific features of European identity interpreting the latter as: (a) a political project and (b) a socio-historical process. In relation to the former perspective, Europeanness can be treated as a politicized identity project, whose impact on European society has often been associated, especially in political sciences, with the finality of the EU's institutional project of integration. From the latter perspective the notion of European identity is best approached as a historical process of social transformation of (national) identities that must be situated amid global and transnational scenarios of 'late modernity'. These two dimensions substantially tally with Krzyżanowski's (2010) conceptualizations of European (social) identities which he treats:

(a) on a strictly 'European level (explaining the concrete interconnection between social and political developments taking place in Europe) and (b) on the level of explanation of social processes in a general (and, to an extent, global) way. (p. 62)

The following section therefore deals with these two aspects focusing, in the first instance, on institutional discourses of European identity and the extent to which they have been reproduced and recontextualized at a citizens' level and, subsequently, focusing on the interplay between macro or global processes and their impact at an European level.

2.4.1 European identity as a political project

The origin of the EU – in the aftermath of a major world conflict whose causes many have seen as rooted in the extreme nationalistic propaganda of nation states at the time (Bauman 2004) – was a political attempt to overcome future conflicts by creating a peaceful and cooperative society among the 'peoples of Europe' where a post-national sentiment could emerge or, at least, where national differences could be reconciled. The EU's narratives (at least in the discourses of the Commission and the most 'progressive' part of EU institutions) have largely characterized Europe as a post-war project aimed at the construction of a polity that would supersede the national dimension. A large cross-section of scholars from political sciences and philosophy have thus regarded European institutions investing in the project of unification with a distinct 'degree of transnational European sentiment' (Kaye 2009, p. 56). In a similar vein, Habermas (2001) has confidently seen the European project as the most notable example of post-national organization and one capable of promoting new civic ideals and a 'civic patriotism' that will eventually bring Europeans together in a post-nationalistic spirit. Likewise, for Eder (2009), Europe embodies a post-national ideal of society, albeit institutional narratives have been too heterogeneous and somewhat incompatible with each other to promote distinctive collective (i.e. European) identities.

On the other hand, from a more critical perspective, historians Malmborg and Strath (2002) argue that, since the Enlightenment, the term 'European identity' has been appropriated by many political narratives, in particular those promoted by the *elites* because of 'the interpretive power contained in the concept [of Europe]' (Malmborg and Strath 2002, p. 3). Seeing the EU's narratives representing a continuation of such discourses Milward, Brennan and Romero (2000) go further claiming that the idea of Europe has been 'exploited' by the unification project to rescue European nation states and to ensure the continuity of their institutionalization. In-between these very diverse positions there is a wide range of views that tend to largely regard the institutional notion of Europeanness as a polysemous construct dependent on social and political contingencies and whose meanings have shifted in time.

At its beginning, for example, the integration of Europe was mainly driven by functional and economic rationales and identity per se was not necessarily one of the original concerns of the political architects of the EU. Even when an 'official' discourse of European identity was introduced with the publication of the 'Declaration on European Identity' in Copenhagen in 1973,[11] the document was more concerned with placing Europe as a 'global' player vis-à-vis other economic trading blocs than actually engaging with cultural, civic or, for that matter, philosophical interpretations of the identity of its citizens. In the past few decades, however, the quest to identify the 'Europeans' and their relation with the EU institutions has intensified considerably in relation to issues of legitimacy of the 'European project' (Cerutti and Lucarelli 2008) and the debated question of the EU's 'democratic deficit' (Majone 1998). In particular, in the 1980s – and in relation to a new phase of the EU's integration – narratives of Europeanness primarily occurred in terms of a Western-centric civilization that existed uninterrupted 'from Plato to Nato' (Niedermüller and Stoklund 2001), thus emphasizing the Latin/Christian 'roots' of Europe in opposition to Muslim and Communist 'others' (Delanty 1995).

A new political phase followed in the early 1990s, which saw the adoption of a social agenda promoting human rights, democracy and diversity in addition to 'free market' policies (Kraus 2011), followed by the lengthy draft of the (failed) Constitution culminating in the Lisbon Treaty and finally, by the EU's biggest enlargement in 2004 which brought into the EU political arena increasingly diversified conceptualizations of Europeanness which were to be (re)negotiated and which shifted the traditional notion of 'the East' as 'Europe's other' (Šarić et al. 2010). The 'issue' of European identity thus became central to institutional discourses which shifted from earlier narratives to new ones emphasizing internal heterogeneity and universal values of democracy and human rights (encapsulated in the 'unity in diversity' philosophy) resulting in a 'move from a cultural definition to a sociological and political construction of a European identity' (Ifversen 2002, p. 3).

A vast body of literature has explored the impact of the EU's narratives on social imaginaries and examined if, to what extent, and how the reception/ reproduction of Europeanness has occurred at the level of the citizen. From a sociopolitical perspective, some scholars have suggested that we could conceive of societal changes brought about by the EU in a framework of 'Europeanization' of society (Cowles, Caporaso and Risse-Kappen 2001, Featherstone and Radaelli 2003). Very concisely, the term 'Europeanization' refers to national structures increasingly being shaped by EU agendas with, for instance, normative, economic and many other fields 'reorienting' towards a European trajectory. In this sense, top-down narratives of European identity have contributed to the circulation and reproduction of discourses of 'being European (citizens)' in public opinion; however, they have also been able to penetrate the public opinion insofar as they have accommodated and have been accommodated by local and national narratives (Mole 2007). Typically European identities have thus emerged in many different forms but substantially they have interplayed with national and other identities in a 'non-zero sum' proposition (i.e. one does not take away from the other).

A model proposed by Herrmann, Risse-Kappen and Brewer (2004) captures such an interplay between identities using the 'Matruska doll' metaphor. Through such a model identities are seen as nested inside each other in a pecking order of 'belonging and loyalties ... so that "Europe" forms the outer boundary, while one's region or nation-state constitutes the core' (Herrmann, Risse-Kappen and Brewer 2004, p. 250). So, for example, while Bavaria can represent one's 'central' identity, Germany and Europe can still be salient 'external' referents.

A less hierarchical and more fluid representation of multiple identities is, however, suggested by some other research. For example, according to Triandafyllidou (2008) and Duchesne (2012) a significant proportion of EU citizens have been able to integrate Europeanness as a component of individual self-understanding in a variety of 'reflexive' combinations coexisting with local, regional and national identities. Along these lines, Risse (2010) suggests one could think of European identity as a 'marble cake' in which 'Europe and the EU become intertwined and amalgamated in the various national identity narratives' (p. 87). For Risse (2010) thus the 'Europeanization' of identities has mainly been occurring through processes whereby the 'core' understanding of what it means to be French, German, Italian etc. converges towards a European 'reading' of it. For example, the French might refer to the French Revolution, the Germans to war memories, the Italians to the legacy of the Roman Empire all claiming their 'Europeanness' while preserving their other belongings. Examining the extent to which narratives of 'post-national' Europeanness (as promoted in normative discourses) are conspicuous at citizens' level Antonsich (2008), however, concludes that while post-national identification with EU-rope coexists with 'national' views, the latter are still the most important ways in which 'people see themselves and the world' (p. 517). In this sense, Mole (2007) suggests that 'national cultures ... continuously reproduce European identity' (p. 211) in a reified 'mirror image' and Risse (2010, p. 10) states that 'Europeanised identities still come in national colours and resonate with the various national symbols'.

2.4.2 European identity as a global process and transnationalism as a new variable

The idea of a European identity can also be understood from a 'global' stance – that is contextualized within macro (socio, historical, political and economic) changes conveniently captured by terms such as 'globalization' and 'transnationalism'. In recent years, a significant body of interdisciplinary literature has recognized transnationalism as an important macro phenomenon emerging in relation to the de-territorialization of cultural, social and economic practices, which are moving away from 'nationally' rooted apparatuses, or which supersede the remit of national institutions (Basch, Glick Schiller and Szanton Blanc 1994, Portes 1997, Smith and Guarnizo 1998, Ong 1999, Portes, Guarnizo and Landolt 1999, Vertovec 1999, Vertovec 2001, Levitt and Schiller 2004, Vertovec 2009). The term 'transnationalism' has been used in political theory with regard to practices of NGOs to highlight the fact that at least one of the actors involved is a non-state entity (Risse-Kappen 1995). In social anthropology (e.g. social geography, migration and cultural studies), transnationalism has covered a variety of concepts typically related to new forms of social interaction resulting from intensified cross-border mobility (whether related to diaspora or triggered by economic factors). At the same time transnationalism has also been appropriated in social movement studies, for example, in relation to cross-border political mobilization (Della Porta and Diani 1999, Della Porta and Tarrow 2005).

The large majority of research on transnationalism has stressed how cross-border connections, which have of course always existed, have particularly intensified of late and been facilitated by cheaper transportation and increased digital communication, and in general by the globalization of practices (Castells 1996a). Profound social transformations have been occurring on a global scale as a result of increased flows of people and other 'social remittances' (i.e. ideas, norms and practices) across borders (Levitt and Jaworski 2007). The literature on transnationalism has generally recognized that

> large numbers of people now live in social worlds that are stretched between, or dually located in, physical places and communities in two or more nation-states [resulting in] even more complex set of conditions that affect the construction, negotiation and reproduction of social identities. (Vertovec 2001, p. 578)

Vertovec (2009) argues that social transformation relating to transnationalism can be examined from distinct conceptual premises. These include treating transnationalism as: (a) a mode of cultural reproduction, (b) a site of political engagement, (c) the (re)construction of 'place' or locality, (d) a type of consciousness and (e) a set of economic transformations. These aspects will be discussed in Section 3.1. with specific attention to implications for 'social morphology' and issues of identity. However it is important to stress the interdependence of these aspects. For instance the social and cultural dimensions of transnational flows of people are strictly related to political discourses as migration inevitably raises the question of membership of a political community (often symbolized by citizenship rights) and thus it is bound to impact on political engagement and choice of affiliations of individuals. Likewise, the transnationalization of economies (see below) has clearly had important consequences for income distribution and the ways that people (are forced to) move across borders or how they 'imagine' their solidarity ties.

Unpacking Transnationalism

The previous chapter has introduced transnationalism as a dynamic and multifaceted phenomenon comprising of interdependent cultural, social, political and economic dimensions. This section discusses such aspects in relation to processes of (de/re)construction of community and their implications for identification dynamics. A discussion is presented which focuses on the changing constructions of belonging to a (national) community in transnational and cosmopolitan imaginaries. In particular examples will be offered of new meanings of (national) language, citizenship and solidarity, on the role of network in the deterritorialization of belonging and how new visions of social orders have been brought about by transnational and cosmopolitan discourses.

3.1 Identification processes in transnational settings: New meanings of community

As elaborated in Section 2.3.1, the discursive construction and reproduction of national identities has relied, inter alia, on cultural and political narratives of nationhood through which citizens have been able to imagine themselves as a 'we-community' (Anderson 2006, Hobsbawm 2010). Building on this model, for the past few centuries, nation states have been able to establish themselves as sociopolitical and economic actors relying on a systemic relation of the 'identities-borders-orders' triad (Albert, Jacobson and Lapid 2001). In other words, national identities have been typically anchored to defined territories, crystallized in structured social orders, sustained by political and legal systems and institutionalized in cultural practices.

The emergence of transnational practices and the exponential growth of transnational ties, however, have increasingly blurred established physical, social and cultural boundaries of nationhood and community belonging. In the wake of intensified cross-border flows, the structured relation of 'identities-borders-orders' can no longer be taken for granted, as national and other narratives are being displaced across different cultural networks, resulting in a dilution of established meanings of community belonging (see, for example, Bhabha 1990, 1994). In Bhabha's view, transnational practices can generate 'third spaces' where individuals can find 'cultural positionality' in reference to a boundless time and space between national territories. This 'in-betweenness' does not reproduce the dominant narrative but rather allows for 'hybridity' which, in some cases, could be interpreted as a 'counter-narrative of the nation' (Bhabha 1994, p. 300). To illustrate the point about the impact of transnationalism on processes of social identification I will discuss changes to three key elements traditionally associated with nationhood: language, citizenship and solidarity.

3.2 Language

Language[1] has played a key role in the 'imagination' of national communities and the construction of linguistic identities. The distinctiveness of a language can emblematically represent the uniqueness of an entire social group vis-à-vis others, while, at the same time, sharing a language can provide group members with a reference for their sameness thus reinforcing their sense of in-group belonging in inter-ethnic relations (Giles and Johnson 1987). Such interplay has often been appropriated by political agendas in the construction of national identities and their institutional legitimization (Hobsbawm 1997, Kroskrity 2000, Wright 2000, Barbour and Carmichael 2002, Anderson 2006, Ricento 2006, Shohamy 2006). The construction of linguistic identities through monistic regimes (i.e. one nation, one-state, one-language) has often been at the heart of nation-state building in modern history (albeit monistic ideologies have often been underpinned by opposite conceptualizations of nation).[2]

As a result, while 'a single unifying language was the best definition and protector of nationhood' (Spolsky 2004, p. 57) as it would ensure the consolidation of the allegiance between the state and its citizens that was needed by the political agendas of newly born nation states, it also contributed to naturalize a close discursive association between national and linguistic identities. As Chilton (2004, p. 9) remarks discussing the institutionalization of the French language: 'If one cannot speak French, one cannot, in the French Republic, be regarded as fully French.' In national discourse, therefore, a national language has often represented both a means for institutions to ensure the reproduction of a national identity and an index for citizens to express their group affiliation. To use Pittaway's (2003a) words:

> [The] essentially top-down notion, that a state can secure loyalty through the dissemination of a common language among a subject population, has been complemented by a bottom-up notion of the relationship between language and state. (2003a, p. 158)

This relationship, however, has increasingly come under strain in the face of transnational flows. The sociolinguistic diversity, that has always existed within national communities, has seen an exponential growth in recent years with societies in most migrant-receiving countries becoming more (linguistically) heterogeneous or 'super-diverse' than ever (Vertovec 2007, Blommaert and Rampton 2011). One of the consequences of living in a super-diverse society is that, while individuals are more likely to engage with a much wider range of semiotic and linguistic resources, patterns of social interaction and identification processes pegged to national features (for instance, the notion of 'native speaker') have largely lost their predictability and some of their social significance as identity markers (Blommaert 2013).[3]

At the same time, along with the increased variety of linguistic identities within national communities, at a transnational level, there has been a conspicuously growing convergence of practices towards the use of a few global languages (primarily English), especially in communication associated with global patterns of trade and commerce.[4] For House (2003) these phenomena have resulted in a *diglossic* societal scenario where a pragmatic distinction can be made between languages that are used for 'non-private communication' (such as English as a lingua franca) and languages used for affective or 'identificatory purposes' (p. 226). Cheshire (2002) corroborates House's view suggesting that English is increasingly representing a marker of global youth identity exactly through the speakers' distinct perceptions of allegiance and belonging to a community on the one hand, and of worldwide communicative expertise on the other.

Heller (2003, 2012) highlights further implications on identities brought about by the transnationalization of economies (see below). In the context of a study of the bilingual Canadian workforce in the tourism industry and the larger context of 'new economy' practices, Heller (2003) contends that there has been

> a shift from understanding language as being primarily a marker of ethnonational identity, to understanding language as being a marketable commodity on its own, distinct from identity [so that] ethnonational consciousness ... now serves

as a basis for economic mobilisation [in a process amid] the tension between local solidarities and transnational affiliations. (Heller 2003, p. 489)

3.3 Citizenship

Citizenship is another notable example of the changes occurring to once fixed systems of (re)producing national identities. For a long time, citizenship was functionally seen as a tool for stabilizing and strengthening the state apparatus. Typically, in nation states, the attribution of citizenship has determined the boundaries of participation in the public democratic debate (through granting the right to vote, freedom of movement, etc.) while, by the same token, social cohesion, allegiance to the 'imagined' national community, and the reproduction of the state apparatus have been ensured through individuals performing their national identities as 'fellow citizens' (Hobsbawm 1997). The consolidation of transnational links, however, has had profound repercussions on the imagination of the political community one is part of. For example, transnational connections (resulting from migratory movements) have consolidated in multiple loyalties which straddle across territorially bounded jurisdictions and which call into question the single allegiance to the 'national' community expected from formal citizenship (Bauböck and Faist 2010). Meanwhile, new ways of understanding citizenship have increasingly emerged and entered public discourses and policies which are crucially redefining the notion of cultural, ethnic and civic belonging and membership in contemporary polities (Stevenson 2003, Mackert and Turner 2017). An increasing recognition of 'cultural identity' as a criteria for modern citizenship (Kymlicka 1990) based on the inclusion of cultural rights and the recognition of differences advocated, for example, by multiculturalism (Parekh 2000) have resulted in some governments extending and/or loosening the traditional principles upon which they grant citizenship rights, allowing for more cases of dual and multiple citizenships.[5]

3.4 Solidarity

The transnationalization of society has not only been reflected in changes to how membership of a political community is formally attributed by states. If we refer to citizenship as one's active engagement with one's civic duties, transnationalism has contributed to an overall redefinition of practices and meanings of civic membership, political activism and solidarity in most modern democracies (Sassen 2002, Kastoryano 2003, Sigona 2013). The micro-solidarity that the nation-state narratives have historically 'scaled up' from household to national levels (Malesevic 2013) is increasingly recognizable in the life of modern political communities through the reorganization of local civic activism along global contingencies. Globalization, for example, has brought to the fore that certain issues – such as environmental risk, migratory flows and organized crime, which obviously do not stop at borders – can affect the wider community and, therefore, can be more effectively debated in a trans-border arena. As Beck (1996) argues there is 'a new dialectic of global and local questions which do not fit into national politics' (p. 226) and which can only be 'properly posed, debated and resolved' (Beck 1996) in a transnational framework. Networks of communication that can span across borders and that can organize themselves around different interests and solidarities therefore constitute an appealing tool for collective political action and group agency beyond national constraints. From an ideological perspective, thus, transnational activism is capable of not only projecting nationalism across borders (as, for instance, in the case of diaspora of stateless peoples) but also transcending national borders to recreate the reference framework for social and political membership at different and wider levels (Bauböck and Faist 2010).

Alongside this interpretation of transnational political engagement, a further important aspect of solidarity relates to the transnationalization of economies. Put succinctly, the last few decades have seen the spreading of neoliberal policies (encouraging a deregulation of trade, wage competition, privatization and a reduced public expenditure) and an ever-growing focus on market interests with multinational corporations accruing their influence on social dynamics (Sparke 2013). The effects of such policies have been highly debated. While the transnationalization of markets has increased economic output and intensified cross world trade, for many (cf., for example, Robinson 2004) such growth has primarily benefitted vested interests, enabling some big corporations' GDP (and influence) to grow to the level of small national governments and to compete with them by eroding some of the traditional functions of nation states (e.g. welfare and social protection). Furthermore, the global financial crises which started in 2007 has added to the loss of job security of a large strata of the world's population, widening the gap between the 'haves' and 'have nots' in most societies.

In the wake of these changes, there has been a polarization of solidarity towards common themes of 'resistance' to globalization perceived as a potential threat

(Castells 1997) whereby most individuals, who tend to identify as 'disempowered' and losing out from transnational economies, have been brought together by different transnational interests rather than by national camaraderie. Grassroots movements such as the 'Anti-globalization' Movement started in Seattle, 1999 and, more recently, 'Los Indignados' in Spain (2012) have shown the ability to harness the potential of transnational connections for purposes of solidarity and common action to counterbalance the 'excesses of capitalist globalisation' (Cheah 2006)[6] In this sense, transnationalism has also been conceptualized as a powerful form of 'globalisation from below' (Portes 1997, p. 296) because the 'social capital' of transnational networks can easily and democratically be appropriated by participants for shared objectives of cooperation or even for more radical and counterhegemonic action in which the transnational element is imagined as the 'transversal' and 'transgressive' 'trespassing' of ideological borders of regulated logics of state and capitalism (DeBardeleben 2011).

3.4.1 The role of networks in transnational and cosmopolitan imaginaries

In the social sciences, the metaphor of network has been extensively used to describe different phenomena.[7] The use of the network metaphor has become especially widespread in recent years in the theorization of social interaction (e.g. communicative practices) enabled and mediated by new technology and the formation of systemic structures in relation to such practices (cf., inter alia, Latour 2005, Dijk 2006, Cavanagh 2007). Terms such as 'social network' have thus been used to describe a group of people connected by shared interests or beliefs as well as the social, organizational, cultural and technological infrastructures underpinning the group interaction. Much academic literature has analysed and discussed the role of transnational networks in the interaction of political and social actors in globalized contexts (see, for instance, Smith, Chatfield and Ron 1997, Della Porta and Diani 1999, Della Porta and Tarrow 2005, Tarrow 2005, MacDonald 2006). In these studies, the conceptualization of network has been especially significant in the spatial representation of communities for its 'open' and flexible structure. Social interaction within and across the network can typically be imagined via the expansion of new 'nodes' in a flexible, horizontal (i.e. non-hierarchical) process which can virtually be limitless as it is not contained physically (Castells 1996b, Castells 1997, Castells 2001). For Castells (2000, p. 14) transnational connections, are 'social practices without geographical contiguity' which have changed the way we think about space. He underscores how, in transnational societies, the meaning of space is no longer anchored in territory and 'places' but instead, it has shifted to the dynamics of 'connections' and 'flows' conceived along the logic of networks. Furthermore, as pointed out by Castells and Cardoso (2005, p. 15), because 'by definition, a network has no centre' the logic of 'core' and 'periphery' (i.e. physical locations and social distances) is downplayed and made less relevant. In this way, individuals tend to experience their location in a social network as a point-to-point dynamic relation and their social interaction as the flows and ties between points/nodes. Significantly, therefore, for Castells (1996b) the power of communication through networks is an effective way of reconstructing social spaces, redrawing the imagery of communities and hierarchies and an opportunity for individuals to re-position themselves in this changed topography.

In a similar vein to Castells, Appadurai (1995, 1996) sees social connections and flows of cultural resources as no longer constrained by physical bounds but relying on 'linked up' local and global dimensions with the opportunity to be enacted via new 'technoscapes'. For Appadurai this can help us reframe social interaction in a new 'relationality' where 'place' is best understood as embedded in a network of connections and in relation to other 'scapes' that make up the network. Appadurai thus sees the redefinition of 'place' opening up social and individual opportunities for negotiating and redefining identities. While he highlights the complexity of 'relating or producing locality' for individuals immersed in transnational networks, he also suggests that they are able to 're-imagine' themselves across borders from new 'translocalities' and in new forms. However, as argued by Hanquinet and Savage (2013) summarizing Appadurai's argument

> global flows do not lead to the homogenisation of location or the erosion of local cultures, but rather they allow a proliferation of spatial signifiers. (p. 6)

Such reconfiguration of signifiers can take place along a local–global continuum whereby experiencing transnationalism may involve several layers of 'glocalization' and may result in different degrees of attachment to cultures, locales and regions (Roudometof 2005). Therefore while transnationalism has raised a new type of consciousness about our connections, places and communities, such consciousness is reflected differently in how actors choose to engage with it, how they organize themselves politically and economically and in how they 'think about and position themselves in society both here-and-there'(Vertovec 2009, p. 24). The next section will outline different theorizations of 'world views' and of 'social orders' brought about by transnationalism and cosmopolitanism.

3.4.2 Transnational and cosmopolitan views of the world

Levitt and Schiller (2004) suggest that it is possible for individuals in transnational fields to engage in a simultaneity of connections spanning from routines and daily activities, to the production of (cultural) identities that reflect their multiple locations. From this perspective Levitt and Glick-Schiller (Levitt and Schiller 2004), define *ways of being* in social fields as opposed to *ways of belonging*. They claim that

> ways of being refers to the actual social relations and practices that individuals engage in rather than to the identities associated with their actions (p. 1010)

therefore suggesting that while individuals embedded in a social field have the potential to identify with any label associated with that field not all choose to do so. By contrast,

> Ways of belonging refers to practices that signal or enact an identity which demonstrates a conscious connection to a particular group ... ways of belonging combine action and an awareness of the kind of identity that action signifies. (Levitt and Schiller 2004)

While for Levitt and Glick-Schiller local and transnational connections can occur simultaneously, *ways of being* and *ways of belonging* are often dependent on the specific context upon which they are enacted. In their words:

> If individuals engage in social relations and practices that cross borders as a regular feature of everyday life, then they exhibit a transnational way of being. When people explicitly recognize this and highlight the transnational elements of who they are, then they are also expressing a transnational way of belonging. (p. 1011)

The element of awareness and reflexivity that differentiate 'being' from 'belonging' in Levitt and Glick-Schiller's argument is also discussed by Beck (2000, 2008), for whom transnational activities and global practices of interconnectedness can be seen as empirical factors in the process of a reflexive cosmopolitanization of society.[8] In broad terms, the cosmopolitan perspective discussed in much literature (see, inter alia, Hannerz 1990, Calhoun 2002, Vertovec and Cohen 2003, Beck and Cronin 2006, Beck and Grande 2006, Calhoun 2006, Held 2010) recognizes the embeddedness of our space into the wider world and it celebrates the plurality and diversity of humans as one community regardless of ethnicity or nationality. In this sense Beck, and other sociologists, see the potential in modern society for the realization of humans as beings living in the

Aristotelian 'cosmopolis'. A cosmopolitan view of society therefore would see all individuals as 'citizens of the world' (Heater 2004) and treat transnational connections as opportunities for social progress through intercultural exchange. For Stevenson (2003) cosmopolitan attitudes transcend culture-centric views and 'see no necessary contradiction between feelings of loyalty and commitment to particular cultures and an openness towards difference and otherness' (p. 57). For these individuals, notions of group and solidarity are much less territorially bound and may result in different understanding of civic communities beyond national ties. For Delanty (2000), more than in the formation of 'global' identities, this understanding of cosmopolitanism can be found, for example, in reflexive attempts to no longer construct national identities in relation to the 'other'. In this vein Beck (2008) suggests that in a cosmopolitan framework identities 'become plural and relate in a plural way' (p. 92) to different national, ethnic and cultural elements. Consequently, identities become a specific combination of a 'creative achievement' of individuality and integration in the global society. They 'are invented, tested and developed' (p. 100), reflexively 'weighted', 'tried out', 'chosen', 'overlapped' and 'rearranged' in a variety of combinations and one 'lives on the strength of the combination' (p. 92).

Another theorization of the different understandings of the world and the different identitarian positionings that individuals can enact vis-à-vis their 'global' awareness is offered by Robertson (1992). Building on sociologist Ferdinand Tönnies' (1952) distinction between *Gemeinschaft* ('community') and *Gesellschaft* ('society'), Robertson (1992) suggests four different 'images of global order' which might describe how individuals make sense of their relations in a globalized world (and/or how the world 'ought to be'). Robertson refers to 'Global Gemeinschaft 1' to define an understanding of the world as a series of 'relatively closed societal communities' (p. 78) which he juxtaposes with 'Global Gesellschaft 1', a frame whereby the world is perceived 'as a series of open societies, with considerable socio-cultural exchange between them' (p. 79). By contrast, Robertson refers to 'Global Gemeinschaft 2' and 'Global Gesellschaft 2' to characterize the perception of the world as a 'fully globewide community' (or, in common parlance, the 'global village') and as a 'formal, planned … organisation' (or a 'strong world government') respectively.

The main difference between the two sets of 'world views' outlined above hinges on the fact that the former set focuses on the diversity of the world (although entailing opposed degrees of 'closeness/openness') while the latter set supports a vision of a tightly integrated world. As discussed by Hannerz (1990, 1996) these different ideologies have different implications for social action taken vis-à-vis the 'global'. For example a 'Global Gemeinschaft 1' would be consistent with the politics of ethnic revivals, while 'Global Gesellschaft 1' can lead to collaboration, harmonization of differences, but also 'liberal nationalism' or a 'hegemonic arrangement among states' (Rumford 2008, p. 143). By the same token, the remits of some religious, peace and environmental movements resonate with the ideals of the 'Global Gemeinschaft 2' whereas 'Global Gesellschaft 2' can be seen (in an optimistic sense) as a consensual and systematic form of democratic world governance while (in the more pessimistic accounts) it has been characterized as a 'centralized' version of identity politics or a global system of reproducing inequalities (Hobsbawm 2007). Thus, as argued by Robertson and White (2003), in modern society there is imaginary scope for individuals to reshape their relation with their national collectivites vis-à-vis the world 'others' by associating with and dissociating from a particular world order – that is by taking a particular stance of globalization. As Rumford (2008) suggests:

> Globalisation has resulted in a circumstance in which we have all come to see ourselves, albeit in many different ways, as existing in some relation the global. What the 'global' is will differ from account to account; we do not all see global in the same way [but] globality, gives meaning to our existence in [the world], and helps us understand the perspectives, struggles, and community attachments which sustain others. The oneness of the world is not incommensurate with our different understandings of it; rather it is a precondition for such a multiplicity of perspectives. (pp. 144–5)

3.5 The transnationalization of the European field

The previous section has outlined a scenario of radical changes occurring at global level in social, economic and cultural fields having significant repercussions on the imagination of community. Taking into account this scenario, this section will discuss the specificity of transnationalism in the European context.

As Fligstein (2007) suggests, two parallel dynamics can be distinguished (at least conceptually) in the transnationalization of the European field.[9] The first set of phenomena at play can primarily be seen as a consequence of the operationalization of the EU project while the second set relates to wider transnational dynamics. The operationalization of the EU project of integration has involved, for example, the introduction of policies aimed at removing customs and tax barriers and harmonizing trade within the Single Market which have enabled free movement of goods, capital, services and people across member states. This has resulted in converging and intensified patterns of economic and social intra-state activities as well as the definitions of new 'spaces' (e.g. Schengen area, Euro area) where borders are no longer in place and have shifted or overlapped and where the 'desirable' trans-state mobility of EU citizens may have contributed to the formation of some transnational social and civic ties (Munch 2001, Rumford 2006). Furthermore, at the political level, the EU system of multilevel governance has institutionalized 'European' organs (such as the European Commission) that are legitimized to take decisions supranationally thus by-passing national sovereignty in a number of areas. This experimental and innovative governance order has contributed to the convergence of legal, financial and political systems towards what is seen by many as a unique form of post-national polity (Ruggie 1993, Eriksen 2005).

However, despite these notable achievements, a truly democratic transnationalization of the European civil society remains, at best, an open process as mobility and the exercise of civic rights is still constrained by national logics. For example, despite its formal introduction under the Treaty of Maastricht in 1992, European citizenship still represents a 'weak' provision because it is not granted by any EU institution and it is subordinate to citizens being nationals of one of the member states in the first place. Furthermore the rights of movement of certain nationals (e.g. Bulgarians and Romanians) into other EU states have been variously restricted and reinstated in time by different states,[10] whereas intra-EU mobility restrictions apply to non-EU citizens whose free movement in the EU is dependent on their status as a family member of a EU national.[11] All of these restrictions add to the incoherent immigration policies of member states and their supranational handling of increasing extra-EU migration into the EU of recent years. In *We, the People of Europe?* (2004) Etienne Balibar has criticized the system of border patrols and detention centres of 'Fortress Europe' as new forms of 'apartheid', advancing the radical interpretation of Europe as a 'borderland' in which the transnationalization of the internal space has been counter posed by the strengthening of physical and ideological external borders (cf. also Balibar 2009).

These issues relate, in large part, to the second set of phenomena concerning the transnationalization of the European field, namely the impact of global patterns of economic, social and cultural mobility, the emergence of cosmopolitan perspectives, the redefinition of political agency and solidarity, (as outlined in the previous section) at a European level. As suggested by Delanty and Rumford (2005) global and local/European processes may or may not overlap – synergically coexist and/or antithetically compete – thus intensifying convergence as well as divergence of social, economic and cultural patterns of transnationalization. The European instantiation of global phenomena has thus been compounded, possibly accelerated but, in some cases, also reversed by the EU's integration process. This interplay has resulted in a highly stratified society in which different transnational elements have filtered down the individual consciousness as ideological components of belonging in different ways (Hanquinet and Savage 2013). In this light Hanquinet and Savage (2013, p. 7) claim that

> the European case can simultaneously be held out as the most striking example in the world of the emergence of transnational institutions and identities, and as the most potent instance of the persistence of nationalism and the limits to cosmopolitanism.

From a similar stance, Delanty and Rumford (2005) argue that European identities can represent postmodern and reflexive forms of 'social self-understanding' and of understanding the transformation of society. These views may encompass forms of cosmopolitan awareness (Beck and Grande 2006) that tend to recognize Europe in its relation with the world (Biebuyck and Rumford 2011). However, Delanty and Rumford (2005) also draw attention to transnationalism as a phenomenon that goes beyond Europe and that involves European and 'non-European' social actors. Transnationalism can thus be interpreted as a subjective perspective or a 'lens' that may reconcile the global and local dimensions into new forms of 'glocalities' contributing to 'a holistic and world-systemic view in which local events are read locally as well as translocally' (Blommaert 2003 p. 612). As suggested by Wodak and Weiss (2005), the availability of collective discourses, social imaginaries and transnational perspectives and dynamics that may potentially drive the process of identification of social actors with Europe and as Europeans[12] must assume the multiplicity of 'different constructions and images of Europe' (p. 128) and different 'ideological dilemmas' (Billig 1988) about Europe. Moreover, by treating the discursive construction of Europeanness on a scale from local to global, one has to recognize the complexity of phenomena at play, taking into account the inevitable emergence of antinomies between the two dimensions (i.e. universality vs. particularity of rights; language preservation vs. lingua franca; etc.) (Wodak 2007).

Forms of identification with Europe and as Europeans can therefore coexist and interplay with narratives of transformation of nationhood and national identities as a political project. In this sense, Europeanness can be instantiated in forms of 'active citizenship' and in the emergence of grassroots European social agency driven by post-national social imaginaries. In relation to this aspect, discourses of Europe(anness) can be driven by the political debate about national versus supranational interests as a key 'nodal point'. By the same token, the different experiences of the 'desirable' mobility of the EU citizens on the one hand, and the experience of extra-EU migrants vis-à-vis 'Fortress Europe' on the other, may result in very different personal experiences of (non)belonging to Europe (Jones and Krzyżanowski 2008). Finally, European identities can be seen as driven by the recontextualization of global neoliberal discourses that impact negatively on some citizens while benefitting others (Krzyżanowski 2003). In this sense, individuals that have to (re)position their identities vis-à-vis global contingencies may construct and strengthen their local and cultural identities in opposition to global threats or may interpret transnational practices as 'ways of being' with little impact on their 'belonging'.

Building on the aforementioned spate of dynamics, the different degrees to which citizens have incorporated transnational and cosmopolitan elements in their interpretations of Europeanness can conveniently be accounted for by notions of 'thick' and 'thin' identities.[13] A 'thick' understanding of European identity is typically oriented towards a particularist approach to cultures and communities that relies on a strong investment in the definition of belonging. In this case, transnational practices tend to be 'situational' (Roudometof 2005) and instantiated primarily in 'glocal' forms of consumption (Hanquinet and Savage 2013) rather than holistic attitudes and beliefs. Processes of identification as European tend to involve the construction of a relationship with the 'Other' in which 'otherness' is recognized 'outside' Europe and is used to demarcate the boundaries of one's European identity (Stråth 2010). A 'thin' European identity, by contrast, is underpinned by an investment in civic values, in the universality of rights and obligations, and it is more consistent with cosmopolitan attitudes 'detached' from specific notions of cultures and belonging. In this case, the 'Other' can still exist but it is recognized and negotiated through inclusion. In this sense, Delanty (2009, p. 77) contends that, from a cosmopolitan perspective, Europeanness can be seen as 'a growing reflexivity within existing identities'. Transposed into the political arena, 'thick' Europeanness tends to perceive European integration as a Euro-centric and bounded phenomenon while 'thin' cosmopolitan perspectives are more closely associated with a post-national understanding of Europe relevant to 'world governance' projects and new social orders. Moreover 'thin' European identities are more likely to inform projects of political agency beyond the national level (Habermas 2003).

Although these different dimensions have been discussed here in rather dichotomous terms they have been analysed in more detail by an important strand of interdisciplinary literature at the intersection of political, cultural and critical studies (cf. Lacroix 2002, Delanty and Rumford 2005, Priban 2007, DeBardeleben and Hurrelmann 2011, Calhoun 2012, Friedman and Thiel 2012) with specific interest focusing on the debate about whether 'thin' or 'thick' identities are necessary or desirable for the success of the European project (see, for example, Davidson 2008). In this respect, one of the most influential views in understanding Europeanness in post-national and cosmopolitan terms has been that of Habermas (2001, 2003, 2009). Habermas' contention is that European identities should be built on a 'thin' conceptual foundation of Europe (i.e. based on civic rather than cultural values) and gradually 'thickened' (i.e. consolidated) through 'constitutional patriotism', a process that Habermas sees taking place through communication in the public sphere and which he regards as essential for the democratic debate and the success of the European project. The concept of the EPS will therefore be further elaborated in the next section.

3.5.1 The European Public Sphere (EPS)

The notion of a 'public sphere' was originally introduced by Habermas (1989) who saw the historical emergence of the bourgeoisie in eighteenth and nineteenth centuries developing a forum

> in which private people, come together to form a public, readied themselves to compel public authority to legitimate itself before public opinion.

In modern discourses the public sphere represents 'a network for communicating information and points of view' (Habermas and Rehg 1998, p. 360) and more generally a site for citizens participation in the democratic dialogue and the formation of public opinion (Wodak and Koller 2008).[14] For Habermas (1989) the public sphere is characterized by the following key elements: openness to participation; challenges to public authority to legitimize decisions and ideal of rational-critical discourse.[15] In this vein Habermas (1997) contends that, for the EU to be a democratic polity, a EPS must exist 'which enables citizens to take positions at the same time on the same topics of the same relevance' (p. 306). Crucially, however, the EPS not only is a site of political deliberation and a democratic 'yardstick', but also constitutes a discursive arena where identities can be created and negotiated. As contended by (Triandafyllidou, Wodak and Krzyżanowski 2009)

> the construction and functions of an EPS involve a continuous interaction and intertwining between different (nationally and transnationally incepted)

ideas/viewpoints and various ethical notions, that are central to the negotiation and legitimisation of different forms of (collective) identities. (p. 5)

Furthermore, the public sphere is seen by many as a precondition for 'claiming' or 'realizing' a wider set of identities (Soysal 1997)[16] including one's Europeanness. For example, for Eder (discussed in Salvatore, Schmidtke and Trenz 2013) the public sphere may provide social bonds beyond the family, 'bridging' the fragmentation of modern society with a democratically and solidarity-oriented social organization. Highlighting

> the creativity of social actors and groups, and ultimately of society itself, in renewing social bonds and inventing new practices, rituals, or narratives of social cohesion. (p. 6)

Salvatore, Schmidtke and Trenz (2013) argue that one of the key features of a modern public sphere is

> the reflexive character of the communicative process [through which] … [m]embers of the public are speakers who debate and deliberate by reflecting not only on their own interests and values but also on their own identity as autonomous agents. (2013, p. 2)

In line with Habermas (2003), Salvatore, Schmidtke and Trenz (2013) regard the public sphere as the social milieu where a European constitutional patriotism should develop which would eventually replace the ethnic bonds of European peoples currently tied to nationhood. Notwithstanding such optimistic views, the extent to which a transnationalized EPS exists remains a contested issue. Some, for instance, see it as just an aggregation of single national spheres (Closa 2001) or primarily conducted from national 'filters' (Triandafyllidou, Wodak and Krzyżanowski 2009). Other views suggest the EPS is limited to educated and professional elites (Fligstein 2007), 'weak 'and 'semi-imposed' by the EU (Splichal 2006) or exclusively reliant on networks of actors or social movements (Eriksen and Fossum 2002). It has however been recognized that 'transnationalisation has the potential to alter structures and processes in the public sphere in a quite radical sense' (Salvatore, Schmidtke and Trenz 2013, p. 3) challenging in particular the logic of democratic deliberations organized around national clusters (Fraser 2007, Fraser and Nash 2014). In this vein, Risse (2010) argues that, even with the shortcomings of being unevenly developed and fragmented, the EPS is contributing to the creation of a transnational 'community of communication' among Europeans where new European identities can emerge. Therefore if one is to find new insights on the meaning and imaginaries of post-national Europe one should be looking at the emergent transnational EPS as an interesting site of debate.

A number of different actors operate in the EPS including the media, political parties, interest groups and NGOs. Several civil society organizations have also emerged which are organized in local and regional initiatives as well as in transnational networks and which focus on different interests and activities (e.g. human rights, democratization processes, environmental sustainability).[17] In the next section I will thus examine how CDA has dealt with different aspects of transnationalism and identities in the EPS and more generally in the European context.

3.5.2 Transnationalism in Europe from CDS perspectives

A significant body of CDS scholars (including sociolinguists and political linguists) have engaged with topics of transnationalism in the larger European field with a considerable amount of research focusing on the development of identities. Furthermore, CDS approaches (and the application of social constructivist and poststructuralist paradigms) have also increasingly cross-fertilized the fields of International Relations and (European) Political studies.[18]

A group of scholars has explored how European identities are represented in and by the media. For example, Bayley and Williams (2012) have examined how Europeanness has been linguistically constructed in the news of Italy, France and the UK offering empirical insights into the different semantic interpretations of 'citizenship'. In another study, Krzyżanowski (2003) analyses how supranational and European identities are constructed in TV talk shows suggesting that European identities can represent an 'adjustment' that 'national, social and cultural groups need to undertake [in response to] new macro-social conditions' (p. 184). The media discourse has also provided a major lens for examining the construction of 'peripheral' European identities in the press coverage of the Lisbon Treaty (Sowinska 2009) and the role of national discourses in the construction of multilingual European identities in national newspapers at the time of the 2004 EU enlargement (Krzyżanowski 2010). Moreover, the role of the media was the focus of a longitudinal study conducted by Triandafyllidou, Wodak and Krzyżanowski (2009) who analysed the extent of transnationalization of the EPS in reporting international crises in post-war Europe in eight national contexts. Triandafyllidou, Wodak and Krzyżanowski (2009) conclude by highlighting the importance of national filters in creating different conceptualizations of Europe as a geographical entity, as an economic space or a cluster of values, which is typically invoked to warrant individual national interests. Furthermore Triandafyllidou, Wodak and Krzyżanowski (2009) argue that different media constructions are reflected in processes of spatio-temporal representations of Europe as either a 'global' or a 'regional' intermediary between East and West while 'the EU as a transnational European actor … did not play any salient role in unifying the European space' (p. 263).

Another strand of CDS has focused on the construction of European identities primarily (albeit not exclusively) from cultural perspectives. In this area Meinhof (2001), Meinhof and Galasinski (2007) have offered insights on the impact of shifting European borders (especially between East and West) on the formation of Europeanness within communities overlapping such boundaries. Furthermore, examining cultural policies against emerging transnational dynamics in European cities, Meinhof and Triandafyllidou (2006) critically questioned the limitations of national frameworks which often assume static relationships between immigration, cultural diversity and cultural policies.

Additionally, the CDS community has extensively dealt with the negotiation of identities in educational, institutional and economic settings vis-à-vis multilingual and globalized societies (including Europe) highlighting the complexity, antinomies and power dynamics involved in the production of linguistic and transnational identities (see, inter alia, Heller 1995, Blommaert 1999, Wright 2000, Pavlenko and Blackledge 2004, Spotti 2007, Blackledge and Creese 2010, Gal 2010a, b, Duchêne, Moyer and Roberts 2013). Focusing on (extra-EU) migrants and examining the EU's multilingual policies and 'national' language requirements, for instance, Wodak (2010) has suggested how these regulatory provisions effectively impact on processes of exclusion of transnational migrants from 'Fortress Europe'. From the perspective of migrant 'voices', Jones and Krzyżanowski (2008) too have provided insights into patterns of transnational identification, suggesting that in many cases migrants make use of multiple 'modes of belonging' to construct individual rather than collective identities where Europe represents a remote (if not absent) 'imagined space' in their narratives.

In particular, Jones and Krzyżanowski (2008) have suggested a framework that distinguishes between the salience of 'attachments', 'belonging' and 'membership' as interrelated dimensions of the process of identification (see also Krzyżanowski and Wodak (2008), Krzyżanowski (2010)). For Krzyżanowski and Wodak (2008),

> The discursive construction of modes of belonging necessarily includes:
> (a) tentative and random attachments; (b) a range of 'feelings' of belonging; and
> (c) legal forms of membership. (p. 102)

Attachment is thus conceptualized as a broad category of emotional 'anchors' (such as physical places and cultural practices) that individuals can potentially draw upon to fully develop into meaningful feelings of belonging in their search for an (ideal) identity position. On the other hand, membership is seen as a sociopolitical and institutional attribution which involves external recognition (as, for example, in the case of citizenship) and which this framework sees typically negotiated in the public sphere and subject to an increasingly debated politics of belonging.

Another strand of CDS has examined the formation of transnational identities within European politics. At the institutional level, Wodak (2003, 2004), for example, has analysed the formation of 'multiple identities' of members of the European Parliament showing how transnational elements of Europeanness (which in this case she equates by and large with 'supranational schemas') are enacted by informants along with their different gender and national identifications/affiliations. Similarly, Krzyżanowski (2010) carried out an investigation of Europeanness among the politicians involved in the 2002–3 European Convention finding that most informants discursively construct a variety of personal and institutional European (post-national) identities through the convergence and divergence of the notions of EU and Europe.

In addition to the investigation of how institutional European/transnational identities are formed, a number of studies have dealt with the formation of Europeanness from bottom-up stances. Among these, for instance, Millar and Wilson (2007) investigate discourses of a cross-section of 'ordinary' citizens focusing on the micro level of everyday talk to gain insights of what it means to be European. Covering, inter alia, issues of identity, local politics, borders and minority languages the authors corroborate other views suggesting that the construction of Europeanness in discourse involves the enactment of multiple affective dimensions of belonging as well as elements of 'pragmatic utility'.

Alongside the many areas of research discussed above, there have been efforts to examine EU-rope and its demos in the context of wider transnational and bottom-up perspectives. For example, Morin and Carta (2014) have merged different theoretical and analytical framework (with CDA being the most prominent one) to examine EU-rope in its external relations with the wider world (viz. in the articulation of foreign policies). Another example is found in Doerr (2010) who, from a critical stance, examines the discourses of members of the European Social Forum as an emergent form of transnational public sphere and, also, as a 'laboratory' for the discursive construction of 'another Europe'.

However, in spite of the many notable examples of work on Europeanness and transnationalism illustrated so far in this and in the previous sections, to date there is a paucity of research within the CDS community on the discursive construction of European identities at grassroots level. The lack of insights on how some 'active' citizens conceive of and discursively enact 'being European'/'doing Europe' from bottom-up and 'beyond-the-national' perspectives fails to grasp some of the ongoing transformation of modern Europe, since, as noted earlier in the discussion, the emergence of a transnational civil society and the development of a post-national sentiment are essential elements for the success of the European project. This research therefore intends to contribute to the advancement of the field of Critical Linguistics with insights on the evolution of European identities particularly in the light of transnational narratives brought about by civic actors.

Operationalizing the Methodological Approach

4.1 Discussion of methods used in this study

The data for this study was collected from EA members between 2011 and 2013 via four moderated focus groups and nine individual interviews. This was further corroborated by some ethnographic work which I was able to conduct as a member of EA's London group. Although I acknowledge the potential conflict between my roles as a member and as a researcher, I believe that the benefits of being an 'insider' and taking an 'emic' perspective (Denzin and Lincoln 1998) (especially in assisting the data interpretation) have outweighed the potential pitfalls. I tried to minimize any potential bias in this sense by making sure, whenever possible, that I had not had any previous contact with the members who agreed to participate in individual or group interviews as this could influence their responses. My participant observation in the field was especially concerned with 'situating' (Gobo 2008) linguistic and communicative practices within social dynamics and organizational contexts in which discourses where produced. These ethnographic insights were also particularly helpful in structuring the interviews, guiding their interpretation and triangulating the results (Krzyżanowski 2011).

The choice of combining focus groups and individual interviews was primarily motivated by the synergy of 'breadth' and 'depth' of data that the two methods can provide and by the different foci on collective and personal dynamics and narratives they allow. On balance the combination of focus groups and individual interviews was therefore aimed at illuminating the many facets of European and transnational identities between social and personal levels.

The use of focus groups in social sciences has increasingly been regarded as a valuable method of data collection 'whenever one is exploring shared (collective) or individual opinions … [and] beliefs' (Bloor 2001). Focus groups can thus provide an effective tool for gaining insights on the construction and negotiation of meanings in a variety of social contexts on account of the interaction between participants that the group discussion can bring about (Kitzinger and Barbour 1999, Litosseliti 2003). Focus groups were thus considered particularly suited to this study as they could best reproduce the genre of discussions normally occurring at local meetings thus providing a familiar and 'natural' context for members.

In addition to focus groups, data was also collected via individual interviews. The rationale for this choice was that one-to-one discussions generally allow for a setting where members do not feel the pressure to conform to group opinions or 'dominant' participants and have greater scope to illustrate their points with personal narratives and anecdotes, which, in turn, can enable the interviewer to penetrate better the 'private world of human experience' of the interviewees (Silverman 1993). In this sense individual interviews were regarded in this study as an important method of investigation that could significantly integrate and corroborate data from focus groups with insights on the individual dimension.

To operationalize the methods discussed above a set of 'primary'[1] topics was identified (via preparatory work, see below). These topics were subsequently discussed at the pilot focus group in London and the pilot individual interview in Rome (see below).

4.1.1 Preparation work

The framing of questions introduced in the pilot group and individual interviews was primarily driven by the research objectives (i.e. defining how 'European identities' are constructed from a transnational perspective). Lead questions asked in the pilot studies (summarized in Table 4.2) were therefore broadly based on the literature on transnationalism discussed in the previous chapter. However, in defining lead questions, I also took into account any ethnographic insights I acquired from within the organization (for instance by attending local meetings and socializing with members) as this gave me a better way to 'understand the social meanings and activities of people in a given "field" or setting' (Brewer 2000, p. 11) and more generally equipped me with a broad heuristic tool to understand the 'common sense of the world' (Silverman 1993) held by respondents. I thus built on these insights to introduce questions from practical rather than conceptual perspectives, for example, by referring to the transnational significance of specific projects, events, practices and the like in which members were involved. Further preparatory familiarization work in this sense was also done by examining the NGO's literature. This included material which was publicly available from the NGO website such as articles, a forum, a blog, an event page, RSS feeds, Twitter accounts and links to the NGO's Facebook

Table 4.1 Examples of lead questions asked at focus groups and individual interviews

Macro topics	Lead questions asked
(Introduction)	Would you like to briefly introduce yourself?
Transnationalism	Can you explain what transnationalism/being transnational means to you? What is 'wrong' with nation states?
EA's activities and scope	Can you explain your motives for joining EA and what your role is in the organization? What do you think the organization's/your own contribution to Europe could be?
European identity	Would you define yourself as European? What would you say makes you European? How do you see your Europeanness in relation to other identities – for example, national?
Eu-rope as a social and a political project	How you would define Europe? Do you see Europe as an equal and democratic society? To what extent (if at all) do you think your idea of Europe is represented by the EU? Do you have an ideal political scenario in mind for the Europe of the future?
Cultural aspects of Eu-rope	Do you see any tensions in reconciling European diversity with the integration project? How do you see language(s) and culture(s) related, if at all, to European identity? Do you think a common language is important in the definition of Europe and the EPS?
(Conclusion)	Would you like to add anything to what we have said so far?

pages. I also examined the material that was circulated electronically to members such as newsletters, pamphlets relating to the launch of specific campaigns and a publication called the *Trans Europa Journal*.[2] In addition I examined a series of videos that the organization posted on YouTube.[3] Overall, such work enabled me to put forward critical questions such as 'What is wrong with nation states?' by paraphrasing provocative propositions found in the literature (e.g. 'the nation-state is not the appropriate political form to promote a responsible politics'[4]). A list of lead questions asked at focus groups is presented in Table 4.1.

4.1.2 The role of moderators

I conducted all interviews and moderated all focus groups except the Cluj focus group, which was moderated by a Romanian speaker (RC) who was fully briefed about the purpose and the protocol of the interview. In conducting focus groups we made sure the lead questions were used as inductive 'entry' or 'anchoring' points to structure the general flow of conversation rather than rigidly determine a protocol of interaction. This means that not all questions were asked in the same order and exactly with the same wording as, in some cases, answers emerged spontaneously during the conversation. Typically, topics were introduced loosely by moderators (e.g. 'do you want to tell me a bit about transnationalism') as that was enough to elicit adequate answers. If, in certain instances, it was felt that answers were too vague or general, further clarification was solicited; for example if a question on transnationalism produced a reply that was interpreted as a simple technical or a lexical definition, then the prompt 'is that what it means to you?' was further asked.

Overall moderators strived to ensure their role was one of 'critical facilitators' (Krueger 1994, Litosseliti 2003) while, at the same time, making participants feel comfortable by providing a clear explanation of the purpose of the discussion at the beginning and by clarifying that there were no expectations of 'right' or 'wrong' answers. In addition, moderators explained to participants they were free to disagree or not to respond should they wish to. Moderators ensured that a well-balanced and informed discussion took place by 'readjusting' the focus when the conversation was drifting or had reached a minor conclusion. Moderators were careful to ask 'open' rather than 'closed' questions, for instance by formulating *wh-* questions (who/what/when/where/why). Moderators also ensured that they did not favour particular participants or express personal opinions.

4.2 Data collection

4.2.1 Data collected via focus groups

4.2.1.1 *London focus group (pilot test)*

A focus group that would serve as a pilot study for subsequent interviews was agreed with two members of the London EA branch through personal contact with the coordinator. The discussion provided a good sweep of data as one of the participants was a senior member with a wealth of experience of organizational practices and discourses and, overall, the interaction between participants generated a reasonably natural flow of exchange. Notes were taken during the discussion to pick up significant non-verbal language (e.g. nodding or moving hands) and further notes reflecting on the experience were taken as soon as possible after the discussion. At the end of the discussion a questionnaire was distributed to participants to collect some socio-demographic data which is reported in Table 4.2.

Subsequent to the London pilot test I approached several local group coordinators in order to extend the study. Local coordinators (who are effectively the gatekeepers of the branch) were contacted by email and through them a call was sent out for volunteers to participate in focus groups and interviews organized locally. My call generated a number of positive responses from members of different branches and, by liaising and negotiating practicalities with the local coordinators, I was able to agree three focus groups within the following branches: Bologna in Italy, Cluj-Napoca in Romania and Cardiff in the UK.

While these branches represent a self-selecting sample of members, they offer an interesting cross-sectional view of the NGO for a number of reasons. Bologna and Cluj (as well as London) represent EA's longest established branches with the highest number of active members. By contrast, members of the Cardiff branch came together more recently to work around specific projects such as 'The Human Library' (see below). Age is another important variable as members of the London and Bologna groups tended to be (on average) older than the other three branches (personal information collected from the local coordinators). Furthermore, from my ethnographic observation at the London meetings and from my discussions with local coordinators I was also able to establish that the London branch has a faster turnover of members than all other branches. Finally, the branches interviewed represented different 'national' make-ups. Although all branches are open to members of any nationality, the Italian and Romanian groups are mainly (but not exclusively) made up of local/national

Table 4.2 Summary of socio-demographic data collected through questionnaires at the focus group in London (pilot)

| Focus group | London (pilot) | |
Participant Code	LO1	LO2
Age Group	18–24	25–34
Male/Female	M	M
Occupation	Researcher	Employee
Nationality	Italian	British
Current Country of Residence	UK	UK
First Language	Italian	English
I Consider Myself:*	5	5

* Multiple options available 1 = A National Of My Country Only; 2 = European Only; 3 = Primarily National Then European; 4 = Primarily European Then National; 5 = Transnational; 6 = Other (Please Specify).

citizens whereas the UK groups show a much more nationally heterogeneous composition with the Cardiff group in particular being primarily made up of international students.

The issue of the language in which focus groups should be conducted was given careful consideration. As the focus groups were intended to recreate the genre of local group meetings the decision was taken to conduct focus groups in the language of the local meetings (e.g. Italian in Bologna, Romanian in Cluj and English in Cardiff). Due to the nature of the linguistic variety/composition of local groups this meant that for some participants the language of discussion was not their first language; however, this did not impede contributions to the discussion, since participants were working/studying in the local language in the respective settings.

A brief account of each discussion and details of participants in all focus groups are given below and also summarized in Tables 4.3, 4.4 and 4.5. Lead questions and interview protocol for these three focus groups and for individual interviews followed the same procedures described for the London pilot group.

4.2.1.2 Bologna (Italy) focus group

A call for participants was put out to members of the Bologna branch by sending an email to the local coordinator. Six people (two males and four females including the coordinator) agreed to take part in the focus group which was conducted at the local office of EA. Some of the participants had known each other for some time as they had been engaged in specific projects, activities or campaigns. All discussants were aged between twenty-five and thirty-four years, four were employed and two were students. Four were Italian nationals, one had a dual Italian and French citizenship, and one was originally Russian but had been living in Italy on a German passport for a few years. Most participants had experiences of living abroad. For most of them English was the best known second language followed by French, Spanish and German. In the questionnaire one participant described herself as 'Primarily National Then European', two as 'Primarily European Then National', two as 'transnational' and the Italian/ French citizen provided the self-description 'Primarily Italian Then French Then European'. The discussion was conducted in Italian which did not prove a problem for the Russian/German participant as her command of Italian was excellent. After some initial warming up by the moderator, the discussion took off easily with lively exchanges. Overall contributions were animated although well-balanced in terms of the time taken up by each discussant and I intervened once

Table 4.3 Summary of socio-demographic data collected through questionnaires at the focus group in Bologna

Focus Group			Bologna			
Participant Code	BO1	BO2	BO3	BO4	BO5	BO6
Age Group	25–34	25–34	25–34	25–34	25–34	25–34
Male/Female	F	F	M	F	F	M
Occupation	Journalist	Researcher	Student	Student	Employee	Employee
Nationality	Italian	Italian	Italian	German/Russian	Italian	Italian/French
Current Country of Residence	Italy	Italy	Italy	Germany	Italy	Italy
First Language	Italian	Italian	Italian	Russian	Italian	Italian
I Consider Myself:*	4	5	3	5	4	**

* (Multiple Options Available) 1 = A National Of My Country Only; 2 = European Only; 3 = Primarily National Then European; 4 = Primarily European Then National; 5 = Transnational; 6 = Other (Please Specify).
** Primarily Italian Then French Then European.

Table 4.4 Summary of socio-demographic data collected through questionnaires at the focus group in Cluj

Focus Group	CLUJ-NAPOCA					
Participant Code	CL1	CL2	CL3	CL4	CL5	CL6
Age Group	18–24	18–24	18–24	18–24	18–24	18–24
Male/Female	F	M	M	F	M	F
Occupation	Student	Unemployed	Employee	Student	NGO Coordinator	Youth Worker/Student
Nationality	Romanian	Hungarian	Romanian	Romanian	Romanian	Romanian
Current Country of Residence	Romania	Romania	Romania	Romania	Romania	Romania
First Language	Romanian	Hungarian	Romanian	Romanian	Romanian	Romanian
I consider myself*	5	5	3	Other**	5	3

* (Multiple Options Available) 1 = A National Of My Country Only; 2 = European Only; 3 = Primarily National Then European; 4 = Primarily European Then National;
5 = Transnational; 6 = Other (Please Specify).

** First Citizen Of My Own Town Then European Then Transnational.

Table 4.5 Summary of socio-demographic data collected through questionnaires at the focus group in Cardiff

Focus Group	Cardiff		
Participant Code	CA1	CA2	CA3
Age group	18–24	18–24	18–24
Male/Female	F	F	F
Occupation	Student	Student	Student
Nationality	Turkish	Romanian	British
Current Country Of Residence	UK	Wales	Wales
First Language	Turkish	Romanian	English
I Consider Myself:*	1/3/5	5	3

* (Multiple Options Available) 1 = A National Of My Country Only; 2 = European Only; 3 = Primarily National Then European; 4 = Primarily European Then National; 5 = Transnational; 6 = Other (Please Specify).

to refocus the discussion. A full summary of data collected via the questionnaire is given in Table 4.3.

4.2.1.3 Cluj-Napoca (Romania) focus group

The group was attended by three males and three females, all aged between eighteen and twenty-four and lasted one hour and twenty-four minutes. Two were students, one was unemployed and the others were in regular employment. All participants were Romanian nationals except one who was Hungarian by birth but had been living in Romania for most of his life. Four participants had been members since the group started while two had only recently joined the team. The discussion occurred in a friendly and jovial atmosphere with many exchanges between participants. Contributions were fairly equally shared in terms of turn taking, with possibly two of the males (CL2 and CL5) more willing to initiate the discussion. Like the Bologna group most discussants had had experience of living abroad. Overall French and English were the best known second languages among this cohort followed by Italian, German, Spanish, Greek and Russian. Three members defined themselves as Transnational, two as 'primarily national then European' and one as 'First citizen of my own town then European then transnational'.

4.2.1.4 Cardiff (UK) focus group

Cardiff represents a newer and smaller branch compared to the other TEN branches involved in the study. Members of this branch first convened in 2011 to work on a specific cultural project for the Trans Europa Festival called 'The human library'.[5] The project consisted of a representation of 'living books' (voiced by actors) which took place at the European School of European Languages, Translation and Politics at the University of Cardiff. Members of the group are primarily students of the School and have met fairly regularly since starting the project. Contact was made with the coordinator as per the previous groups. Three members participated in the focus group which I conducted on 22 April 2012 in a room of the Students' Union building at the University of Cardiff. The session lasted sixty-five minutes. The discussants were three female students, aged between eighteen and twenty-four years: one was a British national, one was Romanian and one was Turkish. All members had lived abroad before and had good knowledge of French (CA1, CA3) and Swedish (CA2). In the discussion, the Romanian member often took the lead and overall she tended to dominate the discussion. On a few occasions I tried to rebalance this dynamic by involving other participants (e.g. by explicitly asking them whether they agreed with her views in order to initiate their responses). The themes emerging from this focus group were clearly influenced by the interests of the participants in terms of culture and language although political issues were also gradually covered more extensively towards the end of the discussion. While in the questionnaire the Romanian member defined herself as 'Transnational' and the British member as 'Primarily national then European', the Turkish member chose three options as detailed in Table 4.5.

4.2.2 Data collected via individual interviews

A pilot interview was agreed through personal contact with the local coordinator of the Rome branch and conducted in the organization's office in Italy on 20 April 2011. The interviewee (coded RO1) was a twenty-eight-year-old male, originally born in Italy but educated in Canada and the UK. The discussion with RO1 was initially conducted as a semi-structured interview based, by and large, on the same questions originally designed to elicit the main topics in the focus groups (see Table 4.1). RO1, however, was very willing to discuss such topics at length and in several cases he took the opportunity to introduce secondary topics too, thus adding to the flow of the conversation. He, for example, wove a general discussion about European identity and transnationalism into specific themes related to the civil rights campaigns he coordinates within the organization (such as a project called People Power Participation and one for the equal recognition of LGBT rights across EU member states). Moreover, in many instances the interviewee took the opportunity to answer questions by introducing personal narratives and giving examples from his own life experiences. The interview format yielded a wealth of data and proved particularly apt to delve deeper on themes of interest that would have not been possible to discuss in the focus group. This format was therefore used for the subsequent individual interviews. Eighteen local coordinators and ordinary members were approached by email through contact details obtained through the organization. A total of eight members agreed to be interviewed (in addition to RO1 who took part in the pilot study). Details of these are provided in Table 4.6.

All the interviews were conducted over Skype, except the London member who was interviewed in a public location in central London. Skype interviews were recorded from screen amounting to a total of six hours and fifty-five minutes. The sound quality was so good overall that the remote interaction did not impinge on the flow of the discussion. The language of the interviews was negotiated in advance with my informants. Whenever possible – that is whenever more than one common language was shared between me and the interviewee – the latter was offered the choice. All interviews were thus conducted in English except the interview with one of the two Berlin members which took place in Italian. During and at the end of each interview notes were taken. At the end of each interview some socio-demographic data was collected using the same questionnaire used in the focus groups (see above). These results are reported in Table 4.7.

4.2.3 Data entextualization

All focus groups and interviews were transcribed using a transcription system loosely based on the HIAT conventions as explained in Appendix. All contributions were anonymized by using codes for speakers (as indicated in Tables 4.3, 4.4, 4.5, 4.6 and 4.7). All discussions and interviews conducted in languages other than English (i.e. in Italian and Romanian) were first transcribed in the original language and then translated into English. I provided the translation from Italian while RC provided the translation from Romanian. RC was also consulted to verify socio-pragmatic and cultural aspects of the text.

4.3 Analytical framework

Although the linguistic analysis within the DHA has been applied in slightly different ways (see, for example, Wodak et al. 1999, Wodak 2003, 2009, Krzyżanowski 2010),[6] by and large it consists of: (a) a thematic (or entry-level) analysis concerned with the content, or discursive topics and (b) an in-depth

Table 4.6 Details of individual interviews

Code	Date	(1)	Member's affiliation	Role	Language	(2)
RO1	20/4/10	F	Rome (pilot) – Italy	Group Coordinator	English*	36'
AM1	9/2/13	S	Amsterdam – The Netherlands	Group joint coordinator	English	80'
BE1	16/2/13	S	Berlin – Germany	Group coordinator	English	52'
BE2	8/2/13	S	Berlin – Germany	Artistic coordinator	Italian	41'
LO3	18/1/13	F	London – UK	Member	English	45'
PR1	24/1/13	S	Prague – Czech Republic	Group Coordinator	English	65'
PR2	27/1/13	S	Prague – Czech Republic	Member	English	42'
SO1	21/1/13	S	Sofia – Bulgaria	Group coordinator	English	61'
VA1	24/1/13	S	Valencia – Spain	Group coordinator	English°	56'

* instances of code-switching in Italian occurred on both sides
° instances of code-switching in Spanish occurred on both sides
(1) F = Interview conducted face to face; S = Interview conducted over Skype
(2) Duration in minutes

Table 4.7 Summary of socio-demographic data collected through questionnaires at individual interviews

Interview Location	Rome – Italy	Berlin – Germany	Berlin – Germany	London – UK	Prague– Czech Republic	Prague – Czech Republic	Sofia – Bulgaria	Valencia – Spain	Amsterdam – The Netherlands
Participant Code	RO1	BE1	BE2	LO3	PR1	PR2	SO1	VA1	AM1
Age Group	25–34	25–34	35+	25–34	25–34	25–34	25–34	25–34	25–34
Male/Female	F	F	M	F	F	F	M	F	F
Occupation	NGO Worker	Unemployed	Cultural Manager	Student	Human Right officer	Admin/ education sector	PhD Student	Journalist	Temp clerk
Nationality	Italian	German	Italian	British	French	American	Bulgarian	Spanish	Dutch
Current Country of Residence	Italy/UK	Germany	Germany	UK	Czech Republic	Czech Republic	Slovenia	Spain	The Netherlands
First Language	Bilingual Italian/ English	German	Italian	English	French	English	Bulgarian	Spanish	Dutch
I Consider Myself:*	4	5	5	4	2/5	1/5	5	5	3/5

(Multiple Options Available) 1 = A National Of My Country Only; 2 = European Only; 3 = Primarily National Then European; 4 = Primarily European Then National; 5 = Transnational; 6 = Other (Please Specify)

Table 4.8 Levels of linguistic analysis. Adapted from Wodak et al. (2009) and Krzyżanowski (2010)

Thematic analysis	Identification of discourse topics, macro semantic propositions and interdiscursive/intertextual relations; identification of keywords and frequent clusters, their collocation and concordance via corpus analysis
In-depth analysis	Identification of main argumentative strategies *Topoi* used to support strategy Identification of means of linguistic realization including Deictic positioning, metaphor, synecdoche, metonymy, trope, membership categorization devices, passivization, other lexical/syntactic and para-verbal elements

analysis aiming to investigate (i) discursive strategies, (ii) topoi and (iii) their means and forms of realization.[7] This model is summarized in Table 4.8 and will be explained below.

4.3.1 Thematic analysis

A thematic analysis or entry-level examination of the data was initially run to map out the content of all transcripts. First, transcripts were read several times to enter the so-called hermeneutic circle (Ezzy 2013). Second, transcripts were coded to achieve a taxonomy of themes and 'nodes' by using Hyper Research software. The main purpose of this analysis was to ascribe topics to categories of discourse and to conflate macro-propositions, themes and sub-themes (Krzyżanowski 2010). Moreover the thematic analysis was used to demarcate the 'boundaries' of discourses and to subsequently help identify 'nodes' as interdiscursive and intertextual relationships (Fairclough 2003). The definition of key discursive topics was achieved both inductively and deductively. Topics were thus organized taking into consideration the 'primary' themes introduced at the focus groups and individual interviews (which in turn were partly based on the literature reviewed, the specific EA organizational literature and the pilot studies conducted). At the same time, topic categories were derived from specific 'secondary' topics brought into the discussion by members and related to discourses specific to the branch or individual(s) interviewed. Results of this topics analysis are presented in Figures 5.1 and 5.2 in Chapter 5, as they are discussed in relation to two distinct dimensions of production.

Furthermore, in combination with the above examination of topics, a basic analysis of all transcripts[8] was conducted via AntConc software (Anthony 2012) to obtain some statistical data on the frequency and use of lexical patterns and linguistic items that could help develop further qualitative insights. Although Corpus Linguistics and CDA are informed by distinct theoretical frameworks, the synergic benefits of combining the two have been explored and encouraged by a large literature; see, for example, Mautner (2007), Baker et al. (2008). In agreement with this body of work, this study has integrated the DHA analytical framework (which in fact is open to mixed analytical approaches) with corpus analysis to compensate some of the potential limitations associated with CDA, primarily the issue of the researcher's subjectivity (see discussion in Section 4.4). It must be emphasized, however, that the results from the corpus analysis were used to supplement and not to substitute the discursive analytical approach advocated by the DHA. The quantitative findings therefore have always been interpreted taking into account different levels of contextualization, (as discussed on p. 20), especially the socio-historical background.

In particular, the corpus analysis consisted of a statistical search to identify the most frequent lemmas or clusters of words in the transcripts, their concordance and collocation (Sinclair 1991, Stubbs 1996). The concordance tool 'KWIC' was used to determine the occurrence of keywords in a context of ten words (five occurring on the left and five on the right) and to identify their semantic and pragmatic use. The collocation tool was used to identify the most frequent left and right collocates of the keywords. Results from this search were used to supplement the qualitative analysis in two main ways. They helped focus on the use of certain keywords (such as the noun *Europe* and the adjective *European*) which were used as 'entry points' to guide the subsequent 'in-depth' analysis (e.g. orienting the investigation towards how members articulated their definition of Europe as a social/political space and a community and how they attributed Europeanness). Moreover results were used in the 'in-depth' analysis for triangulation purposes to support the data interpretations (see, for example, Section 6.3 in Chapter 6 for the role of spatial deictics in the definition of the metaphorical scenario of *spatial dynamics*). To reflect this flexible use, results of the corpus analysis have been presented throughout the analysis of strategies and linguistic realizations (see pp. 75–154) rather than a stand-alone section.

4.3.2 'In-depth' analysis

The 'in-depth' (or argumentation-oriented) analysis of the data evaluated members' statements as logical propositions, in relation to the enunciative positioning and orientation of the speakers and in their intertextual relation with other topics. Moreover the analysis was aimed at investigating the discursive strategies deployed by the speakers. In line with Wodak and Meyer (2009) the analysis treated discursive strategies as 'a more or less intentional plan of practices … adopted to achieve a particular social, political, psychological or linguistic goal' (p. 94).[9] For example, Wodak et al. (2009, p. 33) regard constructive strategies as

> attempt[s] to construct and establish a certain national identity by promoting unification, identification and solidarity, as well as differentiation

achieved, for instance, through arguments of comparison. As Wodak et al. (2009) suggest, however, the use of strategies is often context-dependent and

> although analytically distinguishable from one another, … strategies occur more or less simultaneously and are interwoven in concrete discursive acts.

Consequently, in this study, a taxonomy of strategies was not assumed *a priori* but approached critically, allowing for specific (sub)categories to emerge. As a general principle, however, the analysis of strategies has been oriented towards the heuristic objectives of defining how social actors, objects, phenomena, events, processes and actions were constructed, represented, qualified and positioned in discourse as these were identified as key conceptual aspects as discussed in the theoretical framework (see above). The analysis of strategies therefore was specifically interested in qualities and features that members attributed to Europe/Europeans, from what stances members expressed their arguments, how they articulated and negotiated their different affiliations, attachments, belongings and membership, and finally how political agency was constructed and political actors represented. In this respect, therefore, the analysis has followed the general approach of DHA framework, although adapting it to the specific nature of the data and in the light of the literature revised.

Furthermore, adhering to Wodak et al.'s (2009) model, the analysis of strategies was guided by *topoi* – that is standardized argumentation schemes usually deployed to support strategies, to validate claims and to discursively connect an argument to another to eventually justify a finality. In classical rhetoric[10] *topoi* (Latin *loci*, or 'common places') operate as warrants or implicit premises to the validity of an argument.[11] For example, the statement 'the last Government made a mess of our economy, we cannot afford to let them run the country again' relies on the topos of analogy/likelihood that assumes that an actor is likely to do more of the same in a similar situation. In accordance with Krzyżanowski (2010), as well as universal topics (in the Aristotelian sense) the analysis was also concerned with identifying context-dependent and genre-dependent topoi.[12] The unpacking of this specific 'discourse-pragmatic aspect' (Krzyżanowski 2010, p. 85) of topoi was achieved by interpretive work and via multilevel contextualization (see above), for example, referring to socially or historically shared cognitive frames invoked indexically by participants and/or in relation to the NGO activities. Similar to strategies, a taxonomy of topoi was not predefined, but it was allowed to emerge from the analysis of argumentation schemes. This is reflected in the presentation of results where examples were chosen for their representativeness of one or more strategies or topoi.

4.3.2.1 Micro linguistic analysis

Finally, at the micro linguistic level the analysis identified those linguistic elements which linked utterances with *topoi* and functionally supported strategies. These can include a variety of figurative language and rhetorical tropes (such as metaphors, synecdoche and metonymies); syntactic structures, such as transitive/intransitive, active/passive forms (as these allow for the foregrounding/back grounding of agency); deictic features and other para-verbal features.

With regard to the specific linguistic features studied: figurative language is the use of language whereby one word (or phrase) stands in for another to imply a relationship of similarity. Metonymy refers to the substitution of a word by one of its attributes ('the crown' to refer to a monarch or their properties), while synecdoche substitutes a part for the whole ('wheels' for a car). Another type of metonymic substitution is objectification, in which actors are substituted with a place or organization with which they are associated (Van Leeuwen 1996) (e.g. 'Brussels' for the EU organs), whereas by the process of anthropomorphization an object is given human features as in the expression 'the voice of America'. In the interpretation of socially functional aspects of metaphorical expressions, the analysis has relied on the main tenets of cognitive semantics (cf. Lakoff and Johnson 1980, Fauconnier and Turner 2003, Charteris-Black 2004), for example, on the notions of 'mapping' of 'target' and 'source' domains whereby actors and events are conceptualized and explained in terms of familiar physical and psychological experiences (Lakoff and Johnson 1980). In this light, for example, a common cognitive metaphor of 'Europe is a house' (see, for example, Chilton and Lakoff 1995) entails an understanding of Europe as a construction – that is a physical entity characterized by walls, doors and the like as well as cognitive social implications of sharing with family, dealing with neighbours and so on.

Moreover the analysis has also drawn on Musolff's (2004) concept of 'scenarios' or metaphorical mini-narratives characterized by

> a set of assumptions made by competent members of a discourse community about 'typical' aspects of a source-situation [and the roles of their participants]. (p. 28)

As Musolff has pointed out specific narratives may become common currency in the way we speak about certain subjects and in how we understand certain affairs or processes. Moreover, from a critical perspective, narratives reproduce the selective representations of reality entailed by the source domains, so that, for example, discussing immigration in terms of 'flooding' is likely to reflect (and influence) a negative ideological stance on the subject of people's mobility for its associations with 'destruction', 'catastrophe' and so on.

In this context, for instance, one could recognize different narratives of the European expansion and integration circulated and reproduced in the media and in public discourse over the last two decades. Notably these have included the 'project' and the 'construction' of a 'European house' which sustained discussions of the EU enlargement as 'opening the door to new members' or, in the case of Turkey's application for membership as 'knocking at the EU's door' (Musolff 2012).[13] From a pragmatic perspective, therefore, metaphorical expressions such as the one illustrated above, can act as warrants in argumentation schemes (van Eemeren and Grootendorst 1992) and in some cases they can drive the whole discourse of European integration. Thus, crucially, semantic shifts, can give us insights into related social and political changes.

Deictic words or indexical expressions represent another important linguistic device that was taken into account in the analysis. Indexicality refers to the property of certain elements of language (called deictics) of 'pointing' to meanings like we would physically point our finger to objects (as index is in fact the Latin word for finger). Deictics, more than other words, encode 'the relation between objects and contexts' (Hanks 1999, p. 124) as they can only be interpreted in relation to specific referents or situations. In a narrow sense, pronouns such as *I*, *she*, demonstratives such as *this*, *that*, and adverbs such as *here* and *now* always exist in dual indexical forms (Kaplan 1979) or, in other words, as 'types' with semantic meaning and 'tokens' with denotational meaning. Such deictic terms can only be endowed with meanings if interpreted in relation to specific situations. Interpretation of deictics must therefore be processed on contextual clues which, in turn, can rely on the physical context or draw on social and cultural frames encoded in the hearer's interpretation (Gumperz and

Levinson 1996). In broader terms, therefore, indexicality can be interpreted as 'the pervasive context-dependency of natural language utterances' (Hanks 1999, p. 124) and it can be realized in discourse through different other means. While, for example, a regional accent can index a speaker's identity (Johnstone 2013), this can generate different orders of indexicalities (Silverstein 2003) if an ideological evaluation is associated with a social connotation (i.e. if the regional accent is associated with a specific social practice which then comes to be regarded as an index of 'authenticity'). Furthermore, indexicality can be realized, through specific perspectivization of a message (Renkema 2004), by means of labels, implicatures and epistemic orientations (Bucholtz and Hall 2005) which can reveal the speaker's stance towards 'objects' (e.g. a topic, a person or a relationship).

Chilton (2004) highlights how positioning and indexical anchoring is typically realized along temporal, spatial, personal, and ideological dimensions. For Chilton through deictic expressions speakers can metaphorically construct a 'deictic centre' that defines their ontological orientation to the world and their relationship with society. Indexical anchoring and positioning vis-à-vis the 'deictic centre' can ultimately be interpreted as the speaker's representation of their social identity through time, space and personal relations, i.e. their 'situatedness' (as represented in Table 4.4). For example, as noted earlier, the use of personal pronouns *we*, *us* and the possessive adjective *our* can signal (dis)alignment with one particular group identity. At the same time, as they index inclusion/exclusion, personal deictics can point to a cognitive frame that encodes a 'conventional shared understandings about the structure of society, groups and relations with other societies' (Chilton 2004, p. 56). Likewise, temporal deictic expressions such as 'after the fall of the Berlin Wall' can be understood in terms of a particular historical frame involving wider ideologies beyond the temporal event itself, such as the change of Communist regimes in Eastern Europe. Similar considerations apply to spatial representations where, for example, the adverb *here* and the demonstrative *this country* can symbolically embody a frame entertained by the speaker about geopolitical relations rather than simply proximity. For Chilton (2004), therefore, deictic expressions are salient elements of language that can be instrumentally deployed in political language in the construction of, inter alia, group boundaries and geopolitical spaces.

Building on the above considerations the analysis of deictics has been concerned with: (a) identifying and interpreting indexical expressions that could point to different frames of how members conceived social spaces; and (b) developing insights on how such conceptualizations contributed to members' identification

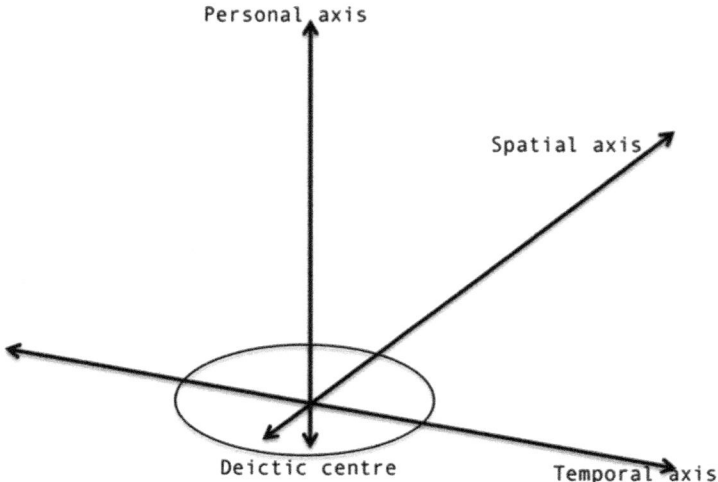

Figure 4.1 A representation of spatial, temporal and personal dimensions constructing a deictic centre. Adapted from Chilton 2004, p. 58.

as European. Decoding the indexical 'value' of certain utterances and linguistic items was achieved via contextual cues and operationalized at different levels of context as proposed by Wodak (2009) and explained in detail on p. 20. For example, the analysis has interpreted the indexicality of *now* in expressions such as 'let's have a break now', 'now, this is the issue!' or 'it's difficult to get a job anywhere in Europe now' on different contextual cues and it has consequently derived different insights into the temporal positioning of the speaker.

Drawing from social psychological (Potter et al. 1987, Harré and van Lagenhove 1999, Davies and Harré 2001) and sociocultural perspectives (Bucholtz and Hall 2005) of language use, this framework therefore appropriates the convenient notion of positioning as an ideological location adopted by speakers in discourse. It thus assumes that discourses and narratives enable the speaker to position themselves (reflective positioning) and the others (interactive positioning) within the social space. As expounded by Davies and Harré' (2001, p. 262):

> The words the speaker chooses inevitably contain images and metaphors which both assume and invoke the ways of being that the participants take themselves to be involved ... Once having taken up a particular position as one's own, a person inevitably sees the world from the vantage point of that position and in terms of the particular images, metaphors, storylines and concepts which are made relevant within the particular discursive practice in which they are positioned.

4.4 Reflections on the analytical framework

It is recognized that the main potential limitation of the analytical framework adopted in this study is the general issue of subjectivity associated with interpretivism. In CDA approaches, as analytical work is highly dependent on the hermeneutic work of the analyst (especially that of reconciling macro with micro dimensions) impartiality may be impinged upon by what some critics of CDA see as an overt political agenda for social change or methodological weaknesses/inconsistencies (Widdowson 1995, Toolan 2002, Jones 2007, Breeze 2011). Such an issue has been addressed as accurately as possible through triangulation with different theoretical approaches and multilevel contextualization; however, this analytical framework subscribes to the poststructuralist view that humans cannot escape structures in order to analyse them (Laclau and Mouffe 2006) and that 'the right interpretation does not exist' (Wodak and Ludwig 1999) because it is mediated by and depends on the background knowledge of speakers and hearers. Consequently, on the basis that '[CDA] does not pretend to be able to assume an objective, socially neutral analytical stance' (Wodak et al. 2009, p. 8), this study makes no claim that findings are generalizable nor entirely free from analyst bias and the limitations of academic discourse as a particular form of social reality which is co-constructed by the researcher.

Results

5.1 Introduction

This chapter presents and discusses the results following the DHA multilevel format used for the analysis (see Table 4.8). The 'thematic analysis' (Section 5.2) offers an overview of key topics; it outlines the boundaries of members' discourses and discusses interdiscursive relations between identity, transnationalism and Europe as they emerged in focus groups and individual interviews. The 'in-depth' analysis (Section 5.3) discusses macro- and micro-strategies, patterns of argumentation and topoi as well as the use of linguistic devices and other linguistic features in representations and constructions of Europeanness. Consistent with the methodological approach that seeks to distance itself from taken-for-granted national categorizations, the results of the data analysis in the next sections are presented at a transnational level rather than by group or branch. This means that while the nationality of participants and the geographical location of interview(ee)s have been taken into account as one of the contextual variables through which discourses were produced (as per model discussed in Figure 1.2), the interplay of nationhood is discussed together with other socio-demographic and contextual variables across 'thematic' and 'in-depth' analyses. Finally, in Section 6 results are consolidated and further discussed in the light of the research aims and to address the research questions.

5.2 Thematic analysis

5.2.1 Preliminary overview of topics and interdiscursive dimensions of European identities

A large number of topics emerged from the content analysis which will be introduced in this section and further discussed in the next section in relation to strategies, topoi and specific linguistic realizations. Prior to the examination of such topics, however, two main discursive dimensions or contexts through which members produced Europeanness during the discussion will be outlined in this section. The first dimension (illustrated in Figure 1.1) refers to members' discussion of 'primary' topics, that is, topics directly related to (European) identity. In this dimension, some members engaged in meta-discussions of identity; they (de)constructed and negotiated meanings, contents and processes of identifications and, by and large, their discourses were concerned with their *identification as Europeans*. The second dimension of 'production' of Europeanness refers to discursive contexts in which, although not invoked directly, meanings of 'being European' were constructed, transformed and challenged by members in relation to a wider variety of 'secondary' topics related to Europe and transnationalism as 'nodal points' (see Figure 5.2). This dimension primarily relates to members' *identification with Europe or with European referents*.

5.2.1.1 First dimension of production of Europeanness

Typically, although not exclusively, the discussion of 'identity' topics occurred in response to the prompt 'do you feel/describe/think of yourself as European' and resulted in members orienting towards two main strategic directions. On the one hand, a significant number of members engaged with meta-definitions of identity, problematizing and critically deconstructing the notion of (European) identity(ies) as will be discussed in the next sections. On the other hand, members were generally concerned with constructing/recognizing themselves as Europeans via explicit claims of belonging, and feelings of connection. This positioning was primarily enacted from personal stances and achieved through accounts and narratives aimed at highlighting either contents or processes of their Europeanness, that is either European elements/traits to justify their positioning or ways in which they felt Europeans. In most cases, members realized their constructions of Europeanness via the following: the invocation of *topoi of interactional experiences*; historical, family, and cultural connections to European referents; and/or the articulation of *relationality* (see p. 20) of their Europeanness vis-à-vis 'other' identities (see below). Most often, therefore, this involved a further negotiation of Europeanness with multiple belongings such as one's city, region and nationhood, as it will be further discussed in the 'in-depth' analysis.

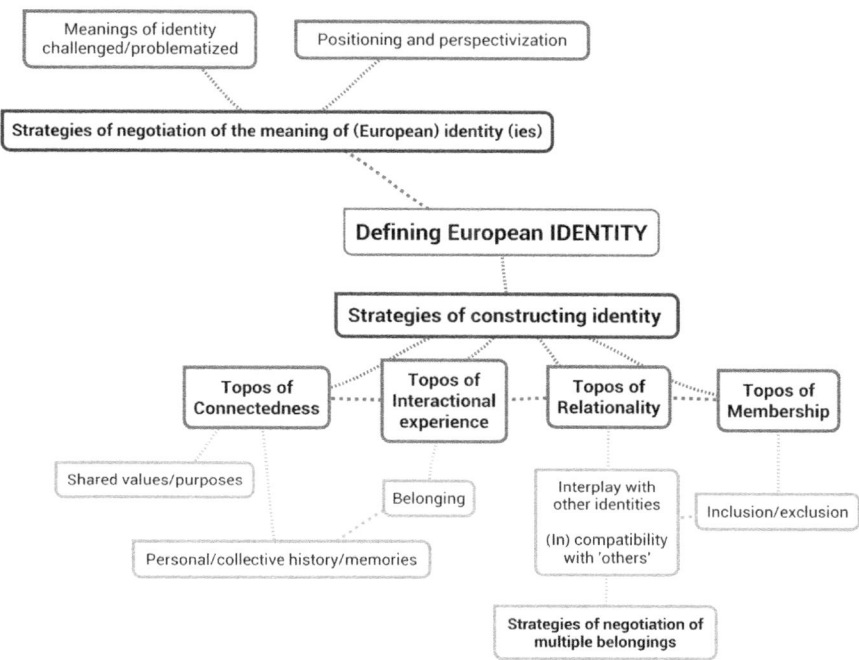

Figure 5.1 A representation of the construction of Europeanness in relation to identity topics.

5.2.1.2 Second dimension of production of Europeanness

As mentioned above, a second dimension of production of Europeanness emerged from the data in which meanings of 'being European' were constructed, transformed and challenged by members in relation to a variety of topics that have been collapsed into the nodal point 'Europe'. Such topics have been summarized in Figure 5.2 in relation to their pertinence to distinct organizational, geographic, cultural, social, economic, and political dimensions of transnationalism (as outlined in the theoretical discussion in Sections 2.4 and 3.2). In many instances, however, topics straddled across different discursive domains; for example, the topic of migration emerged frequently in discourses of global economic flows, cultural encounters, intra-EU mobility, citizenship rights, civic participation as well as social inclusion and exclusion. In these cases, such multiple relations have been represented in the diagram by 'connecting lines'. Within this second dimension of production of Europeanness two strategic orientations were also noticeable: one aimed at the dismantling of nationhood, and the other aimed at the discursive construction of European/transnational communities, spaces and social orders.

In both orientations, transnationalism – interpreted as both a de facto system of cross-border social practices and as an *ideal* sociocultural scenario – represented an overarching frame for members' discussion of European themes without necessarily being claimed as an identity per se (other than being chosen as a self-ascription option in the questionnaire, see below). Through the discussion of 'nodal' themes, members generally tended to represent Europe as a social and political transnational project of the civil society and an open space of intercultural and political debate. Hence, civic frames (e.g. citizenship, solidarity) as well as cultural and historical ones – for example, (re)defining the role of Europe in a changed 'global' topography – clearly represented salient referents for members in their definition of being part of a wider European and transnational community. Most interviewees, thus, achieved representations of their Europeanness as members of an 'expanded' community through meta-narratives of *spatiality* and *progress* (as will be discussed further throughout the analysis). Similarly, in the dismantling of nationhood, transnationalism represented an overarching frame for member's understanding of their activities in a larger remit of global interaction and social transformation against which they generally problematized and deconstructed the meanings of 'national' structures. In these cases, transnationalism was, for example, constructed in discourse as the antithesis of internationalism and intergovernmentalism which were, instead, portrayed as typical top-down and 'mass' understandings of society as 'contained' in and regulated between nations. In most instances, European identity was thus indexed to ideal scenarios of reconfigured social orders some of which related to cosmopolitan and 'global democracy' as it is further explained in the 'in-depth' analysis section below.

5.2.1.3 *Attribution of Europeanness: Usage of the term 'European'*

The two dimensions of production discussed above were also characterized by distinctive patterns of the usage of the term 'European', which, from the corpus analysis conducted, emerged as the second most frequently occurring lemma in the corpus (see Table 5.1). Investigation carried out on the distribution, collocation and concordance of *European* (see Table 5.2) showed that the first dimension of production was characterized by members using the term 'European' as a predicate or as a nominal adjective. As a predicate, European was typically self-attributed as a feeling, a condition and a cognitive process and realized through statements such as 'I feel/am/consider myself European'. In addition, the term 'European' was also used in the attributive form as a nominal adjective as, for example, in the expression 'Europeans have learnt from their history'.

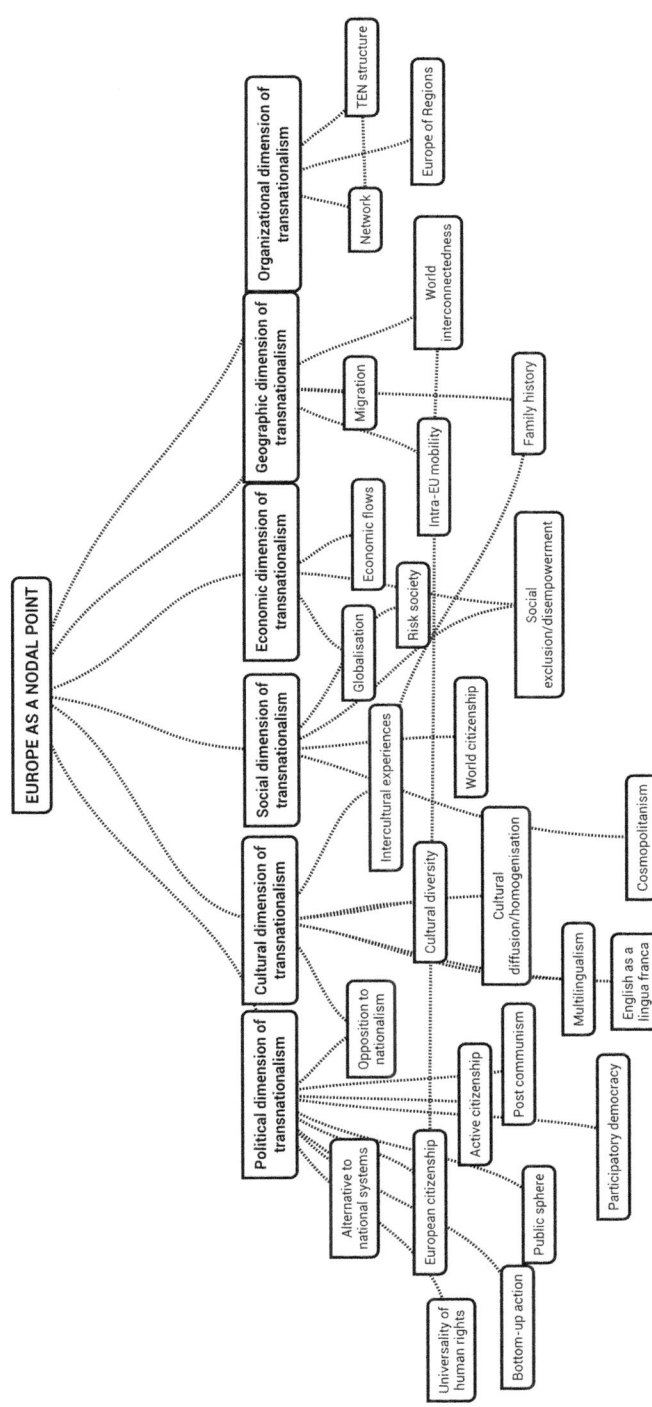

Figure 5.2 'Secondary' topics and their orientation to transnationalism.

Table 5.1 Most frequent lexical items in the corpus by main grammatical categories. Total types analysed: 4083; total tokens analysed: 74852 (Minimum occurrence = 50)*

I (1)	Adjectives	I	Nouns (2)	I	Verbs (2)	I	Deictics (3)
382	European	455	People	2866	be	3118	I
206	English	291	Europe	748	know	1656	it
166	different	277	Thing	705	have	1363	you
101	high	154	Idea	664	think	703	this
98	national	152	Way	439	can	580	we
96	French	148	Kind	359	do	500	they
76	Italian	148	language	331	will	231	my
74	common	109	country	237	say	213	me
74	good	104	example	215	mean	121	these
67	first	93	identity	158	go	116	your
62	political	91	nation	143	see	111	them
61	transnational	89	Sort	133	get	108	their
57	important	88	level	130	work	101	here
57	Romanian	85	EU	125	speak	82	he
54	interesting	84	country	121	want	70	our
50	cultural	70	world	107	feel	54	us
		69	sense	91	shall		
		69	Term	85	learn		
		65	point	67	make		
		64	culture	62	need		
		64	problem	62	understand		
		63	question	58	come		
		61	Time	52	talk		
		57	State	51	live		
		53	Transnationalism	50	find		
		52	Year	50	let		

(1) I indicates the number of instances the term occurred in the text (2) By lemma (3) Deictics include possessive adjectives, personal and demonstrative pronouns and adverbs.

* Lexical items *the, and, to, of, a, in*, which featured as the second, third, fourth, seventh, eighth and ninth most frequent items (respectively) were excluded from the table.

In the second dimension of production the adjective European was typically, but not exclusively, used by members in denominal forms (i.e. derived from or defining the term 'Europe') and differently attributed to various aspects/elements of an ideal sociopolitical system (e.g. 'build a European space of democracy' or 'decisions taken at a European level'). In this second dimension the term 'European' appeared frequently in the noun phrases 'European Alternatives', 'European Union' and 'European Movement'[1] as well as a qualifier of 'citizens' and 'countries'. To a lesser degree, the adjective 'European' was also used by members as a hypernymic qualifier to collectively refer to different varieties of languages and cultures in the continent of Europe. The different patterns of usage of the term 'European' across the two dimensions will be elaborated further below in relation to the analysis of strategies and topoi.

Table 5.2 A list of the most frequent left and right collocates of the term 'European'

Most frequent right collocates occurring with 'European'		Most frequent left collocates occurring with 'European'	
48	European Alternatives	17	feel European
32	European Union	12	as European
16	European identity	8	be European
16	European Movement	7	being European
16	European citizen(s)	6	are European
11	European institution(s)	5	all European
10	European countries	4	is European
9	European Parliament	4	more European
9	European culture(s)	4	very European
5	European Commission	3	Eastern European
8	European language(s)	3	not European
7	European people(s)	3	some Europeans
4	European level	3	what European
4	European policy	3	young European
3	European discourse	3	the Europeans
3	European festival	3	am European
3	European history	2	called European
3	European issues	2	pro-European
3	European thing	2	yourself European
2	European anthem	1	absolutely European
2	European border	1	both European
2	European elections	1	Central European
2	European project	1	classic European
		1	common European

5.3 In-depth analysis

5.3.1 Strategies, topoi and linguistic realizations

As discussed in the previous section, members appeared generally oriented towards the following *macro-discursive strategies*:

1. **the definition of (European)identity**, which in turn was articulated via micro-strategies of
   - negotiation and problematization of the 'meaning' of (European) identity,
   - construction of 'contents' of Europeanness and representation of 'processes' of identification with Europe (i.e. which elements make one European and how those elements are recognized),
   - negotiation of Europeanness vis-à-vis other identities (e.g. local, national, etc.);

2. **the dismantling of nationhood**, articulated via micro-strategies of
   - deconstruction,
   - problematization,
   - delegitimization of national structures;

3. **the construction and transformation of communities**, articulated via micro-strategies of
   - deterritorialization,
   - 'scaling up' of solidarity,
   - transportability of civic engagement,
   - decoupling of linguistic and civic identities.

A table summarizing macro- and micro-strategies, topoi and linguistic realizations has been provided (see Table 5.3 below). It must be stressed, however, that different topoi were sometimes used by members across dimensions to achieve different strategies. For example the *topos of connectedness* was used by several members to achieve representations of a linked community through tropes of bonding and ties (see below) while, at the same time, representations of the open and unbounded nature of modern societies represented a warrant for problematizing and delegitimizing nationhood and national structures. Consequently, at a macro-level, members were often able to dismantle existing spaces while reconstructing new ones and to position themselves in such new spaces redefining their relationality vis-à-vis (new) 'others'. For this reason, although presented separately as convenient categories, distinct dimensions, strategies and topoi should be interpreted in their dynamic interplay as mutually constitutive components of an overall discursive process of transnationalization (as illustrated by 5.3).

5.3.1.1 *On the distribution of strategies and topoi*

By and large, strategies and topoi were equally distributed across individual interviews although most discourses were clearly driven by the specificity of certain narratives related, for instance, to members' personal experiences of mobility or to their involvement with specific organizational projects. These aspects have been highlighted in the in-depth analysis of strategies and topoi discussed below. A few notable patterns also emerged in the group discussions. Members of the Romanian group, for example, conspicuously realized more strategies of legitimization than other members in the construction of their Europeanness, and themes of emancipation and marginalization drove a large

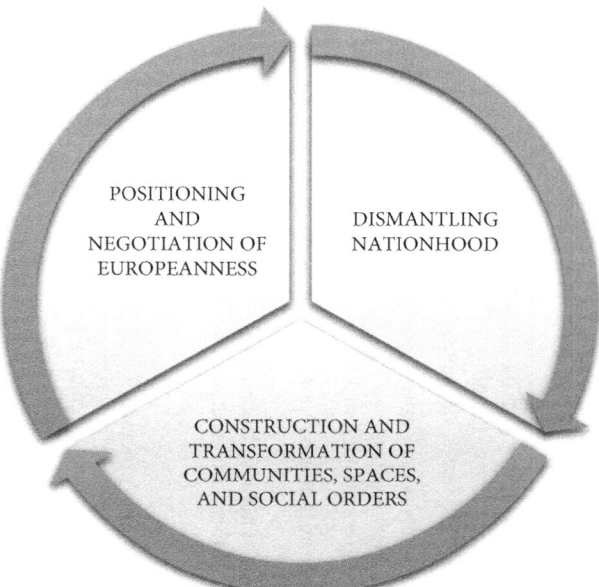

Figure 5.3 A model of how European identity is discursively constructed and transformed from a transnational perspective.

part of the Cluj discussion. By contrast, members of the Bologna group appeared oriented towards deploying more cultural and historical topoi than others in their definition of community. The UK focus groups showed mixed patterns as both the London and the Cardiff discussions appeared focused, on the one hand, on specific branch-related projects and campaigns while, on the other hand, different strategies of construction, deconstruction and transformation were primarily achieved through personal narratives. These idiosyncratic realizations are discussed in the analysis and further interpretive considerations have been made in the discussion (Section 6).

5.3.2 Macro-strategies of defining European identity

5.3.2.1 Strategies of negotiating the meaning of (European) identities

In most cases the question 'Do you consider/define/describe yourself (as) European?' represented the typical entry point to the discussion on identity and the trigger for further elaborations. While most members used this entry point for claiming their identities, the initial concern of some members was to raise issues on the problematic meaning of identities or, in general, to distance

Table 5.3 A summary of macro-/micro-strategies, topoi and linguistic realizations

	Macro-strategies of defining European identity	
	1.a Strategies of negotiating the meaning of (European) identity(ies)	
Micro-strategies	**Topoi**	**Linguistic realizations**
Problematizing/dismissing the meaning of identity(ies); avoiding 'fixed' meanings	Topos of non-categorization Topos of 'thinking European' vs. 'being European'	Dismissive interjections (e.g. Italian *boh*) Hedging (I don't know; 'I'm not sure'), mitigating particles (perhaps) Periphrasis; vagueness; deferral; reversing questions
Perspectivization	Topos of transnational perspective	Verbs and nouns semantically related to vision and location (to see, point of view, perspective, etc.) Spatial metaphor (inside/outside)
Deconstructing/Relativizing the meaning of European identity	Topos of multiple signified/signifiers Topos of Western/Eastern relationality (exclusion/inclusion) Topos of the economic rationales for EU membership	Use of the term 'European' as a predicate and as a denominal adjective Anadiplosis of negative labels Metaphor of the EU as an organic body
	1.b Strategies of representing identity 'contents' and 'processes'	
Strategies of assimilation/ dissimilation	Topos of difference Topos of interactional experience Topos of empathy Topos of culture and history Topos of democracy	Spatial adverbs to indicate cultural proximity/affinity Listing differences and similarities Trope of the 'old world'; metaphor of decline Interpersonal deictics Trope of 'common ground' and 'heritage' Metaphor of 'lessons from history'
Strategies of representing identity formation as an open process	Topos of interactional experience Topos of relationality	Arguments of causality Counterfactual conditional statements

Strategies of representing (inter)connectedness	Topos of family history Topos of network Topos of cross-border experiences'	Metaphor of historical journey ('where one comes from') Para-verbal features showing emotional involvement; Tropes of ties, links, nodes, and connections Metaphor of mapping
Strategies of representing 'in-betweenness'	Topoi of attachment and belonging	Temporal and spatial deictics Expression of uncertainty
Strategies of legitimization	Topos of membership Topos of equality	Metaphor of slavery for emancipation from communism Temporal deictics

1.c Strategies of negotiating multiple affiliations

Strategies of representing mutual compatibility between diverse belongings	Topos of expansion of community Topos of (positive) in-betweenness Topos of multiculturalism Topos of context dependency	Hypernymic/hyponymic implicatures Multilevel representations Arguments of analogy
Strategies of representing difficult or conflictual European/national identities	Topos of insularity/'Britain on the edge' Topos of Turkey straddling across continents Topos of transformation of identities	Inconsistent use of interpersonal deictics Simultaneous inclusiveness/exclusiveness Lexical choices ('alternative')
Strategies of 'otherising' nationality and bypassing national identification	Topos of history Topos of supranational allegiance	Exclusive/antagonistic deictics
Strategies of rearranging hierarchy and relativizing 'core/periphery'	Topos of network and 'interconnectedness'	Metaphor of mapping and 'direct' connections

(Continued)

Table 5.3 (*Continued*)

Macro-strategies of dismantling nationhood		
Micro-strategies	**Topoi**	**Linguistic realizations**
Deconstructing the reproduction of nationality	Topos of historical nationalism Topos of honesty	Agentivization and personification of nations as negative actors; statements of rejection ('I can't do it')
Problematizing/deconstructing national structures	Topos of artificiality Topos of 'natural process of disintegration' Topos of world citizenship Topos of (transnational) flows	Metonymy of border for state hegemony Biological metaphors (life, evolution, decay) Metaphor of container – Trope of 'box' – spatial representations of inside/outside Trope of 'obstacles'
Delegitimizing 'national' responses	Topos of global risk/action Topos of inadequacy	Agentivization and antagonization of states and 'global' actors

Macro-strategies of construction and transformation of communities, spaces and social orders		
Micro-strategies	**Topoi**	**Linguistic realizations**
Strategies of unification and enlargement of community	Topos of network Topos of imagination Topos of shared ideas	Spatial and temporal representations of 'connection' and 'expansion' Agentivization and personification of NGO Botanical metaphor of 'rhizome' Metaphor of mapping – tropes of *schaal* and 'new frontier'

Strategies of 'deterritorialization' of Europe and of 'transportability' of civic engagement	Topos of Utopia Topos of (transnational) active citizenship Topos of 'constitutional patriotism'	Metaphor of 'journey to Utopia' Metaphorization of the term 'European space' Use of rhetorical terms such as 'patriotism' and phrases for example, 'my own country/people' [possessive forms]
Strategy of constructing new forms of democratic community	Topos of experiment Topos of democratic dialogue Topos of values/ideals Topos of diversity Topos of solidarity Topos of history Topos of danger	Metaphor: Europe as a 'lab' Metonymy of 'voice' for citizens Analogy Inclusive deictics/Historical 'we' Trope of 'newspeak'
Strategies of decoupling European identity from linguistic/national identities Strategies of pragmatic legitimization of English	Topos of Europe as a semi-diglossic society Topos of 'languages for communication' and 'languages for identification'	Neologisms ('globish', 'Euro-English') Metaphor of the universality of English

themselves from a simplified use of 'being/feeling' European. In some cases, strategies of problematization and avoidance were signalled by the frequent use of hedging ('I don't know', 'I don't think') and periphrasis in response to the prompt. This is illustrated in the following extract from an interview conducted with BE2, an Italian national based in Berlin, who had been supervising all EA's cultural events:

Extract 1

FZ: and therefore do you consider yourself European?

BE2: I have a big problem with this type of definition (.) I don't know (..) I don't know what it means (.) maybe it's a way of thinking, dunno, perhaps it's not even about being European ... I have a basic problem with the idea of identity I think that the concept of European identity is very problematic because ... the idea of identity gives me this message of something static and immobile, of definition (..) something defined isn't it? Something closed and fixed in time, and I do not think this is a concept applicable to the idea of Europe that inevitably must be something in movement ... and I simply believe that, I do not think it is possible to create an identitarian container for Europe I think it is a wrong approach, well a little bit forced anyway, no I don't think that's the right approach to think about Europe ... I don't know but I do not think European identity is the right idea for Europe.

In this extract BE2 problematized the term 'European' as a meaningful category for his identification appearing wary of accepting an implicit definition of what (European) identity stands for. The member signalled his sceptical stance on the definition of identities through the proposition 'I don't know what it means' and reinforced this stance through the Italian interjection *boh*. *Boh* – which can be loosely translated as 'dunno' or 'who knows?' – is a colloquialism used in Italian to convey confusion, doubt, indifference, unwillingness to discuss a subject or to provide a clear answer, depending on the context. In this case, BE2 used the interjection *boh* to signal uncertainty and difficulty in positioning himself as 'being European', an identity category that he appeared to dismiss in favour of 'thinking' European, an aspect that he regarded linked more to the wider transnational movement he had been discussing earlier. All the same, the speaker hedged such a proposition with 'maybe', thus avoiding 'fixing' a meaning to the quality of 'thinking' European and, overall, indicating a general difficulty to embrace stable or unreserved definitions of identities. Such a strategy of problematization of identity as a category was realized through the *topos of movement* and via the trope of *container*, a recurrent metaphor that is discussed further in this chapter in relation to other members' realizations. Through the *topos of movement* (i.e. Europe is an evolving idea/moving object), the speaker constructed European identity as a dynamic feature of the 'idea of Europe' rather than an essential individual quality. As European therefore BE2 suggested one can only 'think' of Europe but not fix it in a static definition.

A similar view emerged in the individual interview conducted with BE1, the coordinator of the Berlin branch. The prompt on 'being European' generated an initial problematization of the term 'identity', an argument which the speaker supported with some reflexive elaborations on the relational nature of identity and its implications of inclusion and exclusion:

Extract 2

BE1: mmh (..) I have a problem with with this identity thing (…) mmh (.)
[laughs] because identity always means inclusion and exclusion in a way
and so (…) mmh and of course if you ask me yes I'll say I am European but
I am so much more mmh in the same way.

FZ: in what way?

BE1: er (..) I mean the question is (.) is (..) is important for you that you are
Italian or (.) or you don't mind about or is it just about the others this is the
question (..) you know what I mean [hesitates]? … I have difficulties with
this identity thing but, mmh … could you ask me again and I'll think about
it [laughs].

Although BE2 accepted the term 'European' as a category to describe herself, she relativized the importance of such definition with what she saw as the multiplicity of identities that she can claim (a micro-strategy that she realized through the statement 'I am so much more'). Moreover she questioned the meaning of identity as derived from external attributions even dismissing its importance to her by reversing the question ('Does it matter to you?'). Like BE2, BE1's strategy appeared conspicuously oriented towards problematizing the universal significance of identity and avoiding 'fixing' meaning to the term – a strategy that she realized by deferring a definitive answer ('ask me again') and employing para-verbal features (the repetition of the filler *mmh* suggesting uncertainty).

In some other cases, although members did not directly question the meaning of the term 'identity', they constructed different 'layers' of meaningfulness and relevance of 'being European' through different arguments. For example, in the following extract, while LO2 (London pilot focus group) provided more than one justification for his Europeanness he also negotiated different personal meanings associated with Europe:

Extract 3

FZ: ...right, and so would you call yourself European?

LO2: I do think of myself as being European, ehm, but that's simply a way of, I think avoiding having to decide whether I'm British, English or German (.) so it's far simpler for me to simply say that I am European than to sort of say I am half English eh.. whatever [laughs] and in terms of what it means I don't (..) I don't think that I have it (..) that I give it a lot of meaning, actually, to be European (...) I just think that I was born in the continent of Europe, to parents who were born in the continent of Europe, you know, and whose own family was born in the continent of Europe, and that's just about as much meaning as I can give it and I am quite aware that you don't have to go very far back in history to have quite tyrannical and despotic Europe, and and I don't know (.) ehm (..) ehm I don't think necessarily that Europe (..) I mean it could slip back into tyranny and then it could still be Europe, so yeah I'm not sure that I'd give it a huge amount of significance just a little word (..) it's funny [laughter].

In the above abstract LO2 offers different possible interpretations of his Europeanness based on the *topos of the distinction of Europe as a signifier and discrete signifieds*. At first he refers to his Europeanness as merely a convenient label that sums up his mixed background (he was born in London to a German mother and an English father). In LO2's view, 'being European' can thus be an effective way of communicating the combination of different cultural heritages. In this case, LO2 appeared to reproduce his Europeanness at a denominational level as the hierarchical (i.e. multilevel) and non-mutually exclusive relations of national identities, justifying his self-ascription as European on a seemingly practical basis.

Subsequently, the member provided further justifications for his Europeanness, drawing on historical and geographical arguments of the continuity of his family line. In this case he constructed his Europeanness through an interpersonal dimension that drew on the *topos of kinship*, although he appeared concerned with downplaying the salience of this aspect as a 'simple fact'. Notably, LO2 also constructed a further layer of meaning that appealed to social, historical and ideational dimensions in addition to geographical and interpersonal dimensions. In this case LO2 related the 'signifier' Europe to the signified of a democratic and equal society by portraying the Europeans on a historical journey of progress towards better forms of participatory democracy (a topos that the member deployed a few times in the focus group and that will be discussed in relation to strategies of constructing Europe as 'experimental', see p. 139 below) realized, for example, by implicitly contrasting past tyranny with present democracy, intimated through the action verb 'slip back'.

Overall, therefore, LO2's argument appeared aimed at deconstructing the relation between the 'empty' signifier Europe and the signified meanings carried by the former. While relativizing the signified as a 'funny' and 'little' word, he duly explored a range of possible meanings. In this sense, the negotiation of meanings/'signifieds' of Europeanness was linguistically realized by the speaker on the one hand, through his use of the term 'European' as a predicate adjective by analogy with 'being' British, German and so on – and, on the other, through the argument that the term 'European' can represent a denominal form of Europe, itself a term available to ampler inferences including, for example, that of a democratic and diverse society.

Other members negotiated the meaning(s) of identities via strategies of perspectivization, that is, they emphasized their 'perspectives' or their 'way of seeing things' as a premise to make sense of their own and other identities. Some of these arguments were realized through the frequent use of verbs and nouns semantically related to vision and location (such as in English, *to see, point of view, perspective,* etc., and equivalent expressions in other languages). Most often members were able to represent their outlook and to realize their European/ transnational positioning via spatial metaphors. For example BO2 (Bologna focus group) pointed out how she could only give meaning to identities through her transnational orientation:

Extract 4

> BO2: well (…) from my point of view it really is a perspective (..) I mean it is the way I see it, it is a way of seeing problems and issues overcoming our normal (..) usual ways of categorizing (…) coming out of the local but also out of the idea of international, cutting through, so it is a perspective.

The speaker constructed a metaphorical location for herself from which she is able to see (a metaphorical substitution for interpreting and make sense of) the meaning(s) of identities from a transversal/transnational perspective (that she represented as 'cutting through' local and international categories). This premise allows BO2 to construct her European identity through the different 'nodes' of her network (i.e. her different global ties), a strategy that will be discussed under the *topos of connectedness* (see Section 5.3.3.2).

Another representation of transnational positioning as a precondition for making sense of European identity was argued by BO3 as illustrated in the following extract:

Extract 5

> BO3: In my opinion, compared to cultures outside Europe, European cultures have some common features, in some ways (..) I mean, if they [cultures] could be explained, that is deconstructed, in the end I believe people would recognize these aspects of of similarity ... I mean, at least seeing ... try ... trying to see Europe from the outside I think this is what I would see ... I don't know, trying to understand Europe, I've got to see it from the outside and I think that in the end I could see this.

In his argument the speaker relied on a critical perspectivization of Europe to define the common features of its cultures (in BO3's view a salient element of identity). Adopting the metaphor of spatiality and locating himself 'outside' Europe, the member was able to represent his distancing from a Euro-centric perspective as a reflexive attempt to deconstruct cultures. Unlike BO2 in Extract 4, however, BO3 constructed an imaginary 'boundedness' of Europe (implied by the definition of inside/outside). The speaker's use of the adjective 'European' acted thus as a circular warrant for his argument since it enabled him to construct the in/out space and, at the same time, to realize strategies of assimilation (of the inside) and dissimilation (of the outside). In other words, while adopting a transnational outlook, BO3 constructed the meaning of being European as dependent on being 'within Europe'.

5.3.3 Strategies of constructing European identity

5.3.3.1 *Topoi of interactional experience and relationality*

Most accounts suggested the construction of Europeanness occurred through the articulation of its 'relationality' with other elements and other identities. Several members cited experiences of mobility (for study, work, tourism) and subsequent exposure to cultural and social diversity as fundamental factors in shaping and changing their views of society, the way they understood identity and their own identification with Europe. For example, PR1 (Prague individual interview) argued:

Extract 6

> PR1: Yeah, yeah, quite definitely, yeah I am [European]. But again, I was also thinking erm that because I I had never travelled outside Europe and I have

never been outside Europe so I was thinking that perhaps, the fact that I feel European for me has definitely to do with the fact that I travel and live abroad – erm it definitely shaped (..) shaped my (..) my European identity. But I was thinking that perhaps if I (..) if I spend some time outside Europe perhaps I will change my identity and consider myself as a world citizen [laughter] I don't know.

In this case the member positioned herself as European through the *topoi of social interaction and mobility* by constructing an argument of causality which represented her European feelings clearly emerging out of her experience of visiting and living in different places in Europe. By the same token, she represented her process of identification as European as malleable and context-dependant, by offering the counterargument that her feelings would potentially change as a result of experiencing different places – although mitigated by modals or expressions of doubt such as 'maybe' and 'I don't know'. While she portrayed such a process as open to different possible outcomes, her representation of Europe with defined 'inside' and 'outside' suggests her interpretation of the world as divided up in continents, a conceptualization which would explain why experiences 'outside of Europe' would help her develop feelings of world citizenship.

The majority of members represented identity as a rather 'open' (i.e. non-predetermined) process developing out of transnational experiences (the causality illustrated in the extract above). However, a couple of respondents represented such experiences almost as 'catalysts' capable of activating elements of Europeanness that, to some extent, were already part of their identity. The next two extracts exemplify the use of *strategies of assimilation and dissimilation* that were deployed by LO1 and RO1 who, when asked to define their European identity, primarily emphasized in-group similarities among the 'Europeans' and out-group differences vis-à-vis the 'Americans' through the *topos of interactional experience*.

LO1 (London focus group) is an Italian national who, at the time of the discussion, had been in London on an internship with an organization in the field of human rights. He claimed that his interest in EA was primarily related to 'European issues' and the 'juridical aspects of what we [Europeans] are'. His orientation was clearly towards a discursive convergence of Europe and the EU which he described as 'something special in the history of the world'. His alignment with institutional discourses and narratives of the European project was, for example, inferable from expressions such as 'we have created this political organization after the Second World War to create a new world of peace, of human rights culture' in which the pronoun *we* was used in its historical inference to index the institutional project.[2] This stance also emerged in the extract below:

Extract 7

FZ: and do you define yourself as European?

LO1: I define myself as a European and (..) we share different cultures but also a common ground of some cultural elements … on some aspects we have the same points of view (…) I didn't understand this difference before my exchange with this experience in the US but before I was thinking that the Europeans of different nations have, (..) are (.) were very different but it's not that way we have some (..) common aspects like the respect for human rights but also of of some (..) eh aspects of the social welfare that maybe the Americans don't have okay there are differences between Scandinavia and I don't know, Spain, but there is a common ground.

LO1's orientation was towards an interpretation of (European) identity as group distinctiveness. His argument therefore seemed strategically aimed at maximizing intra-group similarities and intergroup dissimilarities drawing on the *topos of difference*. On the one hand, the *topos of difference* was used by LO1 to portray the European group as positively diverse ('sharing differences' is possibly echoing the institutional representation of Europe 'united in diversity') while constructing common denominators – human rights and welfare systems. On the other hand, these very same internal differences were relativized on a global scale to dissimilate the Europeans vis-à-vis the American out-group signalled by the mitigatory '*Okay… but*'. LO1 attributed the 'recognition' of differences to his experience outside Europe thus suggesting that the unfamiliar cultural environment expanded his perspective and resulted in his reshifting the focus of difference (which nevertheless seemed to represent his overall understanding of identities).

RO1 (Rome individual interview) offered a relatively similar account in which he constructed his experience abroad as a crucial catalyst in the formation/recognition of his Europeanness:

Extract 8

RO1: I think European identity is very much about the mind frame, about the way we think, the way that history plays a bigger role on how we would think, how we behave, what mistakes we've made … I think that ironically the easy (…) well (..) first of all yes, I feel very much European, maybe as much as I feel Italian, or possibly even more and ironically I did (…) the

European identity developed when I moved to Canada, and when you're
like in a third country outside of Europe, it's a lot easier to see what you
have in common with fellow Europeans that were also in Canada, so we
would (.) I was in an international college, with people from all over the
world, but it was obvious to me there that I had something in common with
people from Finland or Bulgaria, although we had no shared languages or
food habits, and I thought that culture is about that, but there is something
about finding the same things and, strange peculiar [things?] about
America, for example, and I think identity comes from ... I mean it is also
understood through shared experiences and shared emotions and shared
reactions, so we have very much the same historical cultural background
without really knowing it, and then I moved to Britain, which is a very
Eurosceptic country, where people are very European but they don't think
they are, and people call you European and when I say to people I go to
Europe they don't include themselves, and that even if somehow they are
a lot closer to Europe than they would like to think, but that also helped
develop an identity of (..) and you know again if you met a Spanish person,
or French, whatever in London, he would be someone closer to the way you
think, to your identity and then, meanwhile, the development of a European
policy also helped because they became, you know, places you can go to
work and places that have your own currency and so on, places that have
increasingly the same laws, so that identity goes hand-in-hand with social
and political developments.

Similar to the two previous extracts, RO1 referred to his different experiences
abroad to explain his process of identification as European spawning from them.
The member's strategic orientation was distinctly towards representing identity as
emergent from cognitive and emotive processes of recognition of similarities and
differences. RO1 thus engaged in different arguments in which he constructed
the 'Europeans' as an in-group by acknowledging familiar and unfamiliar traits
('*same and strange things*') vis-à-vis other groups often linguistically relying on the
metaphor of SPACE – for cultural proximity – whereby a European is 'someone
closer to the way you think'. Like LO1, RO1 thus also invoked the *topoi of cultural
background and difference* to construct intra-group commonalities and intergroup differences. Unlike LO1, the speaker elaborated further on the notion of
a European common cultural background and, through the metaphorization
of 'history as a teacher' (invoked via the *topos of history as magistra vitae)* he
portrayed young Europeans as 'having learnt their lessons'.

In this sense, his argument on 'recognizing' himself as European through
shared elements resonates with what Van Dijk (1995) calls 'social (or semantic)

memory' that is a socio-cognitive system of storing knowledge about the past and cultural narratives through the reproduction of discourses and identities. It could thus be argued that for RO1 the process of identification with Europe relies on becoming aware – at a cognitive and emotional level – of such a collective memory and deriving a sense of group connection from sharing these with other Europeans.[3] LO1 constructed his argument through a personal narrative in which the 'alien' context of Canada (which he referred to as a third country[4]) and the European/Eurosceptic context of Britain represented 'reflexive'[5] contexts which helped reveal his own Europeanness. RO1's representation of his process of identification seems thus to point to a mutually constitutive dynamic between elements which are both 'brought along' and 'brought about' by the interactional experience.[6] On the one hand RO1 vaguely suggested the notion of identity as an almost pre-existing (albeit dormant) disposition that would be activated by the context. On the other hand, the fact that the speaker clearly foregrounded places and interaction as key factors in the emergence of Europeanness and the linguistic choice of 'development' would suggest a less deterministic stance. Overall the representation of such an interplay appeared to be reconciled in RO1's argument on the 'Europeanization of places' which, he suggested, could facilitate the process of recognizing similarities/differences and thus of becoming European, a correlation that he linguistically realized through the idiomatic expression 'hand-in-hand'.

The *topos of interactional experience* was also invoked by two Romanian members (Cluj focus group) as the context in which they had to negotiate their Europeanness. In this case, however, the speakers used this topos to represent the relationality of their identities as a difficult process of inclusion and exclusion occurring vis-à-vis other Europeans as illustrated in Extract 9:

Extract 9

CL5: I lost the optimism I had when I was small because it's beautiful that I am a European, that I can travel, and I have a European culture to support me, that I speak a language closely related with Italian and French and that there are Western influences in the Romanian culture, but when you actually interact with most people in the West, being European does not mean a big deal for them.

CL4: That was really my main shock when I came to live longer in the West, specifically in Paris that I had been raised to believe in such a European culture, I had been raised in a family of intellectuals who put a heavy emphasis on a long history friendship, of cultural exchanges between Romania and France, but when I got there I saw that my beliefs or my knowledge about this culture, or about classic European culture didn't matter. The only thing that mattered was the Romanian label, a Romanian badly seen, a Romanian seen as a Roma, a Roma regarded as a thief and so on. It was a long string of clichés that eventually forced me to question very deeply my clichés about the history of a Romanian-French friendship. It is just one example, it might be hard to generalize, but I felt it very deeply. To learn that you are European and then to have it thrown in your face that you are not.

Through the *topos of interactional experience* (in the specificity of relations between 'Eastern' and 'Western' Europeans) both members realized and juxtaposed different constructions of Europeanness. CL5 initially construed 'being European' as the awareness of cultural proximity between the Romanian culture and other Western cultures. The ability to claim his Europeanness on these premises however was clearly devalued by CL5 as an idealization (through the ironical 'it's beautiful') against his personal experience of being denied the validation of such identity by the 'Western' counterpart.

In a similar way, CL4 represented her Europeanness as being rejected by the 'West' through the vivid non-finite clause 'to have it thrown in your face that you are not [European]'. Furthermore, she represented the process of external devaluation of her Europeanness through a 'downward' chain of negatively associated labels (realized via the anadiplosis[7] 'European-Romanian-Roma-thief'). Such processes of exclusion were represented by members in negative terms (e.g. CL4 described it as a 'shock') and this appeared to result in a general scepticism by the two speakers of their personal investment in Europeanness as a cultural construction learnt in their earlier childhood. While the above examples of (de)constructing Europeanness show the relationality of processes in which both elements of internal investment and external attribution must be negotiated, they also suggest that, in some cases, the 'East' can still represent 'Europe's other' and that Europeanness can be constructed through the articulation of such dichotomization.

5.3.3.2 *Topos of (inter)connectedness*

For a considerable number of members the construction of European identity and the articulation of its relationality were achieved via *topoi of connections*, the latter differently understood as feelings, links and ties related to European referents. In most cases such connections were claimed by representing Europe embedded in a worldwide network of social relations with, in some instances, links being accounted for through European heritage.

A few members invoked the *topoi of family history and culture* as initial warrants for claiming a European identity. For example, LO3 (London, individual interview) referred to her transnational upbringing and socialization as the main reason for her European identification as illustrated in the following extract:

Extract 10

LO3: I, I do (…) erm (…) I do feel European although I am limited [slowly] by my lack of (…) I have – I don't have much er foreign language [high tone] so I've got sort of a bit of German and a tiny bit of French, like my – a terrible lack of other languages so although I feel European [laughs] I also feel like I couldn't just travel, like whenever I meet fellow (…) Trans Europa people or European Movement[8] people from around Europe I always notice about how English I am [high tone] [laughs] by my lack of language so, that's purely something that's fixable, but in terms of identity, yeah, I, I feel European I think. The fact that I have so many relatives who live in different parts of the country, in different parts of Europe, erm, that it's just how I was brought up I think (…) to feel European and sort of linked with the history that doesn't necessarily come from the UK, and yeah [softly]

FZ: So, is that what makes you European, erm?

LO3: Partly [high tone] I'm sure it's an aspect of not wanting to just feel British [laughs] So a slight, slight kind of feeling of wanting to be other than being British [softly] I'm sure that's part of it, yeah.

LO3's representations of her own Europeanness were primarily predicated on the warrants of her European family history and her upbringing. The speaker referred to her process of identification as European in affective terms (through the verb 'feel') and through the trope of 'links with history'. The *topos of connectedness* was therefore invoked from temporal and spatial dimensions drawing on the metaphorical representations of movement of one's heritage (cf. the expression '*linked* with the history that doesn't necessarily *come* from the UK').

In addition to these representations, the member constructed her European identity through different representations of her Englishness/Britishness. On the one hand, her national identity was construed as an element of distinctiveness in comparison to other members of the NGO. Moreover by indexing 'being English' to her lack of languages (and constructing this as an acquirable skill) the speaker also mitigated what she pre-empted as a 'limited' Europeanness. On the other hand, her British identity was clearly invoked in a strategy of constructing her 'alterity', that is of defining who she is by emphasizing who she is not (cf. Delanty 2000). In this respect, it was thus possible to recognize the speaker's agentive role in the process of self-definition ('I want to be') that involved the partial otherization of the national referent.

The *topos of family history* was also called upon by AM1 (Amsterdam, individual interview) and realized through the metaphorical narrative of JOURNEY of her family and her own as illustrated by the example below. AM1's account was conspicuous for a general pattern of broken sentences and certain paralinguistic features (in particular her intonation and hesitation) which, along with the use of fillers such as 'oh my God', suggest high emotional involvement in her representations.

Extract 11

FZ: … do you consider yourself European?

AM1: Erm, yes.

FZ: Okay, and what what does it mean to you?

AM1: Erm [laughs] to me it erm, what it means to me? [Confused]

FZ: Hmm.

AM1: Erm (…..) I think for me it's also got to do like in the same way of feeling Dutch or feeling (…) Amsterdammer or, or, something erm I, I think it's got to do with, with my personal history as well [high tone].

FZ: Would you like to tell me about that?

AM1: Erm that my father is Austrian and his parents were from Latvia and erm Czech Republic, Erm and I, I was always, yeah, fascinated by that. I mean I never really got to know my family but then I found out, yeah, I'd say that I started to travel myself and (…) erm and so that already kind of (…) er, it feels er, it (…) it feels a bit random [high tone] that you're born in one country because [laughs] – erm, God, God I'm, I'm making a lot of hand movements here because I don't really know [high tone] [laughs] how to say it but (…)

FZ: That's fine, it's fine (.) take your time …

[She gives an account of her father telling a story about his 'family journey' through Europe to an audience.]

AM1: … so I think that where you're coming from, your own history is really important […and what it] means for me is erm that my family history is in Europe so (…) I feel European and maybe if I, if that wasn't (…) the case, erm, I, I wouldn't have felt that, I don't know, erm.

The speaker initially made sense of 'feeling European' by highlighting the familiarity of different spaces, a strategy which she achieved through the analogy of feeling just European as much as Amsterdammer or Dutch. In her account, she also emphasized the continuity of her European ties along temporal, spatial and affective/intrapersonal dimensions. For example, in a similar way to LO3, AM1 deployed the metaphor of HISTORICAL JOURNEY OF FAMILY (realized through the statement 'where you're coming from ... is really important') to construct her connections with Europe.

Furthermore, Europe was represented by AM1 as a meta-space that could make unitary sense of her identity narrative by making up for not having known her forefathers and by reconciling the uncertainties of feeling 'randomly' located (clearly still a sensitive issue for the speaker which was reflected in her para-verbal language). Her proposition 'my family history is in Europe, so I feel European' therefore seemed to functionally connect intangible aspects of memories within a physically defined European space and ultimately to anchor such space to a fuller identity, providing her with a firmer narrative continuity (Erikson 1980). Despite highlighting the salience of her European connections, AM1's representations of Europeanness appeared nevertheless oriented towards a non-essentialist interpretation of identities. Similarly to other members (see, for example, in Extract 10 on p. 147 below) AM1 recognized that her European identification is predicated on her background, stressing that her claim to Europeanness would be otherwise through the counterfactual conditional statement 'if that wasn't the case ... I wouldn't have felt that' (see also PR1 in Extract 6 on p. 140 for a similar conclusion).

In the last two examples the transnational background of their families is arguably a core variable in the members' accounts. *Topoi of connections and ties* however also emerged as a powerful referent in processes of identification with members who have had direct experience of mobility but not necessarily a transnational family background.[9] For these members, the discussion of mobility and transnational experiences was instrumental in their definition of identity. However, above all, it was the definitions of links and bonds related to their experiences that were highlighted and deemed essential in defining Europeanness. These arguments were typically realized through the *topos of network*[10] as illustrated in the following extracts (Bologna, focus group):

Extract 12

> BO2: ... as far as I'm concerned I have always had difficulties in defining myself
> tied to an identity eh ... certainly the national bond that is really something
> that I've never felt strongly also because of my family background ... never
> felt for Italy therefore the next step could be feeling part of something
> bigger like Europe ... this is something I've been reflecting on since I joined

this kind of association, reflecting on what Europe is and how Europe is not necessarily defined by these geographical boundaries. If I think of it that way, then I can define myself as European ... if defining oneself as European simply means being part of this system then I'm not much interested in it, in that case then I feel stronger ties with the rest of the world as in the past I have worked on projects in Africa, I have minor experiences of international cooperation, wider connections ... however if we look at Europe as a way to expand one's own locality and above all of connecting oneself with the world, then perhaps I feel European.[11]

BO2 referred to the identification process as a 'bond' or a 'tie' (Italian *legame*) arguing that she lacked any strong connections with her Italian identity (through personal communication I learnt that she was born in Northern Italy from Southern Italian migrants). While such lack of bonding with the nation was logically constructed as her main motivation for turning to Europe as a source of identity (through the adverb 'therefore'), she also represented her identity quest as an outward journey ('the next step'). As I have argued in the analysis of the above extract in McEntee-Atalianis and Zappettini (2014, p. 406):

'Acknowledging the multiple meanings of Europe and rejecting the simple geographical or institutional definitions, BO2's overall cognitive scenario appears therefore concerned with imagining Europeanness as a "translocality", a salient anchoring in the process of connecting her with the wider world. Thus, while Europe offers a potential source of identification or a positive tie for the speaker, it does not seem to constitute a fixed identity, but rather it seems to represent a "node" that connects her with the world in a network of multiple belongings and possible loyalties. In her account, BO2 constructs identity as a reflexive and dynamic process, metaphorically represented as a JOURNEY (PATH) that relies on the imaginary of a networked society to provide multiple connections with different communities. Therefore, while one could recognize in BO2's representation the same process of outward motion to the next "doll"/ identity suggested, for example, by the "Russian Doll" model (see p. 30), her realization of Europeanness is clearly not contained by or filtered through nationality but rather achieved by dismissing or skipping the "national level" altogether. Furthermore, as nationality is not significantly invoked by the speaker (other than to be dismissed/rejected), BO2's account does not seem to tally either with the marble cake model. Notably in her argument BO2 appears to use the network metaphor to antagonize the "system" by rejecting institutionalized notions of Europeanness which instead she constructs as "proxy" for her transnational vision.'

PR1 (Prague, individual interview) too represented her process of identification as European/with Europe as connecting with salient anchors, an argument that she realized through the spatial metaphor of MAPPING as illustrated by the following extract:

Extract 13

> PR1: Well, I don't identify as a European, as erm … as Europe as a nation, you know, this is the difference [laughter]. No, no, I don't consider it as a country, you know … not a country, not a fixed thing. It's it's a mixture of other things and and this is why I I identify so much with Europe because erm having lived in different countries and travelled and met people from different countries I take a lot of things or I see a lot of things with which I personally identified and agree or support or you know, like positively identify, I identify as European because there are values things in European cultures and societies which I identify with, but in a way it's more erm in a way maybe it's more erm erm this combination of erm erm of the local level because, for instance, erm I identify with things which which I saw here in Prague, locally but put together as erm an and rise to a more European level.
>
> I: So – it's basically – I don't know if you can call it the combination of these different erm micro environments.'
>
> PR1: Yeah.
>
> I: and still you see them linked together somehow?
>
> PR1: Yes, exactly. Maybe, … erm maybe it is something which is easier to draw on a map rather than to talk you know … perhaps if I draw a map I could put erm erm … a lot of points which would be the places where I lived and the people which I met in this or that place. And then you can link it up together and this is ….this is Europe and this is my identity.

The member initially rejected her identification with 'formal' Europeanness (i.e. derived from an institutional definition of Europe), an argument that she realized by analogy with the problematization of nationhood that she had been discussing earlier in the interview (see Extract 23 below for her argument on the 'fixity' of nations). Instead, she constructed her identification as an 'open' process including referents such as places, people, values and experiences. While these elements were treated distinctly at a local level, they were also used by the member to construct her own individual notion of Europe.

The representation of such process was realized by PR1 through the geographical entailment of map/charting within the JOURNEY metaphor. The expression 'drawing a map' appeared thus used by the speaker for a cognitive rearrangement of the European space whereby representations of her European links and ties – symbolized by lines or roads she had travelled in her lifetime – were consolidated into one. This representation of Europe(anness) highlights a construction of European identity as expanded and interconnected localities (conveyed by the expression 'rise to a more European level') and one in which the agency of the speaker allows for a more personal arrangement of space than that formally defined by borders and hierarchy. In this case Europe is not explicitly contained but rather constructed as a polycentric ideological referent with the emphasis on flows (the lines/roads) rather than on boundaries (see also McEntee-Atalianis and Zappettini 2014 for a similar analysis of PR1's realization of 'mapping').

The construction of Europeanness in relation to the *topos of connections* was also noticeable in the identity narrative of VA1 (individual interview, Valencia), a Spanish national who described herself as transnational in the questionnaire. However, unlike BO1 and AM1's extracts discussed above, VA1's representations of ties and connections as underdeveloped attachments contributed to an overall representation of more 'fragmented' and 'weak' belongings. The topic of identity was raised spontaneously by the member early in the talk when, discussing her one-year work experience in the Netherlands, she elaborated on the relation between Europe and transnationalism as illustrated below:

Extract 14

VA1: for me I mean this is (..) for me this is a question of identity (.) I mean I was born in Spain and maybe I don't feel Spanish you know (..) the feeling of belonging for me doesn't depend on citizenship or where you live or if you're travelling … but for me belonging means not only a place you know (.) it's also belonging to a society belonging to a certain group of people that have similar values to yours (..) I mean I could say yeah I am Spanish and of course if I compare myself to (.) if I compare my habits with other cultures or kind of customs if you want to call it like that and other people people from all over the countries of course I am different (.) there is [*sic*] differences (.) but this but this doesn't mean I belong to Spain (..) I don't know if I want to to to grow my roots or something like that (..) I don't know if I want to stay here you know I don't know I don't know if I want to be in South America or in the north of Europe it's not only the city or the buildings but is also the people is what you give to this society with what you contribute you know (.) I don't know where I belong (…) if you ask me now I belong to my family at the moment and no at the moment I'm not independent yet (.) I don't have a job I don't have my own house and

> now I don't have more options than belonging here so I don't know the
> international experience I had living abroad I didn't feel belonging to that
> countries [*sic*] either … myself I don't know where I belong it's a kind of
> feeling I suppose I will build I will take a little bit from each experience in
> my life of course I will (..) I belong to my place where I was born and you
> know I am a musician I like playing drums so I also belong to my band.

Through her narrative, VA1 reflexively positioned herself 'in-between' stages
of the process of identification, highlighting how her different sources of
attachments had yet to fully develop into firmer feelings of belonging and
groupness. VA1 represented thus identity as a process of connecting reference
objects and consolidating experiences through the metaphorical realization of
'rooting' oneself in a wider social space. However, she controversially depicted
her desire for rooting and her process of belonging as disrupted/interrupted
and somehow caught in between personal choices and external constraints –
her difficulty in positioning herself was signalled by several repetitions of the
utterance 'I don't know' and a general pattern of broken sentences.

VA1's discourses appeared oriented towards the representation of a hiatus
in the process of building her identities, or, in other words, she represented
herself 'trapped' in the progression from 'attachment' to 'belonging' (Jones and
Krzyżanowski 2008) (see p. 45). VA1 constructed her difficulty to locate herself
in relation to a meta-space comprising of different dimensions: a geographical
dimension (specific world locations such as South America/North Europe, or
objects such as buildings); an affective dimension (family) and a social dimension
of groupness (defined by the sharing of values and the moral obligation to give to
society). By contrast, she rejected the significance of citizenship as a formalized
recognition of membership and, through the disclaimer on 'being Spanish', she
downplayed the significance of cultural differences enacted through national
identities.

Amid this scenario, the member discursively marked her social location via
the spatial deictic 'here' and the temporal clause 'at the moment' – two expressions
which point to the specific difficult social-economic conjuncture of Spain (and
more generally of Europe), – a topic that VA1 discussed repeatedly in the
interview and which clearly echoed wider discourses of 'social precariousness'.[12]
It was thus inferable that for VA1 the contingencies of 'here' and 'now' (i.e. the
lack of certainty about the future) were preventing her from emancipation and
a full realization of meaningful social identities through firm ties undermining
the 'ontological security' (Giddens 1991) of her identity. The gap between an
ideal sense of belonging and the social and economic constraints was realized

through the comparative '*I don't have more options than belonging here*' which presents her current choice of belongings in negative terms.

While the majority of members realized their representations of (inter) connectedness as outward expansion – which in some cases would reach out of the European continent – BO6's (Bologna focus group) construction of Europeanness stood out among the others as he invoked the topos of connection to represent a dwindling European society as illustrated below:

Extract 15

> BO6: I just wanted to say something perhaps a bit against the mainstream but maybe today I feel very European because I share with many European youngsters the feeling of decline ... that has ... that our continent is living through and perhaps we feel it more than others and ah ... it's something that I am finding ... really a common element ... which in my opinion characterizes [Europeans] compared to other kids coming from other parts of the world I speak of course of my generation
>
> FZ: OK, can you explain a bit better .. the decline?
>
> BO6: the decline compared to expectations of progress that ah ... that are a little the foundations in the construction of Europe as an institution, as both institutional setup and as a social body, let's say
>
> BO1: but I do not characterize myself with this decline ... (everyone laughs)
>
> BO6: No, but I mean...
>
> BO1: ... old and decadent (in an ironical tone)....
>
> BO6: yes old and arteriosclerotic ... and actually I feel the social communion because [the Europeans'] ancient history was just this ... let's say the world's 'dominant' community and what was happening here in Europe influenced the rest of the world and not always vice versa.

In this exchange BO6 constructed his identity in relation to his awareness of Europe's decline which he claimed to mutually share with other Europeans of his generation. He realized this strategy through the utterance 'I feel the social communion', not a commonly used expression in Italian, but nevertheless reminiscent of Anderson's (2006) idea of 'imagined' communities. Moreover, the member engaged in a strategy of representation of the decline of Europe(ans) through the personification of Europe as a living entity going through the life cycle by drawing on the trope *il vecchio continente* (literally 'the old continent' and equivalent to English 'old world' which is commonly used in Italian to refer to Europe and the history of its civilizations). BO6, thus, portrayed Europe as an ageing individual that has passed his/her prime, supporting this imagery further with the depiction of the European continent as *arteriosclerotico* (a medical term associated with senile deterioration but colloquially used in Italian as English 'barmy').

Through this strategy the speaker arguably aimed at creating empathy and emotional appeal for the waning role of European culture which he regarded as having lost its influence in the world arena and lacking any aspiration of progress. It must be noted, however, that BO6's strategy aimed at representing an empathic connection with the history of the European group was challenged by all other members particularly in relation to the notion of a 'dominant' and homogenous European culture. For example, in the extract above BO1 ironically mimicked BO6's proposition to disalign herself from it. Nevertheless BO6's discourse suggested that his identification process as European was clearly embedded in major historical and social dynamics. The ageing of Europe depicted by the speaker appears to index the centre of world's demographic and economic interests now shifting to other blocks and, similarly, his unattended expectations of progress in Europe could be interpreted as the gradual abandoning of welfare social models in favour of liberal market as a macro-process of the 'new economy' in the last few decades (Jessop 2010). These changes, resulting in a reconfiguration of world 'core' and 'periphery', appear therefore reflected in the speaker's discursive constructions of the de-centralization of Europe ultimately indicating his investment in narratives of decline.

5.3.3.3 *Topos of membership*

As illustrated so far, the salience of identity as membership or formal categorization was generally downplayed by members, for example through arguments that dismissed it as an external ascription (see Extract 2 and Extract 14). SO1 (Sofia, individual interview) also relativized the significance of Europeanness as formal membership, although his argument was principally constructed from an economic perspective and based on the *topos of the rationales for the EU membership* of Bulgaria as exemplified by the extract below:

Extract 16

> FZ: I would like to ask you if you erm, if you um, identify yourself as, as
>   European, erm and er and if so what erm, what that means to you?
> SO1: Ah look ah okay, erm, (..) erm, I'm, er I (...) I do identify as European
>   at one level on another level I do identify as a Balkan, ah you know, as
>   somebody from the Balkans, er and that's kind of important for me and it's
>   important er perhaps because I don't feel the, I don't feel the Eastern leg of
>   the European Union is very much integrated in, in what it is supposed to be
>   integrated, erm so yeah, yeah I do feel yes European with that note in mind.

FZ: Okay can, can (..) can you expand on that erm idea of integration?

SO1: Well …, the big thing of being in, part of ah, er in the EU as such
erm, that is a Bulgarian in my case is that that yeah it's all quotas and
identification that, that, that's why I very much questioned before the actual
membership (…) er, this is one thing erm, so we talk this anyway willy nilly,
erm, as soon as it gets, as soon as you're a member, well you know, travel
is easier and how they move on, you know another one on borders and
da, da, da, it's one thing. On the other, er, you know, er very few people
in my country of origin erm, doubt the, the membership of, of, of okay
it was anything different from just you know, it being done for a political
process you know, for economic purposes basically. Erm, er, this is why, yes
that's returning on the economy thing again, erm, this is why I said that I,
I question the integration of, of Bulgaria for example in, in the EU as such
erm, ahm, on, on everyday level I think there is a sense of identification in
me and other people in general, er which is pretty much er okay these days
for our, on, on the market level I think there is um, I wouldn't call it even
disappointment, I think it's some sort of er, you know just sort of realization
of, of it's why countries such as Bulgaria and Romania are in the EU. So
I think, I think while Bulgaria and Romania are part of the EU because
of, you know of conjuncture reasons et cetera et cetera and dare I say
economic reasons, you know people benefit in some sort of um coincident,
er accidentally you know, within it, whether you know, the, the, the idea of
European identification that I do follow, I develop it, you know sort of like
because of erm, you know it's just there, it's just optional because Bulgaria
is in the EU, you know and I'm like, why not, of course I will develop this
identification focus.

SO1 constructed his argument on the *topos of rationales for the EU membership* of
Bulgaria discerning distinct social and economic purposes of the EU integration
in general. This decoupling gave SO1 the warrant for constructing his European
identity through his (dis)alignment with these different aspects. As he explained
when asked to elaborate on 'integration', he argued that economic rationales
were the main reason for Bulgaria to join the EU. Consequently, for the speaker,
European identity (i.e. the formal entitlement to claim Europeanness derived from
the status of Bulgarian citizenship) ultimately represents a by-product of market
logics and it has been primarily reproduced by Bulgarians from this perspective,
in other words, as an optional, commodified, 'add-on' identity. The speaker
dissociated himself from this identification option through representations of
'banal' mobility and the dismissive expression 'da da da'. While the member
distanced himself from a formalized validation of 'being European' he claimed

his Europeanness in relation to Europe as a project of social integration. However, he highlighted the discrepancy between ideal and factual dimensions ('it is not what it is supposed to be'), an argument that he linguistically realized through the metaphor of the EU as an organic (i.e. properly functioning) body whose 'Eastern leg' is not 'much integrated'. This premise enabled him to take a position as 'someone from the Balkans' an identity that, in this context, appears to supplement a 'weak' European identity deriving from economic rationales and bridges the gap between ideal and factual European communities.

In contrast to most views, members of the Cluj focus group discussed membership (in the specific instantiation of citizenship[13]) as a significant referent for their identification as Europeans. In general, the Cluj members placed much emphasis on topics of mobility as the expression of a newly acquired status of freedom following Romania's accession to the EU in 2007 as illustrated by the extract below:

Extract 17

RC: … would you define yourselves as Europeans? and if you could tell me
what this means to each one of you?

CL3: The right we have now, I don't know, well, I think, that we can travel more
freely now, and somehow we were given more rights to do what we want, to
do what we like … we took some distance from something that bound us,
we are not bound anymore, it isn't hard to dream of something anymore,
like it used to be, now you can learn more easily, as you can be with people
more easily, you can interact with strangers more easily, it's more (..) it's
more ok than before.

CL6: I wanted to say that since 2007, you can really feel better that you
are European, not just that you can travel more, which is indeed really
important, and get in contact with other cultures and all, but you come
into contact with the legislation and all the bureaucratic fields, so to say,
and … a …

RC: Does everyone else feel European because we have the same bureaucracy?

CL2: Yes I often feel equal to others in France, Italy from anywhere and then it
gives you a little more confidence … confidence in yourself as a person, not
as a Romanian, as a European so to speak.

In this case, the three members constructed their Europeanness through the *topos of European citizenship* as a consequence of Romania's accession to the EU in 2007. Significantly, the formal recognition of Romania as a EU member (and of Romanians as European citizens) represented the culmination of a process of political changes occurred in the wake of the collapse of the communist system in

Eastern Europe. The discursive frame constructed around membership therefore carries specific implications for this key transition and for the affirmation of Romanians as Europeans. This was clearly signalled by the temporal deictics *now* and *before* in CL3's discourse, which he used to juxtapose his current status of European citizen ('now') with what it used to be in the past ('before'). In the CL3's representations, therefore, EU membership indexes Romania's emancipation from the communist regime and from the severe travel restrictions that applied to Romanian citizens.[14] From this perspective, the speaker saw his new status of European citizen as an opportunity to overcome the constraints of the past communist regime that limited his civil rights. His claim of a European identity through the formal recognition of membership/citizenship appeared therefore driven by a strategy of legitimization.

Notably, from a semiotic perspective CL3 realized his argument through a vivid representation of 'boundness' that drew on the imagery of slavery and likened pre-EU Romania to past societies where slaves were disenfranchised citizens (e.g. the ancient Roman and Greek societies). CL3 represented becoming a European citizen as the emancipation from such a condition of slavery ('we are not bound anymore') and the acquisition of new rights to participate to the civic life of the European community. In this sense, for CL3, Europe seemed to represent a new salient referent for renegotiating his civic affiliation away from national institutions and closer to the EU institutions which one could arguably interpret as the 'freeing agent' in the passive construction 'we were given rights'.

The temporal dimension deployed by CL3 was taken up further by CL6 (through the marker 'since 2007') to represent her Europeanness enhanced by Romania's membership of the EU. In this case the speaker constructed the experience of dealing with the EU institutions (in the form of legislation and bureaucracy) as a positive example of her EU citizen status and, at the same time, a validation of her Europeanness through the implicit inference that the EU legislation applies equally to all EU citizens. The warrant that all citizens are equal before the law also enabled CL2 to achieve a strategy of legitimization for himself by affirming his Europeanness vis-à-vis other nationals in France, Italy and so on. In this case, the member saw the EU legislation (which, in most cases, applies supranationally) as a 'playing field leveller' because it should grant the same rights and same opportunities to all individuals regardless of their nationality. By anchoring the validation of his dignity as human being and his confidence in a supranational rather than a national legal system, CL2 appeared therefore to invest more positively in his identification as a European citizen, crucially bypassing the national level.

5.3.3.4 *Strategies of negotiation between European and other identities*

As illustrated in many of the previous extracts, the vast majority of members made sense of their experiences and their feelings of belonging by locating (or striving to locate) themselves in an 'expanded' physical and social world. Discourses and narratives of identification discussed so far have generally pointed to the fact that members deployed different strategies aimed at constructing the 'meaning' of identities and their own positioning which clearly entailed the negotiation of a relationality of Europeanness with other referents/identities.

For example, some members constructed their Europeanness in opposition to 'other' cultures of social systems as, for example, embodied by the American 'way of life' or 'non-European' welfare systems (see LO1 in Extract 7 and RO1 in Extract 8). In other cases, certain members claimed their European identity (partly) by 'otherizing' a national referent (see LO3 in Extract 10) or, by contrast, by constructing local, national and supranational identities as equally salient and mutually compatible (as exemplified by AM1 in Extract 11). European identity therefore often acquired meaning in the context of its relation with different identities/affiliations, and how members negotiated such interplay was crucial to the realization of strategies of claiming Europeanness. This section will discuss such aspects in detail starting with some quantitative data on different affiliations derived from the questionnaire.

In the questionnaire the majority of respondents (sixteen out of twenty-six) chose to describe themselves as 'transnational'. While for twelve of them this represented a straightforward choice, four respondents chose 'transnational' together with the following other options (multiple categories were available): 'national only' and 'national then European' (CA1); 'national only' (PR2); 'European only' (PR1); 'primarily national then European' (AM1). The ten respondents who did not choose 'transnational' were equally divided between the 'national first and European' and the 'European first then national' options. Furthermore, two respondents specified a definition other than those available: CL4 defined herself as 'first a citizen of my town, then European, then transnational' while BO6 described himself as 'primarily Italian, then French, then European' (see Sections 4.2.1 and 4.2.2). While these results have been cautiously treated at face value (as I am aware of the limitations of constructing and 'fixing categories) they are taken here as an initial insight into the participants' positioning(s) and have been interpreted in the light of the discursive data.

In a large number of instances, identity categories chosen by members in the questionnaire appeared aligned/consistent with their discursive positioning.

For example a large proportion of members who chose the European/national combination in the questionnaire tended to achieve linguistic realizations that accommodated multiple identities in mutually compatible propositions. For instance, some members derived their Europeanness from the hypernymic implicature of being national (i.e. 'I am Italian/Spanish/etc. and, therefore/consequently, European') or through hyponymic implicatures of being world citizens as in the following extract (Cluj focus group) in which the speaker constructs Europeans as 'tokens' of the human 'type':

Extract 18

CL5: you should … not see yourself only as being from country X, and as a citizen of country X, and just that … just as we are Romanian and the other French, we are all European because we come from the same earth.

While, in broad terms, members represented identities as multilevel affiliations – although showing different degrees of accommodation and not always reproducing them in a linear hierarchical logic – a few members made reference to a more complicated and conflictual interplay between national and European identities. For example, the seemingly contradictory combination of 'transnational' and 'national only' which was chosen by CA1 (Cardiff focus group) and PR2 (Prague individual interview) appeared reproduced to some extent in their accounts, albeit realized within different arguments and through opposing representations of European and national identities. While both members positioned themselves 'in between' these two identities, for PR2 this location seemed to constitute an 'advantage' whereas for CA1 the construction of her location appeared to represent a conflict. The following two extracts illustrate this.

Extract 19

FZ: I'd like to know … if you see yourself as a, as an American and how do you, how does this interplay with your er, er commitment to Europe erm?

PR2: I have to say that erm, I only really feel American when people are telling me I'm American, aha it's not necessarily this very strong being a, you know it's like they say, being outside of Europe, you know, your homeland you feel a lot more attached to it. I mean it's not necessarily the case, like … like I don't necessarily feel, strongly American in the sense of what people understand is American ehr at the same time I also feel that I don't quite feel European either, I feel like it's somewhere, like I feel like I'm very lucky to have like both perspectives and to have experience both and kind of take a lot out of that … I don't know, …, as much as I feel engaged in erm, Europe, (…) I don't think it's also this idea that you give up your national identity to become European … I think that people have many identities, the idea is to really make sure, erm, that European is one of them if you're, if, if you're here, erm because really, I mean I don't think, ah, (…) I don't think that's really ideal especially in the importance of kind of sharing and also keeping different cultures If you want people to er, if you want it to be an interesting rich society of people from different ideas, different views you need to have them keep their, their, their (…) many identities, not just this idea of a flat kind of European. I mean the idea of European in general it's kind of this idea that it's not flat, right? it's like people from all over from, from different places are coming together. So I don't see that as something where like er, your national identity is necessarily inhibiting that European identity, I think er, first some people that's maybe the case but I think the idea is to kind of reach out to people and have this more of a dialogue where people understand that, that it is possible to have both.

PR2's overall strategic orientation was towards the representation of identities as multiple and mutually compatible experiences that are neither exclusively 'transportable' nor necessarily 'activated' by a specific location. Moreover, by underscoring the 'feeling' rather than the 'being' component of identities, she highlighted the transient and non-essential aspect of identity. PR2's initial argument on the interplay between American and European referents of her identity was constructed through a spatial dimension which allowed her to position herself *'somewhere'* in-between *'both perspectives'*. The *topos of in-betweenness* – which in much transnational literature describes ambivalence about settlement and attachment (see, for example, Bauböck and Faist 2010) – appears positively invoked by the speaker who called herself *lucky* to be able to experience that situation.[15]

    Her second argument, that a diverse (as opposed to 'flat') European identity will develop from people interacting and sharing, was warranted by the *topos of multiculturalism* ('if you want a rich society') which regards identities as *resources* and their coexistence as *wealth*. The scenario of 'coming together' clearly echoes narratives of Europe as a 'mosaic of people/cultures' (see Kraus 2008) promoted by late institutional discourses. PR1 thus saw her position 'in between cultures' as a strength rather than a weakness as this enabled her to switch to multiple identification referents without foregoing any of them. Like a few other members, therefore, through her argument the speaker accommodated her European identity with other identities in a 'non-zero sum' equation (one does not take away from the other) representing different identities as compatible and non-antagonist. PR2's identification with multiple referents can arguably be related to her status as a non-EU national and this can possibly account for how she semi-integrated European and national referents in a parallel (albeit non-convergent) coexistence.

A remarkably different stance was enacted instead by CA1, a Turkish national who had lived in Cyprus for four years before moving to the UK.

Extract 20

> CA1: I'm not a part of Europe because I'm from Turkey [rising tone] (.)
> actually it's both part of Europe and at the same time (..) it still isn't in
> the European Union and (..) yes, I've always been keen on studying about
> Europe because of its diversity there's a lot of cultures a lot of languages (…)
>
> FZ: But is it geographical or cultural or what is it about Europe? I mean what is
> it that makes one European in your view?
>
> CA1: I think the common point is history, European history, European
> tradition, … and I think this is the point that makes us European, they share
> the same history.

In this exchange CA1 initially drew on the *topos of Turkey straddling across continents/cultures* to position herself as a non-European as a consequence of her Turkish identity. The speaker realized her 'outsider' identity through a particularizing synecdoche (pars pro toto) which replaces the country (Turkey) for the individual (herself). However she mitigated her initial statement with a further elaboration on the geopolitical boundaries of Europe and, in the following passage, the speaker ambivalently positioned herself vis-à-vis the European group by simultaneously affiliating with and dissociating from it through the conflictual use of the pronouns *us* and *they* contextually referring to the Europeans. While CA1's extract highlights the possibility of overlapping constructions of European and national identities (as also suggested by PR2 in the previous extract), it also reflects crucial tensions. In CA1's torn positioning in and out of the European space one can recognize wider discourses of inclusion and exclusion surrounding the long-debated Turkish membership of the EU and more generally of Turkish identity as Europe's historical 'other' (Rumford 2011). These tensions appear to shape and constrain CA1's discourse and to be internalized by the speaker in an almost 'schizophrenic' pattern of binary belongings and shifting inclusiveness/exclusiveness. In this case, rather than 'running along parallel tracks' as suggested by PR2's 'in-betweenness' (see Extract 19), European and national identities were represented as intersecting while also functioning as antagonists.

A conflictual representation of European and national identities was similarly achieved by CA3, a British national, who in the questionnaire described herself as 'primarily national and then European'. While CA3 characterized Europeanness in relation to mobility and intercultural encounters, her positive evaluation of these aspects was primarily enacted from a national stance. At the same time she constructed a divided representation of British society, a warrant through which she ambivalently called herself in and out of Europe as exemplified by the following extract:

Extract 21

RC: I was wondering if you would call yourself European (..) or perhaps trans-European, I mean how would you describe yourself (.)

CA3: I like to think of Europe as ... ehm ... yeah the experience of living in Europe as being transnational because I think it's very easy to move about and to exchange culture. I think living in the UK our experience is slightly different obviously being an island we are that much further away from it but I think by studying languages that, ehm that sort of distance is bridged because you spend a year abroad and obviously by speaking a foreign language you can sort of go and live in that country, and I think it becomes a lot easier ... I think yeah certainly like the way the UK is concerned people that only speak English I think... there is definitely a distance that they don't feel European or even maybe they don't speak a foreign language but if they are sort of really interested in European cultures ....it's probably as well a political thing some people are very sort of anti-Europe I think it is based on you know the fact that we are separate and people are very keen to guard that whereas other people are much more open to integrating ourselves into Europe and I think in Europe we are also viewed differently ... I think that the UK is in quite a unique position as being part of Europe I think.

In this extract the speaker constructed Europe as a space of free movement and, from a student's perspective, she emphasized positively the 'experience of living abroad'. In this context CA3 appealed to transnationalism mainly as the opportunity to engage in social practices of cultural exchange and language learning. Significantly, though, while CA3 valued European mobility positively, her belonging appeared indexed more to national than European referents and was discursively enacted from a British-centric perspective. Such a stance was signalled throughout her talk by CA3 use of personal pronouns ('we/ourselves') and possessive adjectives ('our experience') that clearly suggest her main group affiliation as British. Similarly, expressions such as 'a year abroad', 'a foreign language' and 'go and live in that country' would equally imply the speaker's nation-centric stance. Furthermore through the *topos of the UK insularity* CA3 represented the UK and (mainland) Europe as 'distant' and 'separate' entities emphasizing the geo-cultural 'uniqueness' of Britain and constructing a marginality of its relationship with Europe.[16] Such a strategy of dissimilation was initially achieved through the simple geographical argument of the UK being an island and therefore physically separated from mainland Europe.

However, CA3 also related the UK's separation to the distinctiveness of its culture through the argument that the UK is 'that much further away from [Europe]' (not necessarily a geographical fact) and that such a gap can be bridged by languages therefore inferring more than geographical distance and relying on a scenario of 'contained' national cultures. The *topos of insularity* was further used by the speaker as a warrant for her representation of views of the European project in the British society split between what have often been characterized as 'Eurosceptic' and 'Europhile' attitudes. Although CA3 offered a neutral representation of these two sides through the lexical choice of 'people', she consistently aligned her group membership with the British referent and its distinctiveness (her in-group positioning, for example, supported by the expression 'we are viewed differently'). At the same time, in the final proposition of Extract 12, the member discursively placed the UK within Europe albeit through the disclaimer on its 'uniqueness', a representation that, in relation to the extract, seems to reinforce a metaphorically peripheral positioning of Britain in relation to Europe and the speaker's own ambivalent location 'on the edge' of European identification.

PR1 offered another example of a conflictual interplay between national and European identities albeit from a very different positioning than illustrated in the previous examples. PR1 is a French national, who, at the time of the interview, had been living and working in Prague, having previously lived in the UK and Romania. When the member (who chose 'European only' and 'transnational' in the questionnaire) was asked directly about her European identity she replied:

Extract 22

PR1: I definitely feel European (.) erm I and I would identify myself as
 European erm
FZ: Would you define yourself as European only?
PR1: [Laughter] Well if it's the type of the context, of course, but it's true, for
 example I had recently this this kind of struggle (..) in the summer I took
 part in a summer school in Budapest [on the integration of Roma] and erm

so of course at at the beginning, the first lesson, the first class everybody
introduces himself or herself – So everybody says 'Yeah, hello I'm blah,
blah, blah. I come from this or that country.' And erm I don't know I maybe
it's because … I didn't feel comfortable saying I'm from France; so I said
I come from the Czech Republic. Because actually I am currently living
there and this is the country where I have just come from. So I felt very (…)
and the and the other side I am a French citizen and I grew up in France
so it's the country where I spent most … most of my lifetime [laughter] so
I cannot I cannot deny it either. But I realized okay why why do we have
always to introduce ourselves with a country of origin? Why … what is it
the first thing we say 'Hi, I'm [name] I'm from France.'? You know it's erm
why that? So I still haven't come a solution [laughter]. And it's true that
most of the time when I introduce myself if … if I have to say erm if it is
related to … to nationality, yeah I would say probably I'm from France.
But erm I I am still I fight through that in saying it. Then if I have to define
myself I would say I I feel a European citizen. But of course, if I meet some
other [laughter] … I'm hoping to say 'Hi I'm [name], I'm from Europe' I
don't know it's a bit ridiculous I think [laughter].

In the above extract, through a personal narrative, PR1 constructed multiple
identity options for herself (a European citizen; a French citizen/someone from
France and someone from the Czech Republic). While she acknowledged the
context dependency of their relevance she also represented the enactment of
different identities in terms of a *struggle* highlighting thus the tensions between
free choice, external constraints and the relationality of the 'other' (Jenkins 2014)
in her process of identification as European and the negotiation of European
with other identities.

On one level, PR1 constructed her struggle as the dilemma between her ideal
aspiration of claiming herself to be European and being called upon to claim an
identity based on national referents. Therefore, although the speaker suggested
that she would choose the European identification to best describe her feelings,
contextual and interactional constraints forced her to claim a national identity
as a convenient label to introduce herself. On another level, in defining her
national identity, PR1 also referred to the struggle between, on the one hand,
those conventional elements that would make her French (citizenship, culture,
etc.) and, on the other, her problematic acceptance of 'being French'. While the
member discussed this topic a few other times in the interview through the *topos
of honesty* (see strategies of dismantling nationhood in Section 5.3.4 for details of
'the moral dilemma of calling herself French') in this case the perceived negative

meaning associated with claiming a French identity is specifically inferable in relation to the controversial decision adopted by the French government in 2010 to shut down a number of Roma settlements and expel the residents.[17]

Although the member did not explicitly elaborate on this aspect, it would be reasonable to assume this was the most likely reason for PR1 to distance herself from being associated with France given the specific relational setting in which she had to call herself French, viz. a seminar on Roma integration. The Czech demonym was thus used by the speaker as a 'resource identity' which enabled her to resolve the impasse of wanting to dissociate herself from the negative French nationality on the one hand, while having to take up a national identity for her interlocutors on the other. PR1 realized the strategy of claiming a Czech identity through the pragmatic implications of the construction 'to come/be from' which can refer to both one's birthplace and residency. In PR1's discourse therefore the specific enunciates 'to feel European', 'to be French' and 'to come from France' appear to index: (a) different degrees of salience of identities (from an ideal aspiration of belonging to an 'imagined' European community to the formal attribution of French citizenship) and (b) different degrees of agency (as well as different external contingencies) that allow for the negotiation of multiple identities. By the same token, PR1's representations suggest the dynamic and tense interplay that European and national identities can embody and the general context dependency of identities.

BE1 (Berlin individual interview) was another member that, negotiating her different belongings, overtly questioned and rejected the national identification (in this case as a German) because of its negative connotation; this is exemplified by the extract below:

Extract 23

BE1: Yes I think for me I don't really identify as being German no not at all but this is also because of the German this is also because the German history they really don't have many good things to talk about but I identify with the really really small 300 people village I come from so this is quite easy to identify with the village I come from and then I identify as a Berliner now because I'm living in the city and I identify more [with Berlin] which is quite strange because it so much bigger as being European than being German but I think this is really more to do with my work with European alternatives.

FZ: This is really interesting because basically you're saying yes you are local and then you sort of bypass this national identity.

BE1: Yeah, but I think this is really just because of the German identity (..) for example I was so often in Italy before for longer times, and also thought it would be so nice to be an Italian woman, which is strange because it's another nation, but for me they really have [unclear] more positive than the German nationality, for example, (..) I think I just have a problem with the German in a way, due to history, which is quite strange because now, in the crisis it happens quite often that if you are German people say 'come on, but you're in Germany, and you've got money, and you can find a good job, so come on' but really, I can't be proud of it because I see the crisis from outside more than inside.

FZ: Am I correct in thinking that perhaps being European is also a way for you to make up for the bad image of being German.

BE1: No, no, I never had such a good feeling about being German.

FZ: Okay

BE1: So, so, no, it's not (..) is not because I feel so strongly European, no it is (..) no (.) I don't know (.) I can't (.) no (..).

As BE1 negotiated her multilevel affiliations it became apparent that she rejected a German identity as a negative referent. Initially, BE1 engaged in a strategy of delegitimization of the German identity through the *topos of history* realized in this case through the propositions 'they don't have many things to talk about' and 'I can't be proud of it'. Through the moral evaluation of a past which, in her view, marred the attractiveness of 'being German', the speaker clearly dissociated and excluded herself from the German community through the use of the pronoun *they*. Moreover the uneasiness of being German was also made discursively relevant by the speaker through the context of the current economic crisis. In this case, although she could potentially identify with a positively connoted German referent, PR1 indicated again her rejection of Germanness. The speaker realized such a strategy though her metaphorical external positioning (inferable from the expression 'I see the crises from the outside') through which she empathized, from a non-German stance, with other Europeans who have been affected by the crisis.

Despite the delegitimization of Germanness, the member indicated her desire to belong to an expanded community and she thus constructed her identification referents in a motion of spatial progression from the local to the supranational level. In her argument the speaker indicated that, although she is able to 'imagine' national communities (e.g. she could imagine 'being' Italian), her process of expansion rejected the national level on account of the specific negative indexicality of being German (a negative attribution that, however, she did not apply to her village or to Berlin). While BE1 did not make explicit the cause of her 'shame' associated with Germany (inferable from lack of 'pride'), it would be reasonable to attribute it to the Nazi past war crimes. This, however, was not taken further in the interview as she adopted a strategy of avoidance which was signalled by the broken phrases 'I can't, no...' suggesting she was dealing with a sensitive issue.

5.3.4 Macro-strategies of dismantling nationhood

Dismantling nationhood was achieved by members through discursive strategies aimed at deconstructing, problematizing, challenging and delegitimizing cultural and political meanings associated with the 'signifier' nation. The negative framing of nationhood was typically achieved by members in reference to the structure of 'nation states' and their crystallization in 'national' elements (such as borders) or established social representations of national groups and nationalities (the idea of being French, German and so on). Members predicated the negative representations of nations as artificial constructs on two main argumentative schemes: one based on a critical revisionism of nation states as cultural hegemonic projects and the other exposing the current inadequacy/ unresponsiveness of national structures (such as governments) vis-à-vis global flows. These strategies emerged explicitly especially when members were asked to elaborate on their understanding of transnationalism and in some cases it was elicited through the prompt 'what's wrong with nation (states)?' on the back of general negative stances on nationhood as illustrated further in Extract 14, Extract 15 and Extract 16.

5.3.4.1 *Topos of nationalism*

Several members realized strategies of dismantling nationhood through the *topos of nationalism* which challenged the general attachment to national referents. For example PR1 referred to nationalism in the wider meaning of a dangerous ideology as well as of its 'banal' forms of reproduction:

Extract 24
FZ: … and erm and I would like you to perhaps explain to me a little bit what what you think erm transnationalism is?

PR1: Yes. Erm so that's a bit tricky [laughter]. Erm well first of all I, I really cannot identify with the idea of of nation and nationalism – not only nationalism as a negative ideology but nationalism as such; whatever

definition you give it. Erm I I don't really, personally, I don't really
acknowledge the fact that there are nations and they correspond to some
kind of criteria. For me it's something which is quite abstract – and I agree
it exists as a kind of erm let's say [unclear] use it for erm some research or
to analyse something but in the everyday life I cannot actually identify with
this concept. So that's why actually transnationalism even though it contains
the word nationalism [laughter] – is closer to how I identify myself. Because
it's … it's exactly this transcending this idea of, this very restrictive idea of
nations …

FZ: What's wrong with nations?

PR1: Erm (pause) what's wrong with nations [surprised/high pitch + laughter]?
I don't know what nations are for … I think the problem with nations and
especially the way they have been constructed, you know there are different
ways they have been constructed but the results are exactly the same to
me, – is that they force you to live in this … to identify with this very
unique category which is why … they force [you] to identify with the same
criteria … and also to act as the person who identifies with this criteria …
you know the language and the religion or erm also to identifying with your
homeland, you know …

FZ: Would you then identify more with a local or regional community?

PR1: Well, for sure it is less dishonest. Because I think national identities is …
are really dishonest. If I say I … I am French; in a way I am lying because …
well I am because, as a matter of fact I am [French I] because I grew up
etcetera, etcetera, but I … I mean it means that I identify and that I embrace
the French nation. And I … I am sorry, but I do not [laughter]. So maybe I
embrace part of it, but not all of it and maybe some … I don't know … maybe
not at all you, you know … so I think at least this more … this more local
identification through your city or … or your village or … or both or region;
at least it is more honest. … you know last time I was having a lunch with a
Czech erm partner in Embassy – and … and we talked about this actually
and I told him how is it possible to identify with such a big country with sixty
million inhabitants, you know as in this idea of imagined community; yes,
okay, but how completely can I do it? It's not honest, I cannot do it.

PR1's strategies of dismantling nationhood were primarily predicated on the
topos of the reproduction of nationality. PR1 assumed that 'nationality' (as an
essentialist identity) is (re)produced through what she calls 'nationalism as
such' (that she regards separate from the ideology of national supremacy). For
PR1 'nationalism as such' constitutes a structured system of cultural and social
rules where 'nation' represents the main anchor/referent of group identity which

one is expected to validate in discourse (a perspective similar to critical views discussed in Section 2.3.1).

The speaker's strategies of dismantling nationhood appeared thus aimed, on the one hand, at characterizing nations as meaningless/negative referents of community and, on the other, at rejecting the personal reproduction of nationality through 'banal' self-categorization (i.e. the reproduction of discourses of nationality as a defined social category). Referring to transnationalism in opposition to nationalism she signalled her 'distancing' from the idea of nation and her 'closeness' to that of transnationalism representing such cognitive and affective orientations through the spatial metaphor IDEAS ARE PLACES, which represents the degree of relevance ('meaningful/meaningless') in terms of proximity ('near/far').

The speaker's rejection of nationality emerged more clearly in my request to unpack her argument of dismissal of nation (which caused her some surprise and hilarity or nervousness). In this case her strategy – initially aimed at characterizing nations as artificial and purposeless constructs and realized by the speaker as her rejection of the 'fact' that there are nations as tangible entities – went on to depict nations as negative agents as they constrain individuals to forcibly fit the category of 'nationals'. In the speaker's view, therefore reproduction of nationality is an artificial process of (self-)ascription of externally predetermined elements rather than developed out of a free choice. The main discursive tool used by PR1 to achieve the negative representation of nations in this process was through their agentivization, that is, their characterization as actors capable of determining, or at least influencing, one's behaviour and constraining one's choices, thus implying an asymmetric power relation between individuals and hegemonic structures.

In this context, the agentivization of nations rely on their interpretation as cultural and social structures (instantiated for instance in linguistic and religious practices etc. transmitted by family, schooling, state institutions) through which the reproduction of national identity occurs. This characterization and a critical appreciation of the process of (re)producing nationality seemed to warrant PR1's rejection of nationality as a 'constraining uniform' and to question her allegiance with the national community.

Such a positioning/stance was reinstated by the speaker when asked if local/ regional communities would be more appropriate categories that she could identify with. In this case, the speaker constructed her argument around the 'moral dilemma' of defining herself as French. In other words, she questions to what degree the term 'being a French person' captures her true bonding with the

French nation, rather than being a convenient label. Through the *topos of honesty,* PR1 seemed to suggest that all identity categories are available to individuals on a 'honest/dishonest or real/artificial continuum' that is, a moral evaluation of how they reflect one's feelings of groupness/membership and which appears directly related to physical proximity – a representation consistent with the 'near/far' metaphor of spatiality adopted earlier.[18]

Premised on the *topos of honesty,* the reproduction of Frenchness was perceived by PR1 as a forceful expectation to claim herself as something untrue. As in her earlier argument, the speaker is here implying awareness of the process of identification as the reproduction of belonging to the 'imagined community' clearly echoing Anderson's argument that a large community of strangers will feel a nation because they can imagine so (as discussed throughout Sections 1 and 2). While PR1 recognizes (through the pragmatic implications of 'I'm sorry') that there are social expectations of calling herself French (i.e. reproducing the sociocultural structures she was born and raised within, or in other words, 'being a French person'), her investment in these narratives is nevertheless not enough to reproduce her Frenchness as this would make her an 'impostor', something that on moral basis, she 'cannot do'.

Such a 'moral dilemma' was further represented by PR1 through the trope of personification of nation (i.e. the imaginary of nations as living entities), a rhetorical device that has been often adopted in many national and nationalistic discourses (Hobsbawm 2010). PR1 deploys the metaphor of 'embracing the nation' to construct a conflictual relation with her fellow citizens (the French imagined community) and, through some hedging, mitigating and conflictual propositions, she ultimately seems to (partly) reject the expectations of 'imagining herself French'. Through her moral critique of nationality the speaker thus not only challenges the historically established system of imagining oneself as part of a community described by Anderson (2006), but significantly she ultimately challenges the cultural system of reproducing nationality in discourse (what Hall (1996) regards as fundamental in the continuity of nations).

The critical deconstruction of nationality was also achieved by LO3 (London individual interview) through a negative characterization of nation states. When asked to clarify her stance, she argued along similar lines to PR1:

Extract 25

FZ: Can I ask you what is wrong with nation-states?

LO3: [Sighs] What's wrong with nation-states? It's a very good question. I think that erm (…) it's, it's the rigidity of them. It's the fact that there's this, this border that, that's been decided that that's, that's what your identity is erm and (…) and that it's pitting different nation-states against each other and, and suggesting that there's a, there's an interest for people within it that is, that is opposed to people's, er the interests of people outside it erm … and, and it is arbitrary.

LO3 delegitimized nation states through the conflation of different arguments and topoi. The *topos of artificiality* was used by LO3 to critically portray nations as closed and hegemonic systems of power, a representation which she supported with the trope of 'border' as a symbolic negative referent of containment and coerciveness. The term 'border' was employed synecdochically for the exercise of public power in nation states and it was given syntactic prominence as the agent/cause in a series of propositions in which, through historical inferences, nations were delegitimized on moral grounds for their dominance over people (i.e. for instrumentally constructing groups and fomenting their rivalry, imposing divides and ascribing identities). In LO3's argument 'borders' were thus used as the grammatical agent in a series of representations of negative actions (cf. 'it's pitting', 'it's opposed'). Unlike PR1 in Extract 14 who problematized nationhood as her moral difficulty of reproducing habitus, LO3 achieved a strategy of delegitimization of nation states relying, inter alia, on the *topos of container* (inferable, for instance, from the binaries 'people within/outside). This topos is discussed further in the next section below as it was invoked by several other interviewees in synergy with the *topos of flow*.

5.3.4.2 Topoi of flow and containment

Several strategies aimed at the dismantling of national constructs were achieved by members through specific realizations of the generic *topos of flow* that represented the movement of society, ideas, and so on. For example, BE2 (Berlin individual interview) drew on the imagery of the natural flow of historical events to dismantle nationhood primarily in reference to the 'inevitable' process of state disintegration. This is exemplified by the following extract:

Extract 26

FZ: I wonder, just as a provocative question, what's wrong with the nation-state
BE2: Oh well I think boundaries are a construct, this is not me who says it,
they are a construct, but a well-established construct, that, from a physical and political construct, has also become a cultural construct, so I think it is now difficult to go beyond this idea, and to take down the nation-state, and I think that it is not even necessary … it will happen, it will be a natural

process, I mean the disintegration of the nation-state is happening anyway, and it will happen because it is almost a biological process. I believe that the nation-state is becoming more and more obsolete but exactly for a natural process, fundamentally, occurring more in a network of cities than in a cluster of nation-states.

BE2 responded to the prompt 'what's wrong with a nation-state' with an argument that problematized nation states as artificially bounded units relying, like PR1, on a critical interpretation of nation as a historical and sociopolitical construct which has been reproduced culturally (although he supported this claim with a non-specific external source – 'it's not me who said it'). The speaker proposition that 'it is not necessary to go beyond the nation-states' would at first appear to contradict the premise on the artificiality of nations and even more the NGO's support for a transnational organization of society. However the speaker's main strategy here was to represent the dismantling of nation states characterizing it as a natural process occurring within an 'ecology' of society.

To construct his argument, BE2 relied on the *topos of flow* through which he represented the world as naturally interconnected. Furthermore he deployed the metaphor of THE WORLD IS A LIVING ENTITY to represent social phenomena in terms of natural processes. Depicting the world as a living body with its own biology, therefore, for BE2 social structures are liable to decay with the passing of time just like any living entity, this imagery evoked clearly by the verb disintegrate. At the same time, through his discourse BE2 depicted the degradation occurring to social structures as if they were part of a biological process of evolution whereby changes have functional purposes. The use of the word 'obsolete' is therefore to be interpreted not only in reference to the meaning of 'inadequate for the times' but also as 'no longer functional for the organism'.[19] Through this frame the speaker was thus able to contextualize the natural demise of nation states due to their functional inadequacy along an evolutionary line of progress and transformation (signalled by the progressive/future verbal forms 'is happening/ will happen'). This frame, highlighting the naturalness of the process, allowed the speaker to construct the NGO and its activities as somewhat involved in the process of dismantling but not necessarily the main agents. Later in the interview this representation was discursively reinstated by BE2 who referred to the organization activity as 'experimental' thus building/capitalizing on the conditions brought about by the disintegration of the nation state (see Extract 24 below).

Further strategies of dismantling nationhood were also achieved via the *topos of containment* which members deployed to represent nation states as units contained by artificial boundaries.[20] For example, CA2 used the trope of 'box' to explain her idea of transnationalism and to represent/negotiate her identities in these terms:

Extract 27

> CA2: … I guess I can call myself a transnational but obviously we also impose our own limits, our own boundaries, so…
>
> FZ: In what way, can you clarify?
>
> CA2: …ah … that … this thing that I am Romanian … OK so we were doing this exercise yesterday, picking a book title for our books in the human library [a cultural event that the Cardiff office had been organizing] and … and we were supposed to talk about our identity, and I was saying, okay, I am Romanian, but I don't like to think of myself as only Romanian, and to limit myself ..and to put myself in a box, within the boundaries of Romania, within the boundaries of Bucharest, and I like to consider myself as a world citizen actually not necessarily a European citizen.… so I guess this is transnationalism … we don't have to… we shouldn't at least from my point of view stick to only one box the Bucharest box or the Romanian box and then we should like distance ourselves and see the world from a more general perspective from the bird's eye view perspective.

In her argument, the member constructed her multiple identities through the frame of the 'world citizen' and the cosmopolitan ideology of one world where no division between humankind should exist on the basis of social and geographical borders. As discussed in McEntee-Atalianis and Zappettini (2014, p. 407):

> 'CA2's identification as a world citizen represents a "way of belonging" in the world community which emphasizes the interconnectedness of individuals and in which the taxonomy of identity based on geopolitical boundaries is seen as artificially constructed and imposed upon individuals.'

The speaker therefore appeared to use the CONTAINER metaphor (in the specific form of the 'box') to challenge the idea of a social order tied to locality and defined by clear-cut in/out dimensions. By deconstructing the 'boxes' (and their pre-constituted order) the speaker effectively deconstructed the salience of denominational communities such as nations. As suggested in McEntee-Atalianis and Zappettini (2014, p. 407):

> 'In this sense, it appears clear that the metaphor of spatiality deployed by CA1 draws on Beck's (2008) critique of nation-states as "containers" of societies, that is, as defined and bounded spaces of social interaction and where the boundaries have negatively come to represent the limits of new possibilities

of extended interaction. Moreover the metaphor of "containment" appears to drive her whole argument about "identity politics" that is the self-imposed limits of self-categorization. By deconstructing the boxes not only does the speaker deconstruct the salience of locality but she also rejects the "container theory of society" … and appears to refuse "ticking the box".

Moreover, CA2 appeared to challenge Herrmann, Risse-Kappen and Brewer's (2004) Russian Doll Model of European identities as discussed above (p. 51) that regards identities hierarchically stacked and embedded. Instead, in CA1's invocation of the 'bird's-eye view', one can recognize a spatial positioning that suggests her distancing 'above' and 'outside' the world 'boxes'. In this sense, the narrative of transnationalism arguably gives the speaker a reflexive opportunity to see the 'bigger picture' and to position herself in relation to it.

The 'container theory of society' was also challenged by RO1 (Rome individual interview) who (as in the previous two examples) drew on the trope of containers and the *topos of flow* to realize strategies of delegitimization of national structures aimed at showing the inadequacy of states vis-à-vis global flows, as illustrated below:

Extract 28

RO1: Yeah, transnational is just (..) a move beyond the idea that you know nations
are the sort of units of everything in which life happens and that, at best there
are relationships between nations (.) but the idea that life moves across nations
both my sort of work life and personal life ehm is a representation of that …
[he goes on to discuss travelling in many different countries for work in the
last few weeks] … so this is what transnational life is about so it's not any more
seeing going abroad as you know travelling to another country you know and
discovering something new but it's seeing the normalization of life in its every
stage love, work, leisure happening across borders with erm obviously the
complication that the world is not ready for that the world is still very much
based on national institutions and to give an example of that from my life I
can get married to my partner in London but I can't get married to my partner
here [in Italy] and if I get married to my partner in London I cannot come
back and live in Italy with my partner because marriage is not accepted and
he's not a European citizen, so he would not have a permit to stay so it's very
much the example of transnational life being there but nation-states putting
obstacles towards this transnational life flowing…

RO1 was engaged in an overall strategy of negative representation of nation states for which he used the *topos of movement* to juxtapose the 'flow of life' with the rigidity of national barriers. By contrasting the natural flow of transnational life on the one hand with the institutional organization of the world as defined by artificial national structures on the other, the speaker's goal was to show the inadequacy of the latter and, ultimately, to delegitimize them.

From a linguistic perspective the speaker realized this representation through the metaphor of LIFE IS MOVEMENT in which citizens interacting through increased cross-border mobility are metonymically referred to as life itself ('life moves across nations') and, therefore, positively connoted. Through his argument, the speaker also normalized practices of border crossing as naturalized 'ways of being' – that is, ordinary everyday life experiences encompassing different fields (love, work, etc.) and devoid of any exotic association. Against this backdrop of positive representations of 'vital' and 'natural' movement of society the speaker was able to characterize nation states as negative agents which regulate the natural free motion of life by applying artificial barriers to control movement (i.e. by enforcing border compartmentalization). RO1, thus, drew on the metaphorical concept of NATIONS/STATES ARE CONTAINERS ('units in which life happens') to criticize a purely intergovernmental notion of a world system (i.e. the idea that 'at best there are relationships between nations') that hasn't caught up with 'real life', his argument resonating with critiques of the container theory of society (Beck 2008).

In his argument, RO1 interpreted transnationalism not only as trans-border mobility of people and exchange of cultures, but also as the organization/regulation of such societal interaction as operated through institutional structures. RO1's discourse represented these dimensions in a tense relation of movement. While people and life were represented 'on the move', institutions were characterized by their inability or unwillingness to catch up with the former. This crucially allowed RO1 not only to portray nations as backward institutions but also as negative actors interfering with the flow by containing and regulating it. This depiction of borders as obstacles seems to challenge a typical representation of borders as necessary tools to regulate the 'flow/flooding' of migrants as found in many national public discourses (see, for example, Van Dijk 2000, Gabrielatos and Baker 2008). Furthermore by highlighting the tension between the free flow of life and the regulated order of society, RO1 raised the complexity of negotiating institutional and personal identities such as same-sex spouses, a matter in which (inter)national and supranational remits of legislation overlap conflictually.[21]

5.3.4.3 *Topos of inadequacy and global risk*

Another set of strategies aimed at challenging nationhood was predicated on the *topos of inadequacy of national structures* and the *topos of global risk/action*.

In general, these topoi were deployed by members to contextualize national initiatives against a global background, a premise which often enabled them to realize strategies of delegitimization aimed at discrediting nation states as no longer capable of performing their traditional functions of providing security and prosperity for their citizens.[22] For example, LO3 (London individual interview) referred to the *topos of global challenges* to represent nation states as non-credible actors or indeed 'non-actors' as shown in the following extract:

Extract 29

> LO3: I find as er (…) you have increased erm cross-border markets and environmental concerns, er, I think that … I think the argument clearly isn't that nation-states are getting less powerful but I do think there's a lack of … there's a, a reduced legitimacy of nation-states – given the fact that you have transnational corporations, you have global climate change, you have all these issues that are being avoided by nation-states because they can say, they can kind of claim powerlessness and claim that it's not in their interest to do something, because if they do something and no one else does then obviously that [unclear] competitiveness.

LO3 delegitimized nation states by embedding the sovereignty of their decisions into a global scenario made up of major actors and contingencies (generically nominalized as 'markets', 'corporations', and 'climate change'), a warrant that she constructed as a factual notion ('the fact that you have'). LO3 achieved her strategy of delegitimization through the argument that nation states do not constitute simply ineffective actors but also wilful non-actors while retaining their power. LO3 realized her argument though the passive continuous construction 'are being avoided' which, in this case, did not appear to be aimed at obfuscating the agent (nation states) as much as at foregrounding their non-action as well as the highlighting the sense of urgency.

Strategies that challenged and delegitimized national solutions also emerged prominently in the discussion conducted with the Romanian group where a few members invoked the *topos of global risk/action* (i.e. 'there is the need for globally concerted action vis-à-vis global problems'). As illustrated in the example below, CL5 (Cluj focus group) brought to the fore the issue of transnational organized crime while discussing the activities of the Cluj branch:

Extract 30

> CL5: Moreover, we believe that, nowadays, problems can be solved better at a transnational than national level (..) we just had an event yesterday about

the mafia (.) how can you stop the mafia at the national level when the mafia is transnational? It launders money in various countries from an account in Italy to an account in Romania, it brings garbage from Romania to Italy and then if governments don't collaborate they each stay with their problems while the mafia remains transnational, supranational.

As LO3, in this case the speaker referred to global challenges (in the specific instantiation of transnational mafia links) to construct the inadequacy of national apparatuses. In this case, rather than through a straight proposition, the delegitimization of nations was achieved by CL5 through the pragmatic implication contained in his rhetorical question 'How can you stop the mafia?'. Against this scenario, CL5 supported instead a response at the transnational level that he specifically saw instantiated in the concerted action of his (and other) NGOs, national authorities and the EU institutions. Like in Extract 15, CL5's proposition relied on the representations of opposing good and bad agents: on one side the mafia was personified as a cross-border actor (through the expressions 'it launders/it brings garbage') and, on the other side, a broad and hybrid 'us' group made up of the larger transnational civil society referenced through emphasis on the pronoun *noi* (we) (which is normally omitted in Romanian as such information is already carried by the verb declination) and that must thus be interpreted as highlighting the transnational agency of the group.

5.3.5 The construction and transformation of communities, spaces and social orders

Members realized a number of strategies aimed at the construction and transformation of feeling part of a collectivity. By using different arguments that emphasized different organizational, political and cultural aspects of groupness, members represented multiple communities of relevance[23] and associated with one or more of them. Discourses of mutual engagement and sharedness contributed, on the one hand, to representations of EA as a community of practice, of interest and of action, while on the other hand most members clearly indexed their activities to wider social, political, and cultural ideals thus constructing their belonging to wider imagined European/ transnational/ world communities. In most cases, thus members constructed their European identities between social and organizational dimensions through topoi of network, values, democratic dialogue and solidarity, which will be discussed further below.

5.3.5.1 *Topos of network*

The topos of network was used by members to represent the interconnectedness of their activities and to achieve strategies of unification and expansion of community. In some instances these strategies were achieved primarily from an organizational perspective as exemplified in the following extract (Cluj focus group):

Extract 31

> CL2: We have colleagues in Italy, England, France that I talk to every day,
>   and … we do activities together (.) the festival is transnational in the sense
>   that certain events are happening in several cities … in Cluj, London at the
>   same time, and … it is transnational, because there is a close cooperation
>   between young people from various countries and not because somebody
>   above gives an order or something …, but it is a continuous exchange
>   of ideas and possibilities for action … there really are no borders in
>   our work, … there is never any problem traveling (.) except for money,
>   of course, but otherwise, the Internet is available anytime and we can
>   communicate, transmit anytime.

CL2 highlighted certain practical aspects of community interaction representing events occurring seamlessly across time and space (e.g. he highlighted the simultaneity of communication inside the organization and the fact that the Trans-Europa festival takes place simultaneously in different cities). While these aspects were discussed primarily in relation to work practices (suggested, for example, by the term 'colleagues') he also stressed the NGO's non-hierarchical structure ('nobody gives us orders') and the agency of individuals engaged in a common purpose of cooperation, suggesting thus that for EA members the salience of being networked is more than being a community of practice (Wenger 1998). The aspects of engagement and connectivity underscored by CL2 represented the main drivers for most members' representations of feeling part of a 'node' on the network and, above all, of their ability to participate in the creation and the expansion of the network itself as conveyed by these two extracts (Valencia and Prague individual interviews):

Extract 32

> VA1: For me one of the most important things is to work locally because
>   in grass roots things have to start from below … you've got to make
>   people aware (…) I think it's very important for organizations like EA to
>   have this kind of transnational conscience … to raise awareness among
>   people … at the same time I think it's very important to network you
>   know like you have to work from the most loc-local level to the most

international and transnational level it's kind of yeah I am working here but you know things get connected between small groups all around Europe and you know the voice can be stronger for what we are defending or whatever.

Extract 33

PR2: The network is working on (..) in terms of reaching out to individual people and kind of informing and connecting, because I think that, you know, in a lot of ways there is a lot of information, ahem, about er this kind of EU project, this EU idea out there, is the idea of getting people engaged, getting people interested … and so for me again like this is what I like about the network, that it really is working on this erm, again on a very local level and then kind of expanding from there.

In the above extracts, both members characterized their activity as taking place within live communities of interest and action which, for example, VA1 connoted positively through the attribution of a 'transnational conscience' and a 'voice' which personifies EA as a living entity capable of moral decisions. PR2 achieved a similar representation through the proposition that 'the network is working' thus depicting the NGO structure as an actor of its own. Furthermore through the metaphor of network and interconnectedness the community was not represented in a predefined but in an ongoing process of transformation and capable of expanding, propagating and reaching out to other members. In these representations it was also clearly noticeable how members had an important investment in their role as active citizens that is being agents in creating connections and enlarging the network.

While the two examples above illustrate a construction of network primarily from an organizational perspective, other members used the *topos of network* to conceptualize changing social structures and social orders and the very idea of community. In a significant number of cases realizations drawing on the topos of network enabled members to construct social interconnectedness and to imagine the European community linked beyond borders and embedded in a glocal system of connections. For example, discussing the topic of transnationalism during the interview, EA's Cultural Director BE2 (Berlin individual interview) highlighted this aspect by engaging in a vivid representation of networked physical and social spaces through a biological metaphor:

Extract 34

BE2: Internationalism always presupposes a two-way closed relation whereas
… transnationalism pushes one to think in a more horizontal more

rhizomatic way not in a one-to-one closed fashion but this idea of crossing
that allows me to move, think, reflect both geographically and culturally
through several nations without forcing me down a path without having to
go from point A to point B I can move between A and Z in different ways
that have new relationships and of course I'm talking of relations between
nations and communities between the local and the global this I believe this
is what transnationalism is I believe it's a way of thinking.

The main strategy achieved by BE2 was the representation of the world's
different communities interconnected by culture and not bounded as self-
contained units. In his account, BE2 relied on the metaphor of NETWORK,
which he realized via the interdiscursive reference to 'rhizomatic' thinking.[24] By
invoking the *topos of network* through the botanical metaphor, BE2 appealed to
a natural and biological interconnection of the world (see Extract 16, p. 181, for
a strategy of dismantling nationhood achieved via a similar realization). From
this perspective, he represented cultural exchange as the 'lymph' that circulates
uninterrupted through the rhizome/world and that should not be interrupted by
artificial containments such as its crystallization in national cultures. Trading on
this premise, BE2 construed (his) identity as a fluid relationality with the world's
cultural flows and, furthermore, he highlighted an agentive element in his ability
to choose the path/interaction one wishes to follow.

This depiction points to a cosmopolitan outlook on the world where
transnational flows are naturalized (as the rhizome) and nations are somewhat
portrayed as artificial barriers. In BE2's account on the multi-directionality of
paths linking the local with the global, a particular spatial configuration was thus
recognizable which tends to emphasize connections as the relations between
units rather than the units themselves (cf. Castell's conceptualization of network
discussed on p. 63). Moreover, the representation of identities as 'options' that
one could choose and rearrange for oneself echoes Beck's interpretation of
reflexive identification processes in a cosmopolitan society (see p. 41).[25]

5.3.5.2 *Topos of imagination*

The *topos of imagination* represented an argumentative scheme that members
frequently deployed to construct an ideal European community especially
through metaphorical representations of society as moving, expanding and
progressing in space/time. For example, AM1 (Amsterdam individual interview)
constructed a dynamic relation of movement between multiple communities/
identities through the spatial/geographical metaphor of 'mapping'. In particular
AM1 used the trope of *scale (Dutch schaal)* to construct the European space

and the imagined boundaries of the European community as an expanded (g)
locality. Through the trope of *schaal*, AM1 drew on the concept of (linear) scale –
the ratio between a distance on a map and the actual distance on the earth – to
represent her 'mental map' of Europe, as illustrated below:

Extract 35

FZ: Okay, so how do you go about this new Europe that you want to erm,
create …

AM1: There is this concept (..) schaal verharding (.) no, what, what's it called in
English, concentric circles idea [slowly] [unsure] or the, the, that you up the
scale [high tone] that you go from, from one (…) community to a bigger
community erm (…) in Dutch it's schaal you know (…) scale enlarging
[rising tone] (…) erm (…) [brief discussion on the spelling of schaal]

FZ: Okay and (..) I mean how does one feel connected at European level, I
mean what is it that makes you European in this (..) upscaling as it were?

AM1: That, it's the idea that if you can erm increase that scale in your head
from, from a region to a nation then, then you should also be able to (…)
see it erm in a, in a bigger scale, and I think that (.) that there, it's, I think
it is erm (…) it is really the, the borders that you, that you have in your
head [laughs] I would say that (…) erm (…..) that after, after your your
nation-state the next logical step is Europe because that's the continent
you are on or something and after that it's the world but I dunno if it's the
final step [laughs] perhaps we could go to, to a different planet! Yeah, I
think so that that's, that that would be the next logical step but that is so, er,
incomprehensible [high tone] for people, the world is so big – that erm in,
in, in Europe people can find erm (…) er, we say they could (…) er, Europe
kind of (.) is the new (…) the, the new frontier.

Like some other members, AM1 relied on the metaphorical scenario of
communities progressing in space (realized through expressions such as
'you go from … to' and 'the next step'). Notably, AM1's strategy was aimed at
depicting European identity as one stage in the dynamic process of expanding
the imagination of community. While this imagery is partly consistent with the
Russian Doll Model (see above), AM1 also represented the motion of expansion
of communities as limitless (i.e. towards 'one planet' or beyond); her argument
therefore resonates with cosmopolitan visions of the world as one 'global village'
or a 'Global Gemeinschaft 2' (as discussed on p. 67).

AM1 realized her argument through the *topos of imagined community* (i.e.
Anderson's theory on the construction of national 'we–ness'). Drawing on this
topos, the speaker argued the possibility and desirability of expanding one's

perception of community by shifting the imagination of borders (linguistically realized through 'upping the scale') and by backing her claim with the warrant that if one can think of a regional or a national community then one should also be able to imagine a wider European/world community.

Reproducing membership of local communities on a larger scale or territory was represented by AM1 as a primary cognitive process and consequently, in her view, what makes one European is the idea of seeing oneself as a member of a larger community. In this case the speaker's representation of 'border' was notably different from that adopted by other members, for example, in strategies of dismantling nationhood (see LO3 in Extract 26) in as much as that the signifier 'border' supported the notion of enlarged community and was assigned more positive than negative connotations. Furthermore, the representation of communities historically moving towards larger configurations was enhanced by the use of the term 'new frontier'. Such a term not only suggests the physical edge of boundaries but is distinctly related to notions of exploration/pioneering and visionary social reforms.[26] AM1's strategy seemed therefore to achieve a redefinition of space and community in expansion and to construct Europe as a proxy for the ongoing narrative of human wealth and social justice.

Representations of Europe as an imagined space also emerged conspicuously in the interview conducted with BE1, who is the coordinator of the Berlin branch and also an anthropologist in the field of migration and social movements. One of the most prominent aspects of her discourse was an explicit metaphorization of Europe through the *topos of Utopia*[27] as illustrated below. Utopianism (i.e. an ideological commitment to constructing a better society) has historically been the basis of various civil political and cultural movements in and outside Europe and it has generally represented a central imaginary for all societies '*n order to answer basic questions relating to their identity and orientation to the world [which] extends beyond the institutional forms of society with a vision of an alternative society*' (Delanty 2009, p. 19).

BE1's metaphorical representation of Europe as a (non)place through the *topos of the Utopian ideal* represented a major linguistic device that clearly permeated her vision and ultimately made sense of her discursive and social goals as illustrated by the following extract:

Extract 36

BE1: Ehm I see Europe well ehm I have a special view on Europe I think because I don't see it as a geographical space because ehm the things we're talking about we're handling with [*sic*] are are not geographical if you talk issues of migration for example so ehm [pause] well yeah

FZ: Okay yeah so if I were to ask you what Europe means to you … what defines Europe of course from a transnational point of view?

BE1: Europe I mean when we're talking about Europe to me it's more really kind of imagination of the wish of how we can live together it doesn't work in reality at the moment but it's an idea we have to go to … I think that the idea of this ideal of having a shared place to live in makes me European and yeah … yeah [pause]

FZ: Okay … shall we call it a … an imagined community?

BE1: Yeah you can call it an imagined community

I: Or is it really about place?

BE1: No no no no it's no no no it's no it's not about place no it's not mmh

FZ: Or maybe not a physical place maybe an ideal place as you called it

BE1: It's a kind of utopia if you ask me yeah [a utopia] we should go to

FZ: And in this … well let's call it utopia then, who can participate I mean can anyone be European …? who can be European?

BE1: In the utopia everybody who wants to be European can be European I think [long pause] yeah yeah I think it's more it's a more … not a geographical or political one it's more about divisions but you know this utopia could be everywhere I also could be talking about the whole world but Europe is a place I can think about Europe is more or less an ideal about it so everybody who's interested in this field is sharing with me this idea of Utopia and they can take part in it … yeah I mean the European Union is not a utopia it's not an ideal … Europe for me is more well what I was talking about before so it's not a geographical thing so …ehm m-my Europe, my image of Europe is quite bigger then EU countries and it's really more about this shared ideal of a peaceful shared place

FZ: Okay okay and would you say this is what brings trans-Europeans together

BE1: I'm quite sure yes yes … but this ideal could be everywhere I mean it could be somewhere in Africa it's just a shared yeah a shared ideal yeah that's it

FZ: Okay so okay and do you think it is by chance that it's in Europe physically or are there also historical reasons or …

BE1: No of course there are historical reasons it's not just about sharing this this utopia it's just place focused you know but I mean this what I well let's call it utopia and this is really about shared values and shared idea of a peaceful place and this could happen everywhere but of course there's a process in Europe and you have this idea of Europe of this peaceful place after the Second World War and of course and it also due to certain issues it is what it is and am happy about it and just to to put it away from this geographical thing … mmh, I mean if you if I were living in New York I

would engage in the same things I'm doing here I'm quite sure because
it's a human idea and yeah what I mentioned before this integration and
migration thing of course it matters if there are African people in Berlin,
Africa is part of Europe in this moment it's connected of course.

During the interview, BE1 achieved different strategies of deterritorialization of
Europe through the *topos of Utopia*. While at the level of literal meaning BE1 often
characterized Europe as an ideal society rather than a physical place through
propositions that frequently downplayed, if not dismissed, the geographical
dimension; at a metaphorical level BE1 often relied on representing Europe as a
'place' and her commitment to a better European society as the journey towards it.

These two levels of meaning were articulated in an argument that can be
summarized as follows: there is a moral obligation for individuals as citizens
to achieve a better (i.e. more just, equal, and peaceful) society and because
IDEA(L)S ARE PLACES and PURPOSES ARE DESTINATIONS, progress
towards the goal is made by moving towards the desired place. As she often used
the terms 'place' and 'space' interchangeably in her talk, the metaphorization of
spatiality adopted by BE1 may entail different representations of the European
ideal society as more or less contained. All the same, filling the gap between a
socially divided Europe (as the point of departure) and an all-inclusive society
(as the ideal destination) represented, for BE1, a metaphorical path to follow
which provided her with a sense of destination and purpose for her journey.

In BE1's spatial conceptualization of Europe therefore the path to a bigger-
and-better-than-the-EU European society constituted a powerful referent for
her orientation to Europeanness so that the process of 'getting there' appeared
just as salient for her identity as the destination itself. Significantly, BE1's dual
representation of the European space as both a destination and a journey
contributed to her construction of European identity as the dynamic interplay
of the two and an unfinished product given the unattainability of Utopia.

Moreover, through her strategy of deterritorialization the member also
constructed a tense representation of Europe and the EU as somewhat
divergent projects. A few times in the conversation the speaker signalled her
partial dissociation from the institutional vision of Europe, highlighting the
discrepancy of real and ideal scenarios. BE1 thus clearly expanded the notion of
Europe outside the geographical boundaries of the institutional project through
a series of arguments predicated on cosmopolitan views and the topoi of *global
citizenship enacted locally* and *universality of ideals*. Through these topoi, she
was able to imagine Europe as a universal (rather than territory-specific)

ideal and therefore to envisage its implementation in any physical space even outside the European continent. BE1 therefore constructed a 'transportability' of Europeanness that for instance enabled her on the one hand to reconstruct Africa as part of Europe and, on the other, to recognize the EU project as a favourable context for implementing utopian visions.

The topos of *imagining a better society* was also taken up by AM1 (Amsterdam individual interview) during her discussion of the reasons for joining the organization. AM1 referred to (transnational) Europe as 'an idea' that she realized she was sharing with others, as illustrated in the extract below:

Extract 37

AM1: I erm (…) erm, well, … the title of my thesis [was] European
    Alternatives [high tone] … and when I was looking for [laughs] erm if there
    was already something else called that, then I found – found out that the
    organization was called that, but I hadn't heard of the, of the Trans Europa
    Festival also and that was actually an idea that I had years ago … so I think
    it's er, for me it felt like, 'Oh yeah okay' [high tone] so that's, it also kind of
    feels like my own baby or something [laughs] Like now I don't know how
    to say it but it's erm I can really connect with, with the whole idea behind
    it because erm, yeah, it had, it had popped in my mind before as well and
    I think that's maybe also interesting in these times that are, that there
    are different people in Europe thinking the same idea, like what, er, let's
    experiment with this European thing.

Although AM1 referred to the cognitive aspect (an idea) of imagining transnational Europe, she clearly highlighted the affective dimension of her interest and the strong degree of personal investment in such project through the metaphor of 'her own baby' which suggests her close relation with the idea. On the back of this representation of sameness, the member engaged in a strategy of representing the process of connecting herself with other like-minded people and developing their shared ideas further thus relating her imagination to the construction and the expansion of the network. Therefore, while the process of identification represented by AM1 seemed to rely on the recognition of shared elements of imagination with other 'trans Europeans', it also involved a strong element of agency and openness to the potential outcomes of the Trans-European project and ultimately it seemed to drive her vision of community. Such a definition of community was linguistically realized, inter alia, through the open and inclusive indexicality of the pronoun *us* in the cohortative realization 'let's experiment with this European thing'. Furthermore 'different people' in the proposition 'there are different people in Europe thinking the same idea' suggests a wider and diversified community involved in 'doing' Europe.

5.3.5.3 *Topos of (transnational) 'active' citizenship*

In members' accounts, representations of their active participation in the construction of a European civil society emerged conspicuously as referents of Europeanness. In this sense, members' identification as Europeans seemed to derive primarily from the exercise of active citizenship and their investment in being active agents in the process of 'doing' Europe. Furthermore, active citizenship was interpreted in light of a culturally open citizenship, that is, from the premise that any individual should contribute to a participatory democracy and the democratic life of a community regardless of their cultural background or any formal membership. This point was discussed by PR2 (Prague individual interview) as illustrated below:

Extract 38

PR2: Erm, (…) the idea of transnationalism for me really means this idea
of (..) that people independent of geographical borders are still coming
together saying that we have a common idea, a common voice and we have
a common purpose … this idea that everyone, you, you're not locked by,
by where you are geographically and where you're kind of home is. Erm,
I mean it's especially an issue for me because I guess that though, even
though I am not European by birth, living here for a long time I can still
contribute in some way and it doesn't matter if I'm living I Prague or I'm
living in Berlin or I'm living in the UK, I can still contribute to this idea of a
greater overarching community.

PR2's construction of community was initially realized through an argument of convergence of transnational interests through the metaphor of journey and entailments of movement ('people are coming together'). In addition, the member constructed a widely inclusive 'we'-community through a strategy of unification that attributed different commonalities to the group. Against this background, the member was also able to claim an active role in the construction of the European community, despite the disclaimer that she is not European by birth.

Such an argument was supported by the *topos of active citizenship* through which the speaker represented civic participation decoupled from cultural or geographical containments – such a deconstruction realized via the metaphorical entailments of 'home' for culture and 'locked' for physical places. By relying on the warrant of deterritorialized civic action, PR2 was able to represent her local contribution as meaningful to the imagination of an expanded community.

Other members represented their engagement as active citizens/agents in EA through the metaphorical scenario of 'experiment'. Through this scenario several members constructed Europe as a 'laboratory' with the right set of conditions for developing a better society through transnational forms of democracy thus characterizing their activity within EA as the opportunity to test such experimental forms of civil engagement. This representation emerged, for example, when LO2 (London focus group) discussed his main motivations for joining the organization as illustrated below:

Extract 39

> LO2: I originally joined EA because I was really interested in this idea of what happens next politically and culturally and socially after... after this sort of century where we had an organization of the world into nation-states …
> and I was interested in what happens next so my expectations were (..) ehm of, very much more experimental way of looking at political organizations because there are (…) because there are (..) there really is the question of moving beyond the nation-state moving beyond erm ways of organizing erm politics and and is ... and I think it's often been very easy erm when talking about Europe … people just think about Europe … just being a big state, just being a very big state and not have that sort of ... additional creativity to think that it's not simply one big state but actually it is something different, it's not a state any more and that in those senses those are the aspects I, I wanted to play with and experiment with more and have sort of more creativity with and so in that sense ehm ehm ehm, I, I, I think there's more that could be done.

LO1 engaged in a strategy of construction of Europe as a new polity drawing on a specific *topos of the advancement of democracy* which he referred to a few other times throughout the discussion. Through this topos, LO2 represented democracy as the development of the political organization of European societies, that is, a historical process of moving from power exercised by dictators or monarchs to more democratic forms of sharing and representation (cf. Extract 3 in which Europe was represented at risk of 'slipping back into tyranny').

In this sense, LO2 had argued earlier in the interview that modern European politics has been reliant on the paradigm of nation states that is, organized around territory and ethno-cultural criteria for citizenship and participation in political life, a notion that he repeatedly problematized. By contrast, he represented active citizenship as an opportunity to develop the European society out of the nation-state system into newer and better forms of democracy. Such a proposition was argued along spatial and temporal dimensions, realized respectively through the expressions 'the question of moving beyond the nation-state' and 'what happens next'. For LO2, therefore, the personal salience of Europeanness seemed grounded in his civic commitment to social change and in his ability to be an actor in such a process of transformation.

The scenario of experimentation emerged in BE2's (Berlin individual interview) discourse too as a warrant for constructing a mobile European space/ community as illustrated below:

Extract 40

BE2: I see the European space as an interesting space of experimentation.

FZ: OK, in what sense?

BE2: In the sense that perhaps it has the dimension, the cultural and political
    conditions for putting in … for implementing this idea of transnationality
    for the time being only in Europe because … although for me it will have
    to develop by necessity beyond the European space expanding for example
    to the space south of the Mediterranean … many see precisely in this idea
    of Europe, in this feeling of belonging to Europe … just a first step in being
    able to experiment with the idea of transnational citizenship beyond that
    of national citizenship. … And the way I see it is just like this a space for
    a first test – I like to call it a first exercise of sharing – because it has the
    right geographical dimension to … to be able to be able to try it let's say…
    however it will be possible to do it also outside of Europe although for now
    it's easier in Europe as we already have the institutions.

Like LO1 in the previous example, BE2 characterized Europe as a new political system which has the right conditions for the enactment of transnational active citizenship, that is, a form of community membership separate from nationality.

For BE2, therefore, rather than being a formal membership attributed top-down on ethno-cultural grounds, transnational citizenship should be claimed through active participation in the political life of the 'imagined' community. Moreover, for BE2 such a model should further emerge from the formation of a public sphere, the sharing of a political culture and it ought to include any individual who is willing to participate in the life of the polity. Through his argument, BE2 achieved a representation of Europe as an ideal civic community whose members derive their sense of belonging from the investment in the idea of transnationality. Furthermore, while on the one hand BE2's representations were aimed at anchoring the process of political transnationalization of Europe to the EU institutions (whom the speaker aligned with through the pronoun 'we'), on the other hand a strategy of transformation was recognizable, aimed at moving and expanding the transnational community beyond EU-rope. As other members, BE2 represented such a process as a bottom-up, one-directional motion ('step') initiated locally and propagated further out by geographical proximity in an almost inevitable cosmopolitan progression.

BE2 was able to construct his argument of movement and expansion through different levels of abstraction of the term 'European space', a strategy also deployed by other members (see, for example, Section 5.3.5.2) that, in many cases, allowed for transient and movable boundaries of the European community. In the extract above, for example, the European space (initially constructed as an ideal scenario of transnational democracy) is subsequently characterized as geographical Europe and finally conflated with the EU, thus constructing different overlapping communities of relevance. Nevertheless through the representation of Europe as a 'lab', or a metaphorical environment for running a transnational pilot test that would have to be replicated worldwide, BE2 emphasized the salience of participating in a project of community building from grassroots and, furthermore he embedded the experience of constructing a European *demos* in the wider context of belonging to a global community.

Several members deployed the topos of *active citizenship* to construct their identification as Europeans through their political engagement. For example, when asked about his motivation for joining the NGO, RO1 (Rome individual interview) replied:

Extract 41

> RO1: Last year I left the UK to come back to Italy because I wanted to get involved in politics after spending so many years away my main interest remained Italian politics which I was appalled of and constantly ashamed of while being outside and I thought that I could sort of use the ability I developed outside my own country so there was this sort of almost innate feeling of patriotism and it came out of this stronger kind of often (…) subconscious feeling that you had to do something that's been on your mind that you have to do it for your own people (…) that said I think the Italian identity is only transitory (..) it is only for the time being 'cause I do see the European alternative as a much bigger one but it's somehow less shared for the moment.

RO1's political commitment was a recurrent theme throughout the interview and it seemed to represent for him what Aristotle termed a *bios*.[28] In other words, his identification process appeared to be driven by the construction of ties with fellow citizens around common civic interests. RO1 justified the motivation of his commitment to politics primarily in emotive/biological/ genetic terms ('almost innate'/'subconscious feeling'), and through rhetorically laden possessive expressions such 'own people', 'own country'. Furthermore, unlike any other member, he referred to 'patriotism' a lexical choice that clearly underlined a strong community attachment and involves a sense of pride and responsibility towards his nation.

While RO1's political commitment stood out among most other participants and, in many regards, from the NGO discourses too, his reclaiming of a bond with his 'own people' however appears to be dependent on the short-term contingency of 'appalling' and 'shameful' Italian politics. Therefore, while he portrayed the Italian society as the object of his current political commitment to social justice, he appeared to be equally willing to redirect his commitment to a new, bigger, more relevant purpose and to share such a commitment with a larger community. In other words, he uncoupled his democratic identity from nationalism in the direction of Habermas' 'constitutional patriotism' (2003) that would make Europe a sound post-national project.

In this case, the member constructed the *transportability* of his active citizenship (i.e. his political engagement as a source of identity) through a strategy of transformation of his civic allegiance to a new and bigger 'imagined' community, a strategy that he realized through the pragmatic relativization of his initial expression 'that said'. Furthermore through such an argument of transition, RO1 represented Italian and European identities in antagonizing terms over time; their mutually exclusive interplay is suggested by the adjective 'alternative'. The member here clearly represented the transitory nature of Italian identity vis-à-vis the European/transnational referent through temporal expressions such as 'for the time being' and 'for the moment' which suggest a transient stage in the process of transformation from one to the other.

The *topos of active citizenship* emerged also in the Cluj focus group where a few members used it to construct Europeans as a larger community of citizens and, at the same time, to downplay or dismiss their attachment to the nation:

Extract 42

CL4: What I mean is that we see ways to solve problems and ways of action without taking into consideration the national state or institutions, but we think how the ordinary citizen, one like us, a citizen of Cluj when they come up with an idea, how to present it to someone who has power, but someone who does something for all Europeans, because we are all European citizens.

In this extract CL4 constructed an argument that represents active citizenship as the direct relationship between civic actors at a local level and the EU institutions. Through this argument, the speaker achieved different constructions of groupness signalling her belonging to different communities of relevance. Along with her initial orientation towards the organizational identity ('we see ways to solve problems'), CL4 explicitly identified herself as 'a citizen of Cluj' and as a European (which consistently reflect the self-ascription she gave in the questionnaire 'first a citizen of my own town, then European' – see Table 4.4). This construction crucially appears to sidestep the level of identification as national, with, in fact, the significance of national institutions overtly dismissed by the speaker. The legitimization of this direct allegiance between local and European levels seemed to interdiscursively relate to the specific construction of Europeanness emerging from the Romanian focus group that was interpreted as an index of equality/emancipation (see 5.3.3.3). In this sense, while CL4 could enact her multilevel active citizenship, she bypassed the national level reinforcing her allegiance with local and European institutions.

5.3.5.4 *Topoi of transnational democratic dialogue and equal participation/representation*

Along with the topos of active citizenship, the *topos of democratic dialogue* was often invoked by members to achieve, inter alia, micro-strategies of unification aimed at the self-representation of a cohesive community of citizens engaged in a democratic dialogue between themselves and with the EU institutions.

In a few cases, strategies of unification were realized through the metonymical use of 'voice', a trope semantically related to democracy via, for instance, 'freedom of speech' and 'debate'. Often the trope of 'voice' was invoked by members synecdochically, as pars pro toto, to represent the collective action of citizens wanting to 'be heard' by (the EU) institutions. For example, these representations emerged conspicuously in the interview conducted with VA1 (Valencia individual interview). In many instances during the interview, VA1 constructed a feeling of commonality through the trope of 'voice' and the *topos of equal participation* (i.e. the Aristotelian principle of justice whereby, in a democratic system, equality among citizens is based on their number, not their worth) as exemplified by the following extract:

Extract 43

VA1: The way Europe is now conceived … it doesn't it doesn't eh … it doesn't have to be with this political and economic system and this setup you

know it's not democratic you know like I don't think all – all the countries
inside the … the E-European European Union system are treated with
the same opportunities so I don't think they have the same voice … inside
EA is different yeah maybe not but all of us have the same ideas but we
can discuss it and we can agree something … because when in European
Alternatives we have transnational meetings our voices can have the
same value whereas (…) at institutional level the things that Germany
says will be that (..) [laughter] you know they're not going to discuss with
other countries … [she gives a long example of political fragmentation
among Spanish political parties] so this idea of a single voice is like we're
all different but we have a process of decision made by participation and
democracy and we finally manage to have one voice although each one has
their own ideas and this is what makes you heard by institutions because if
we were like thousands of different voices what would happen in the end
is that we wouldn't manage anything and this is why I was comparing it
with the situation in Spain … this is also what happens with this European
citizens' initiative when we all have a common goal and we try to reach
some changes in the law and this … and this you can only manage because
of the different voices make one.

In the extract above, VA1 initially represented the EU as an unequal
economic association of countries and she aimed at delegitimizing this setup
through the *topos of equal participation/representation*. The member realized
her strategy through the synecdoche of 'voice' (that anthropomorphizes
states as disempowered/discriminated against humans) arguing that the
intergovernmental arrangement of the EU favours the more economically
powerful countries. This proposition was further elaborated by VA1 in relation
to Germany, which she perceived as the dominating actor in the current financial
crisis. This negative representation set up a comparative framework through
which VA1 was able to contrast the grassroots approach and to portray EA in a
positive light, as democratic, through the proposition that within the NGO all
'voices have the same value' (i.e. have the same power).

In this case, VA1 realized her construction through the same synecdoche of
'voice' in reference to members and by contrasting the plurality of opinions at
grassroots level with their restricted representation at institutional level. The
speaker was thus able to portray the NGO as a non-national civic actor that
'talks with the institution' in a recontextualization of the institutional discourses
of 'Plan D' (see p. 12). In contrast to the delegitimization of the EU setup,
however, the speaker used the trope of 'voice' to legitimize the group action and
to construct it as a cohesive force. On the back of this different representation,

the construction of the European society in VA1's discourse appeared focused on the notion of power distribution and organized around (positively connoted) transnational rather than (negatively connoted) national interests.

Through the trope of voice, VA1 achieved an overall representation of Europeans as a community of citizens exercising their democratic rights transversally and bottom-up. Such a trope was also instrumental in the juxtaposition of (closed) intergovernmental and (open) transnational conceptions of Europe. Whereas in the former, VA1 represented power instantiated in a few national representations (EU countries) and exercised unequally, in the latter she represented the power of 'voice' as evenly distributed within EA and, at the same time, capable of being consensually mobilized into a cohesive aggregate (realized through the unifying expression 'different voices make one').

Although VA1's use of 'we-European citizens' was primarily enacted from an organizational perspective, it appeared to index the wider scope of transnational civic action, for example, in her reference to the citizens' initiative campaigns which, in some cases, have been carried out by EA in association with other civil actors.[29]

5.3.5.5 *Topos of values*

The discussion of (shared) values, principles and beliefs also contributed to the members' discursive definition of several European communities of relevance and their identification with one or more of them. Although some members referred to values in vague terms and had to be encouraged to define them specifically, several members explicitly named human rights, social equality and democracy as perceived fundamental community referents. There was however little consensus among members on the extent to which such values connote European identity as will be elaborated in the next few extracts. For example, in the Bologna focus group, an exchange between two members suggested that the topos of values was realized mainly through a temporal/historical frame to achieve different strategies of representing themselves as Europeans.

Extract 44

> BO4: For me what unites Europe a little (..) I was born in Russia then when I was 13, 14, my family and I emigrated to Germany and now I'm living in Germany well in theory [she laughs] and for me Europe, Europeans are aware ah ... of what their history is, of where they're going and for me they represent certain values the ... the democracy okay some states more and in some states less ... but compared to Russia however ... yes but these democratic values make the difference and perhaps unite somehow.

BO2: It really is a historic question … democracy is [well?] rooted, perhaps
the problem though is that we don't question ourselves on the meaning of
having democracy as a value I mean one takes for granted that there is a
democratic system and so for me, yes more than really being a shared value
it is … dunno.. it's almost a a a I don't know a historic legacy not sufficiently
processed.

In this passage BO4, a Russian-born, German-naturalized student who, at
the time of the interview had been living in Italy for one year, engaged in an
argument that constructed Europeans as a rather cohesive group on an historical
journey (realized via the spatial representation 'they know where they're going').
By perspectivizing her argument from a transnational stance – via a brief account
of her multiple ties with Russia, Germany and Italy – the speaker positioned
herself externally in relation to the European community (signalled by reference
to Europeans with the pronoun *they*). From this external standpoint she used
strategies of assimilation and dissimilation juxtaposing Europe with Russia to
represent Europeans united by the values of democracy and mitigating internal
differences ('more or less').

In her exchange with BO4, BO2 initially aligned herself with her interlocutor's
views that democracy is a distinctive European value. BO2 also reproduced
BO4's proposition on the historical continuity of democracy in the European
community, an element which she represented as heritage, thus drawing on the
metaphorical scenario of family in which cultural assets are passed down by one
generation to the other. In this case, while BO4 appeared to draw on the *topos of
values* from the 'inside' perspective of family, she also reflexively characterized
democracy as an unfinished process suggesting her positioning as a European as
someone with a duty to make such heritage her own.

The topos of values often emerged when members discussed the reasons for
joining the organization. Arguments aimed at representing the sharing of common
values were commonly offered as one of the main reason that had brought them
together. However, a number of distinct representations also emerged which
reversed the causality of such process. In other words, some members referred to
European values as emerging from, rather than justifying their engagement in the
organization's activities. This aspect, for example, was highlighted by PR2 (Prague
individual interview) as illustrated by the following extract:

Extract 45

PR2: Well it's funny, because this thing comes up all the time of this idea of
this shared or common values and what that means, erm, I'm somewhat

more hesitant to use this term 'common values', like er, for me it's er, maybe more so this idea of erm, a common purpose like it doesn't necessarily have to be attached to any set of values even though having a common purpose oftentimes there are common values of course come out of it (..) but this idea about er, people are all working towards the same goal, erm it doesn't mean that we all have the same opinions on all of them, but the goal in terms of working towards a better, in this case, a better Europe and what that means (.) socially, politically, erm, culturally, all of these things, of what it means to how we can, we want to get this kind of common idea of making things better … Erm, for me personally like I think like yes that is the idea like erm, if there is this common purpose of people working together, people wanting the social equality, people wanting to share cultures, or people wanting kind of erm a certain level or a certain quality of life, if that's what being part of Europe or being a European can mean, like then, then that's great.

PR2 clearly represented values in different terms from the previous example (see BO2 and BO4 in Extract 42). While both representations in Extracts 42 and 43 constructed values as 'holders' and 'drivers' of the European community, they emphasized two distinct facets of such ideals. On a spatial/temporal dimension PR2 portrayed the European community along a future orientation (through the preposition *towards*) highlighting the key role of common intentionality/ agentiveness of members. She engaged in strategies of deconstruction of established meanings (i.e. the decoupling of values from community) and reconstruction of meanings (via the association of Europe with specific social and cultural ideals). By contrast, BO2 and BO4 focused on the past dimension portraying values (such as democracy) as part of a narrative close to that of a European civilization (although, to some extent, both members mitigated these representations).

Consequently, on the one hand, Europeanness appears to be restricted by certain historical, geographical, and cultural elements while, on the other, it was defined in more loose and universal terms (suggested, for example, by PR2's use of the generic term '*people* striving for common goals'). In broad terms it was noticeable how some members deployed the topos of values to 'bring along' Europeanness in their discourses whereas others tended to represent Europeanness as brought about by a mutual project. Furthermore the extent to which these values could be regarded as European and/or Western/universal represented another controversial point for the definition of community and membership. For instance, BE2 (Berlin individual interview) argued:

Extract 46

> BE2: The point is when one talks of shared values do these values that unite
> us really exist? This is the first question that arises I do not think they do
> because these values are different between neighbours and often extending
> a value, a moral to one common European root I think is even more
> complicated and I think it's a bit of a discourse that can ... that risks of
> ending up in more reactionary discourses when one speaks of common
> Christian roots which is clearly still a discourse ... the issue of values for me
> immediately raises a question mark are there really values that make this
> idea of Europe shared?
>
> FZ: Some members would answer democracy human rights ...
>
> BE2: This applies on paper though ... as an ideal because then if you look
> at individual states in Old Europe say Hungary these concepts become
> a bit obsolete and sure you're right democracy is certainly a value one of
> these values undoubtedly however the next question is is this democracy
> a European value ? I believe it is a Western value. ... So this is my point if
> these values that we called shared do exist I think they do go beyond the
> geographical boundaries of Europe.

BE2's main strategy was to challenge a Euro-centric view of moral values arguing that such shared values do not exist nor, if they do exist, can they be assumed to be contained within the borders of Europe. BE2 realized his strategy by supporting his argument in two ways. First, he refuted that shared values can be found in the European community on the premise that values are 'family specific' (thus representing Europe as an enlarged neighbourhood in which he included himself). Secondly, he rejected the desirability of extending common (e.g. Christian) morals through the *topos of danger* (i.e. the risk of regressing to conservatism). BE2 realized his argument by formulating rhetorical questions at the beginning and the end of his proposition ('Are there really shared values?'). As I engaged with such a question, BE2 deployed a different argument. While he conceded that shared values might exist as ideals – a point that he mitigated with the example of Hungary – through another rhetorical question he also detached Europe from democracy, constructing the latter as a more loosely defined 'Western' value. While the deterritorialization of democratic values from Europe dovetails with BE2's vision of experimental transnationalism likely to be replicated and expanded beyond Europe (see Extract 30), his characterization of democracy as 'Western' falls short of a complete universalism (as it implies a West/East division). These antimonies were found conspicuously in the interview conducted with PR1 (Prague individual interview) as illustrated below:

Extract 47

PR1: – so, so I think what (…) what unites people in this group is really the idea that we share some values and we acknowledge that these values are universal and that we want to spread them or support them; not only in our own country, not only in the country where we live but also erm everywhere. And we have a kind of empathy with erm with people from other countries erm having these sorts of issues … facing similar issues (.) and I I think it's really this idea of erm of universalism maybe

FZ: … so basically it's not it's not just European values (..)because you called you call them erm universal values?

PR1: Well, I erm (…) maybe, (..) maybe these are European values even though I am not sure I can say that [laughter] because what I think, they might be similar but I think I think it's values which erm we would like to give them this universal so erm erm how to say (..) erm this (…) universal (..) meaning maybe or erm –

FZ: Okay. Can you … can you give me an example?

PR1: Yeah I don't know, for instance erm the value erm the principle of equality you know … erm so we want … I am not sure (..) I wouldn't (…) [laughter] I don't know what to say it's a European value but it's a value which we would like to see everywhere [high tone].

PR1's construction of Europeanness in relation to values involved strategies of unification and strategies of transformation. These were realized through the prevalent use of the term 'values' in its meaning of 'ethical principles/ ideals guiding one's actions/goals'. On the one hand, PR1 achieved a strategy of unification of the group through the proposition that group members share similar values. On the other hand, a strategy of transformation was also achieved by PR1 which was aimed at projecting the expansion of such values along prospective spatial and temporal dimensions which were inferable as beyond organizational remits or geographically defined Europe ('everywhere').

In PR1's argument the definition of groupness seemed to rely both on the awareness of sharing certain values and, at the same time, on her desire to turn such values into ideal drivers of the group activities and the expansion of such community of relevance. In other words, PR1 envisaged an ideal enlargement of community relying on transferring what is shared within the NGO to the wider society. This however rested on PR1's rather problematic premise that self-constructed universalism as some sort of higher moral ground ('we acknowledge that these values are universal') and warranted her contradictory proposition of wanting to spread universal values (which one must assume are already established and accepted).

PR1's elaboration thus seemed to highlight the ideological dilemma of defining values as devoid of specific European connotations while effectively construed them as a discriminant of groupness (e.g. in her use of the pronoun *we* indexing the Prague branch and possibly the whole NGO and distinct from the generic 'people from other countries' albeit empathically connected to them). These ambivalent representations of European/universal values appeared to be the cause of her impasse (signalled by some circumlocution and hedging) in the last part of the extract above.

5.3.5.6 *Topos of solidarity*

A number of constructions of the European community were achieved by members through arguments that defined the moral boundaries of solidarity and the notion of common good among the European community, with some members especially emphasizing issues related to wealth distribution. For example BE1 (Berlin individual interview) argued:

Extract 48

> BE1: I think [equality] is quite important in a way because being European can mean you're really really really rich and you live in a rich country but also it can mean you (..) you live in a poor country where old grandmothers have €40 to live on for the month so it's incredible (..) I think this is something we have to work really really hard … this is just what people have to recognize what it means to live in a shared Europe a shared place.

BE1's construction of being European was clearly predicated on social and economic conditions among community members and it was realized through different arguments driven by what she perceived as a gap between ideal and actual conditions and by her commitment to fill such a gap. The speaker thus constructed an argument for change through the *topos of economic solidarity* which implies inequalities must be reduced through the sharing of resources.[30]

By using the *topos of economic solidarity*, BE1 achieved diverse representations of the European community and of Europeanness. On the one hand, the speaker constructed the meaning of being European in relation to a community with striking income inequalities, an argument that she realized through the generalized juxtaposition of poor/rich countries and the singularization of extreme examples. In this sense, she used the term 'European' as a predicate adjective to extensively include any economic subject within geographical Europe. On the other hand, through the *topos of solidarity* the member constructed an ideal meaning of being European as a collective commitment to a different society or a utopian shared place, which is consistent with her metaphorization of 'Europe as Utopia' (see Extract 35).

Very similar views were expressed by AM1 (Amsterdam individual interview) who explained the notion of (economic) solidarity by analogy with the Dutch system:

Extract 49

AM1: For example in the Netherlands there is erm one part … that is really poor and everybody pays the taxes and the money gets redistributed and nobody really thinks about it because we're all Dutch and there is this (..) so there is this solidarity … and then the European argument is of course, well, you can, well, it's, it's the scale thing again, like how it works in a nation-state, it can also work like that in, in Europe, the, the countries that have a bit more money they re-redistribute that to parts that are erm poorer … Yeah, but then what you ask of your people is that they feel solidarity with those other countries and it's easier for those people to feel solidarity for a region in their own country, because everybody feels, yeah we're Dutch, we have this history together and erm, yeah, we speak the same language or, you know, erm you, people accept more that they're erm, er, fellow citizens and erm in Europe this erm the, the institutions are, and the laws and everything erm (…) also put that in place for all European citizens and erm we have the right to vote but people don't accept [emphasis] that because they don't feel, yeah they don't feel it.

AM1 used the analogy with the Netherlands and the 'scaled-up' imagination of community (see Extract 25) to argue how the concept of solidarity in nation-states should apply to the European society. In this sense, she envisaged the same fiscal functions performed by states being reproduced by the EU institutions on a larger scale with net contributors supporting net receivers. However, AM1 also highlighted the difficulty of realizing what Habermas (2003) termed 'solidarity between strangers'[31] and ultimately the limitations to the emergence of a European demos. This 'empathy gap' was, for example, realized by the speaker through the use of the verb 'feel' to connote Dutchness as 'felt' more intensely than Europeanness (cf. also the use of 'your people' or the qualifier 'fellow' in relation to Dutch citizenship that would support the representation of national camaraderie). Moreover, AM1 realized her argument about the 'empathy gap' through different characterizations of national and European identities as 'thick' and 'thin' identities (see p. 46), respectively. On the one hand, she highlighted how the perception of (Dutch) nationhood is based on 'thick' or cultural referents (history, language) whereas, on the other hand, Europeanness was represented from a 'thin' or civic perspective (laws, institutions, right to vote) as a wider community that has not yet fully developed.

While several members invoked the *topos of solidarity* in a similar way to AM1 and BE1 (in Extract 38 and Extract 39), SO1 (Sofia individual interview) appealed to the *topos of solidarity* to sceptically distance himself from the NGO mainstream interpretation of transnationalism and from the EU project which he saw at risk of reproducing an authoritarian ideology. SO1's elaboration is exemplified by the following extract:

Extract 50

> SO1: Well erm (…), for me transnationalism is erm, (.) the new, sort of (..) how to say this, the new speak ehr, I would say of er (.) of a of an older word er which is internationalism … I understand why it's being done, er, there are many countries transnationally, or internationally who currently are at odds with er, erm, er ex-Soviet past for example, … so, so I understand the general framework, these days to speak of a, a European co-operation erm mutually et cetera, et cetera and ways to solidarize, solidarize between countries and different groups (..) ehr (..) however … erh, my, my worry about transnationalism has always been that erm, it sort of ehr, um zeros in on to the socialist past for example of the Eastern Block countries that are involved in European Alternatives … I think … transnationalism is a way to erm, to reignite again er practices of er co-operation between er, pretty much oppressed groups or groups that are involved in the oppression of other groups ah, that are involved in, against the oppression of other groups, erm, and ways to ehr, uhm rearticulate er (…), a global group of policies.

Drawing on the *topos of solidarity,* the speaker constructed an argument that portrayed the transnational ideology as potentially dangerous. He realized his strategy through the trope of 'newspeak', an Orwellian reference (Orwell 1949) to a totalitarian socialist regime where language is redesigned to control thoughts and to reinforce the dominance of the state. In other words, for SO1, transnationalism can potentially be the 'new speak' for internationalism, a term that, in this context, the speaker attributed with a specific negative connotation in relation to Bulgarian communist history.[32]

SO1 used this specific topos as a warrant for his argument that likened certain transnational rhetoric about the European integration to the same discourses of international socialism. Through such a warrant he expressed concern (albeit mitigated) about historical recursivity or, in other words, about the fact that, despite the modernized wording, Europe could become just a mega-state where citizens would be disempowered subjects just as much as they used to be under communist past, a social and political scenario that he clearly perceived negatively and which he warned against.

In this case, one could grasp the historical reasons at play in SO1's negotiation of his identification as a member of a transnational/European community. Unlike the Cluj members, who saw their Europeanness as an almost unreserved validation of their post-communist location (see Section 5.3.3.3), for SO1, the communist legacy appeared to be part of an ideological negotiation between, on the one hand, being committed to new forms of democratic socialism in a community of Europeans and, on the other hand, cautiously embracing the more institutional vision of such a project for fear of a recontextualization of dominant discourses (cf., for example, his objection to Europeanness as a consequence of Bulgaria's formal membership of the EU as discussed in Extract 16).

5.3.5.7 *Topos of diversity*

As noted in previous sections, the generic *topos of diversity* was deployed by members interdiscursively with other topoi to achieve different strategies. For example, in Extract 7 and Extract 8 it was illustrated how members drew on narratives of interactional experience to construct the external diversity of Europeans vis-à-vis Americans through the *topos of difference*. From a different perspective, internal diversity was called upon by PR2 (through the *topos of multiculturalism*) as a positive context for constructing her multiple national/ transnational affiliations (cf. Extract 19).

In addition to these discursive realizations, several strategies driven by *topoi of (internal) diversity* also emerged from the analysis through which members achieved different representations of the transforming European community. For example, the topos of *living with differences* was invoked by LO2 (London focus group) in his elaboration of transnationalism as the 'celebration of diversity' (and counter posed to the rejection of national homogenization) as illustrated below:

Extract 51

    LO2: I actually quite like this transnational thing (..) you're not trying to raise
        differences between people but, actually, you're saying that, actually, erm,
        it's great that there are differences and actually (.) what we, we, we, are
        simply doing is looking for ways to organize, so that different groups can

live productively and in peace with one another (.) we don't necessarily
have to raise the differences you know we (..) that's what the states have
operated throughout the last few hundred years, and it resulted in genocide
it resulted in em (..) eh oppression, (..) let's not try to reproduce that idea on
a greater level, let's say, actually, that's where we got it wrong, let's embrace
our differences and let's live with our differences and that's good, that's great,
that's productive, ah…

From a historical perspective, LO2 invoked the topos of diversity as a warrant
to both delegitimize states (in the attribution of causality between suppression
of differences operated by nation states and genocide) and to construct an
argument in favour of a social order with an enlarged and yet diverse community
of citizens. This strategy of construction was realized via a fluid and largely
inclusive meaning of the pronoun *we* which carried different indexicalities:
at one level, the pronoun *we* pointed at the organization and its activities and
helped LO2 to portray EA as an agent in the construction of a desirable society
of peaceful coexistence of groups.

At another level, the indexicality of *we* which the speaker appealed to was
inferable in a larger historical remit of a European conscience (e.g. in the
expression 'we got it wrong'). Such understanding appeared thus to be key in
constructing the historical continuity of Europeans and, at the same time, in
driving the imagination of wanting to be part of a self-transforming community.
On the one hand, therefore, the *topos of diversity* was instrumental in the
representation of a rupture with the past (via the delegitimization of the social
order of nations) while, on the other hand, it served to legitimize the activities of
the organization and its members (which LO2 attributed with the continuity of
the historical *we* as Europeans).

5.3.5.8 *Topoi of language(s) and multilingualism*

Topoi of languages and multilingualism[33] played an important role in how
members discursively constructed an imagined community of Europeans.
A number of different arguments predicated on the *topos of multilingualism*
emerged when members were prompted to express their views on the relation
between identity and language(s) and if and how that related to the definition
of Europeanness. Overall two major strategic orientations emerged from such
views which related to somewhat distinct civic and cultural interpretations of
Europe.

On the one hand, the topos of multilingualism was invoked by several members
who were adopting particular cultural stances to achieve a representation of

Europe as a positively diverse society where languages (connoted as proxies for cultures) were represented as tools for fostering transnational interaction and intercultural dialogue among citizens. In this vein, individual multilingual abilities were constructed as important components of one's Europeanness, as they could facilitate intercultural encounters in the European space, the latter mainly conceptualized as a social context of increased mobility. For example, the *topos of multilingualism* was invoked by CL4 (Cluj focus group) in relation to his personal experience of travelling in Europe and interacting with other cultures (see strategies of interactional experience on p. 140 for similar constructions). Conceptually, CL4 constructed his belonging through the representation of Europe as a 'familiar space' via the metaphor of home as illustrated below:

Extract 52

> CL4: Languages make you free … I for example I went to various countries and had to get along with people who didn't know another language and then look, I learned Hungarian in a few days, enough to handle getting directions … and I started with hello, so, but without knowing anything before, I kept interacting with people, I learned how to say right, I want to go there … [language] gives you freedom to go anywhere, and you still feel at home.[34]

The individual interview with LO3 (London) provided another example of how the topos of multilingualism was deployed to represent and accommodate the cultural diversity of the European community. As an English native speaker, LO3 constructed an argument of solidarity with other Europeans whose first language is not English and who tend to converge to English as a lingua franca, especially in EA transnational meetings. Recognizing her own head start and advocating the need for British to learn more languages, she expressed her stance as follows:

> LO3: '[speaking English only] highlights an arrogance of forcing everyone else to speak your language … and it's just erm, it's just a sense of (…) I don't know it's just … like having friends that you don't make an effort with, making them always come to your house rather than you go and visit them, that kind of thing'.

In this case, LO3 achieved a representation of Europe as an amicable community in which mobility and language accommodation allow for exchange and interaction between friends. Although positively connoted, such representation is somewhat different from CL4's in the previous example. While CL4's use of 'home' entailed a sense of belonging to a common space, LO3's representation seemed to support an understanding of Europeans as a community where different cultures live side by side although each separately contained in their own 'house'.

As well as from cultural perspectives, the topos of multilingualism was frequently invoked by members from civic perspectives, in reference to linguistic practices in the general remit of the EPS, for example within and related to the organization itself, and, to a lesser extent, in relation to (internal/external) practices of the EU.

In both these contexts, languages and multilingualism were typically discussed in relation to issues of communication and democracy with most members recognizing important tensions between ideational and practical dimensions of multilingualism in the making of Europe (i.e. how to best ensure linguistic democracy and preserve cultural diversity while transnationalizing the EPS and deepening the integration process).

These tensions have been highlighted in a paper that, drawing on the data and analysis of this study, has discussed the negotiation of multilingual ideologies in members' discourses (Zappettini and Comănaru 2014). This paper argued how a large number of members appeared oriented overall towards the representation of Europe as a quasi-diglossic[35] society in which communicative and identitarian functions of language were divorced (see, for example, House (2003) discussed on p. 58) and, at the same time, how members appeared concerned with constructing arguments strategically oriented towards a general legitimization of the use of English as a convenient tool of communication in the transnational political arena.

Building on this insight, the following discussion will focus on how members typically achieved these arguments via different micro-strategies of separation, justification, pragmatization and accommodation. For example, in an exchange at the Bologna focus group, two members achieved a strategy of deconstruction of the English language into separate entities with distinct communicative and identitarian functions:

Extract 53

BO1: in my opinion we really need to distinguish, there are two languages, one is for work and everyday communication, globish, right? and then there's English.

BO6: indeed, there's also the Euro-English of bureaucracy that has got nothing to do with Shakespeare's language, which is the language of the English.

The overall strategy adopted by the two members was to decouple communicative and identitarian functions of English into new and old forms/varieties ('globish' and 'Euro-English'[36] and 'classic English', respectively). While the former were attributed mere communicative functions as a lingua franca, the latter were seen as 'personal languages' retaining their salience as referents of cultural identification (e.g. 'classic English' was associated with the English heritage via the reference to Shakespeare).

A similar argument grounded in the distinction between identitarian and instrumental functions of English was constructed by RO1. However, more than BO1 and BO6 (see extract above), RO1's strategy was aimed at downplaying the identitarian connotation of English and at highlighting instead its potential role in the integration process, as exemplified by the extract below:

Extract 54

RO1: Well, I think that my dream, my vision is that Europe be united politically and for this to happen … we need to have a language in common … I think [English] should be encouraged ... and yes it would give an advantage to English and Irish speakers but ... I think sometimes it goes like that, … some groups in society have advantages over others and the role of the state or of an institution like the EU is to make sure that these natural advantages do not make those people step over others ... I'm really a fan of English not because I see this as a sort of cultural imperialism, because by now English has nothing to do with England any more or with the UK …

FZ: Can I just ask you to explain what you mean by English is no longer related to England do you mean the English identity?

RO1: Yes, that's exactly it, I don't see it as an imposition of cultural imperatives from the Brits, you know, by now English is the language of Europe… by now, you know, if aliens came to the Earth, by now, they'd probably try and talk to us in English… it's the language of old England it is the language of the US but it is the language of the EU too…

RO1's argument was predicated on the ideological warrant that a common language would facilitate processes of democratic debate and ultimately promote the emergence of a European polity. This warrant was offered by RO1 as a statement of necessity (supported by the modal verb 'need'). From this premise, the speaker constructed an argument of 'pragmatic legitimization' of the widespread use of English within the NGO and beyond. Through his argument, RO1 achieved a strategy of constructing a *universality* and *modernity* of English by representing it as a global language devoid of specific geographical and cultural connotations or ownership.

This strategy was realized along a temporal axis (signalled by the expressions 'by now' and 'anymore') which the speaker used to represent a socio-historical evolution of English away from definite associations with a culture or a territory. Furthermore, RO1 appealed to a cognitive schema of universality of the English language through 'the hyperbolic and futuristic imagery of "aliens" expected to be able to communicate with humans, an effective linguistic device that allowed him to contextualise issues of communication among Europeans in a global, indeed universal, context' (Zappettini and Comănaru 2014, p. 414).

In his argument, RO1, on the one hand, challenged one important aspect of nationhood (the association between languages and cultures), while, on the other, reinforced his support for the civic role of a common language as functional to the expansion of community, an argument that resonates with some discourses of the construction of civic nations (cf. footnote 36 on p. 57) and which seems to dismiss the EU's rhetorical construction of multilingualism as the equality of languages.

In this sense, a number of constructions emerged in members' discourses that seemed to challenge the representations of multilingualism and European identity promoted by institutional discourses (see Zappettini 2014). For example, at the focus group conducted in Bologna, the debate about whether and how a shared language would contribute to a stronger sense of community or to a better identification with Europe generated different arguments as illustrated in the four-way exchange below:

Extract 55

BO6: ... since politics works by proxy ... the language too can be a proxy for the representation of rights (...) which language is not an issue, it could also be Chinese, it is a problem though if language is associated with the national character, that becomes ... at the political level, in the imagination ... the language can be a barrier ... if it is dragged by its hair [into politics] just so that it represents an obstacle

BO1: I think that, for all of us to be able to feel European, language is an obstacle ... if I spoke the same language as a German I would feel closer to the German ... so, for the sake of argument, if we spoke the same language it would be easier to feel European

[BO6 shakes his head]

BO1: I think so ...

BO3: More to the point, European politics without a European language is impossible I mean you can ... you can blame Europe using your own language but you cannot advocate European politics without a European language because one thing is, how do you say, to express political and social contents and another thing and ... well ... and thinking of the milk quotas, when you have to stand up for a right that you were denied maybe you can do it by translating Venetian [laughs] into Italian into English, but to have a policy, I mean in the end probably you cannot have a European public discourse without a language.

BO6: But it is not necessarily so in the sense that all that's been done by European institutions, which is a huge thing, has been done without considering this issue, anyway, ... but now a big problem arises, that is the fact that since there is a big push from the bottom at the political level and a large shared discussion on the web I can comment on an Italian blog but I cannot comment on a German blog.

BO4: I can! [All laugh]

BO1: Exactly, that's an obstacle.

In discussing the lack of a common language as a potential obstacle to the development of the European community, BO6 and BO1 took opposite views. BO6 initially constructed language as a means for democratic debate. As such, his argument was that any language (e.g. Chinese) would guarantee the exercise of democratic rights (an argument that he rested on the premise 'politics works by proxy') highlighting the communicative aspect of languages. However he conceded that the politics of language can instrumentally mobilize the association of language and nationhood (the identification aspect), a proposition that he realized via the reference to the imagination (of being a community) and the Italian idiomatic expression *tirata per i capelli* (which roughly translates as 'dragged by its hair' and is used to suggest involving someone in some action against their will or when something irrelevant is introduced into a discussion).

BO6's view that language is primarily a means of communication was somewhat challenged by BO1 who, on the other hand, emphasized the function of language as marker of groupness via the analogy of affinity with German and, albeit hypothetically (Italian *per assurdo*), she positively evaluated a similar scenario for Europeans. BO3 took the discussion back to the pragmatics of language in the EPS arguing a distinction between 'reactive' and 'proactive' enactments of citizenship suggesting that the latter can only be achieved through a common European language.[37] The member invoked the *topos of active citizenship* (discussed in Section 5.3.5.3) to construct an argument aimed at showing how democratic participation can be hindered by practices that require linguistic mediation and, by contrast, promoted by a direct means of communication.

BO3 realized his argument by associating civic participation with linguistic practices/abilities (drawing from the 'milk quotas' example that had been discussed earlier in the focus group) and by contrasting what one 'can do' with what one 'cannot do'. BO6 responded to BO3's argument through a similar evaluation of languages enabling different degrees of democratic participation in the EPS. While BO6 realized his argument via a similar 'can/cannot do' contrast, such an argument was predicated on the juxtaposition of top-down versus bottom-up perspectives. While BO3 initially somewhat aimed at dismissing BO6's proposition on the necessity of a common language (by offering a positive evaluation of what had been done by the EU institutions), he agreed with BO6 on the warrant that there is an increasing need for citizens to be able to speak a common language in order to participate in the democratic debate about European issues.

This exchange points to the relevance of language issues in the definition of the EU-ropean community (Wright 2009) and, in particular, to the role of English as a lingua franca in the EPS, a question that Wright (2000) has referred to as 'the elephant in the room' with respect to how it has been dealt with by the EU institutions. The extracts discussed above suggest that, although members recognized the 'symbolic capital' (Bourdieu 1991) embodied in languages – see, for example, BO1 ironically emphasizing her knowledge of German as empowering her in Extract 45 – they appeared overall more willing than institutional powers to acknowledge the need to approach the question of linguistic justice without the ideological legacy of nation-state building that regards languages as inextricably associated with cultural identities or as political resources (Wright 2000).

6

Discussing and Summarizing the Findings

6.1 Strategies and topoi

The results have suggested a complex and very dynamic picture of how European identities were constructed, challenged and transformed by members. Different strategic orientations were recognized in members' discourses towards the (de)construction and negotiation of meanings of (European) identity, the challenging and dismantling of nationhood, and the construction of new (imagined) communities, spaces and social orders. These strategic orientations must be interpreted as overarching discursive drivers or frames that oriented members towards specific micro-strategies and linguistic realizations (as discussed in Section 5.3).

Moreover, the analysis has shown how members often realized different micro-strategies simultaneously in the discussion of any one topic, so that, for instance, the delegitimization of national apparatuses and the transformation of meanings of nationhood frequently occurred concomitantly when members 'explained' transnationalism and/or Europe.

The analysis has also highlighted how members produced Europeanness in different discursive contexts (see Section 5.2.1), for example, through the articulation of 'identity' and 'European' topics, via both civic and cultural topoi, relying on personal and reflexive dimensions as well as on wider discourses of Europe, and transnational and cosmopolitan narratives.

Furthermore, the analysis has suggested that, in many cases, processes of identification *as* Europeans interplayed with and relied on members' identification *with* European referents.

At one level, strategies of constructing identification *as* European were deployed by members and predicated on both cultural and civic topoi. These were aimed at claiming some European credentials. For example, in arguments constructed on cultural topoi, some members anchored their identification as

European in the specificity of their family background or in the recognition of similarities and differences emerging from interactional experiences related to mobility. In the construction of Europeanness predicated on civic topoi, other members referred to a European tradition of democracy and the welfare system or, in the case of the Romanian focus group, to the newly acquired status of European citizens. At the same time, in this context of production, the data analysis has shown that a large proportion of members took a generally cautious, if not sceptic, stance on embracing clear-cut and static definitions of (European) identity, an attitude often signalled by epistemic markers such as 'I think' or 'I don't know'. Frequently, claims of Europeanness were articulated through the negotiation of its relationality with other identities and in the general context of global and post-national understandings of society and groups whereby identities were meta-defined along 'thin' interpretations of the term (see p. 46). Consequently, as illustrated in the analysis, the meaning/value of formally ascribed and externally validated identities was often downplayed or dismissed, with the term (European) 'identity' in some cases deconstructed as an 'empty signifier'.

At another level, strategies of constructing identification *with* 'European' referents conspicuously emerged in the data. These strategies were a means through which members achieved different representations of their belonging to (a) transnational communities(y). In this case too, members predicated such representations of community(ies) on both cultural (e.g. linguistic and ethnic diversity) and civic (democratic participation, social equality) topoi. In this dimension, however, a sense of identity was primarily forged around the experience of contributing to a common project through action, participation and solidarity. Arguments were primarily articulated around elements of the 'nodal' point Europe (see Figure 6.1) or via organization-specific contexts.

Significantly, most topoi invoked by members were informed by cultural, civic and historical conceptualizations of Europe as both a society and a community with different degrees of internal cohesion/diversity and different degrees of external interconnection with other communities. In this sense, these topoi can aptly be interpreted in the light of a larger ideological taxonomy of views that members held about their individual, social and political belonging to a 'Global Gesellschaft/Gemeinschaft' 'order' (see pp. 41–2). The data has suggested that while most members shared a view of the world as a 'Global Gesellschaft 1' – that is as made up of a diversity of societies with much sociocultural exchange between them (see, for example, topoi of (inter)connectedness, of diversity and of interactional experience) – they hardly supported a vision of society as one single integrated system of planned governance ('Global Gesellschaft 2'). At the same time, a considerable number of members pointed to their understanding of the world as a rather integrated community (a 'Global Gemeinschaft') and their perspectives of such global awareness often acted as a warrant for what they perceived as being part of a collective action in the interest of such community of relevance (see, for example, topos of solidarity and topos of transnational active citizenship).

In members' discourses, therefore, Europe represented multiple referents and appeared driven by what Robertson (1992, p. 395) sees as two related dynamics of globalization: the 'implosion of the world [and] the explosion of situated cultures, institutions, and modes of life'. In other words, in members' views of the world, Europe could be read as the local instantiation of a global interconnected multicultural society as well as the local instantiation of an enlarged civic community of relevance. For most members, therefore, identification as European emerged from their association (or dissociation) with such different conceptualizations of Europe and it was often instantiated in representations of their interaction in a space of social and cultural diversity, and/or their participation in a modern project of 'constitutional patriotism'. These representations contributed to an overall definition of Europe as a dynamic society/community whose boundaries of interests often overlapped other communities of relevance.

6.2 Linguistic realizations

The 'in-depth' analysis in this chapter has highlighted a diversity of linguistic realizations through which members achieved their strategic goals. Two specific features, which have emerged from the data as particularly significant in members' discourses are discussed further below: (a) the metaphorical scenario of spatial dynamics; and (b) a set of temporal, spatial, personal and ideological realizations whose indexicality pointed to distinct frames/interpretations of Europe, transnationalism and nationhood.

6.3 Metaphorical scenario of spatial dynamics

A large proportion of informants realized their arguments through the use of figurative language, such as metonymical and metaphorical expressions (cf. Section 5.3). While some of these expressions were deployed by members occasionally and idiosyncratically, the analysis found that a large proportion of tropes and metaphorical expressions were embedded in/belonged to metaphorical source domains of network, journey, movement, container and biology (see Table 6.2). In addition, results for the frequency of N-grams[1] of the keyword 'Europe' in the corpus (see Table 6.3) showed that 'Europe' was associated with a conspicuous pattern of spatial prepositions (in, across, outside, around, to, part of, in the continent of, from), as well as geopolitical qualifiers (Central, Eastern, Western, federal) and with terms semantically related to cognitive and ideological dimensions (idea, shared, fortress, etc.). These different insights coherently suggest a larger metaphorical scenario of space dynamics which members often draw upon to explain transnational social processes related to mobility and which, at the same time, acted as an overarching driver of members' narratives of Europe and community.

On the one hand, members invoked the scenario of spatiality to construct the world interconnectedness, to represent social interaction as unbounded movement and flows and to discursively deconstruct national structures through, inter alia, entailments of national boundaries as partition, containment and so on. On the other hand, as illustrated in the analysis, the scenario of *spatial dynamics* was also instrumental in constructing and defining the 'European space', a term which members often used metaphorically to represent and explain social,

Table 6.1 Summary of the main source domains and linguistic realizations related to the scenario of 'spatial dynamics'. Adapted from McEntee-Atalianis and Zappettini (2014, p. 406)

Scenario of spatial dynamics	
Main metaphorical domains	**Typical linguistic realizations**
Network	• Connections/lines/ties/nodes • Point-to-point distance • 'Horizontal' architecture • Place/space crossing
Journey/ Movement	• Path/destination • Mapping/orienting/scaling • Flow/energy/expansion • (Artificial) obstructs
Container	• Boundedness/closeness • 'Box ticking' • Outside/inside
Biology	• Natural/living entity/system • Growth/evolution/collapse/age

political and cultural meanings of Europe. While in some cases the European 'space' coincided with institutional visions of a functionally integrated economic and political system, most members invested the term with a symbolic meaning of an ideal/utopian society with new forms of participation and solidarity. Several members, thus, made sense of their activities and their own Europeanness through metaphorical frames of *expansion* and *progression* of community whereby they represented themselves and Europe as a civic community in the making, expanding and 'reaching out' to the world crossing over (national/artificial) boundaries. In this sense, rather than a 'house' containing states, nations and cultures as commonly found in institutional discourses (Musolff 2006) the 'construction' of a European space emerged as a powerful discursive referent for members' imagination of themselves as European and relied on the 'horizontal' architecture of the network and its 'nodes'.

Table 6.2 List of most frequent *N*-grams (2–6) of the key word 'Europe'

Frequency of clusters and collocates co-occurring with the term 'Europe' in the corpus analysed

69	in Europe	3	is Europe
42	of Europe	3	old Europe
15	about Europe	3	shared Europe
13	outside Europe	3	the Europe
11	across Europe	2	all over Europe
10	federal Europe	2	beyond Europe
9	to Europe	2	fortress Europe
9	part of Europe	2	from outside Europe
9	(in) the continent of Europe	2	groups all around Europe
9	(in) Eastern Europe	2	inside Europe
8	idea of Europe	2	of what Europe
8	think Europe	2	over Europe
7	that Europe	2	see a federal Europe
6	around Europe	2	states of Europe
6	with Europe	2	talking about Europe
4	for Europe	2	that in Europe
4	from Europe	2	the lingua franca of Europe
4	see Europe	2	the old Europe
3	a Europe	2	think that Europe
3	a shared Europe	2	this idea of Europe
3	all around Europe	2	time outside Europe
3	and Europe	2	to see a federal Europe
3	as Europe	2	United states of Europe
3	central Europe	2	want to see a federal Europe
3	ideal Europe	2	Western Europe

Moreover, as well as a web of sociocultural experiences, family ties and the organizational structure, in members' discourses, the term 'network' crucially indexed the exercising of active citizenship and a civic commitment to developing democratic participation. Civic initiatives initiated at a local level and then often carried out on a European scale were thus represented by members' as an activity of 'reaching out' and 'connecting' with other citizens contributing to the imagination of building and expanding the European community. Besides, the network was often interpreted as a tool of bottom-up democracy that could reduce social distances by enabling citizens to reorganize social orders through 'horizontal' (i.e. non-hierarchical) interconnectedness. The European community was therefore often represented as a community on a historical journey of progress towards better forms of participatory democracy to be achieved transnationally (cf. the expression 'the need to go beyond the nation-state').

It must be noted that, in the characterization of Europe as a transnational space, only a few members appeared to conceptualize distinct geopolitical 'cores' and 'peripheries' of Europe[2] (see also, for example, the topos of insularity of Britain on p. 170), while the majority of interviewees were able to represent the European space as diffused across the network. At the same time, however, through their discourses, members produced new forms of centrality and peripherality via representation of marginally located social actors vis-à-vis institutional powers (e.g. in binary representations of citizens and states, transnational corporations and individuals, etc.). In this respect members construed Europe and the EU institutions as equally convergent/divergent concepts. On the one hand transnationalism was equated with intra-EU mobility and active citizenship was understood as a tool for fully developing a civil European society somewhat in line with institutional discourses. In this sense, even from a bottom-up perspective, the data has shown the strong institutionalization of European identities, reflected, for example, in the use of the term 'Europe(an)' deployed by members (see Table 6.1). This would suggest that, in the exploration of European identities, the 'situatedness' of one's Europeanness must take into account the distinct normative, social and cultural definitions of Europe produced at institutional level. On the other hand, several members highlighted how their grassroots commitment should result in what they believe is the creation of a transnational public sphere to be expanded well beyond Europe ('an experiment to be replicated'). Therefore it was noticeable that most members understood the transnationality of their activities in a larger remit of global interaction and social transformation, whereby transnational active citizenship was frequently discussed and represented in terms of world citizenship and universality of rights. In this case, although it was not entirely dismissed, the EU project was relativized as one early expression of such a new world order.

Identification with European and transnational referents, therefore, emerged as an overall dynamic, if fragmented, process in which the transportability of members' civic commitment across the network allowed for the deterritorialization of the political project from physical Europe and a general 'movability' of identities. European identity thus was not only constructed by most members as the product of the internal transnationalization of Europe (i.e. the institutional project of political and economic integration of nation states) but also discursively derived from the active creation of Europe as a centre of transnational political and social interests emerging bottom-up. In this sense the salience of feeling European for the majority of members did not just seem to lie in the external validation of a status (such as citizenship) as much as in their agency to imagine and actively enact such citizenship.

6.4 The indexicality of Europe and nationhood

The analysis has shown that, in synergy with the scenario of spatial dynamics, members frequently realized their discursive strategies through the use of temporal, spatial, personal and ideological deictics to mark a multiplicity of referents such as actors, spaces and objects. For example, one of the foci of the analysis was the indexical use of possessive adjectives and pronouns (e.g. *we/us/ours* and *they/them/their*) since, as emphasized in Section 2.3.1, these can typically correlate with the definition of boundaries and group demarcation/differentiation. The analysis of these elements has strongly suggested that in members' discursive representations there were no unified 'we-communities' but rather a multiplicity of often coexisting and fluid affiliations to different communities of relevance. In some cases, the indexicality of 'we' pointed to the organizational sense of groupness whether at the level of the local branch or more transnationally (e.g. 'our events', 'our work'). In a similar way, the 'we-citizens' implied by 'our institutions' was often realized from the perspective of a local administration, the national apparatus or the EU system. Furthermore, some members anchored the meaning of the 'we-group' to a generational belonging (e.g. 'our generation), an awareness of a socio-historical condition (e.g. 'our situation') or simply the condition of being humans (e.g. 'our emotions'). On the whole these referents would suggest the flexibility of members' perception of their 'we-ness' on a local to global continuum that allow them to simultaneously position themselves at different deictic centres (see below).

At the same time, *they/them/their* were also used in discourse to index different referents such as cultures, nations and governments. The majority of members did not antagonize these groups vis-à-vis a defined *us* but rather they appeared to reproduce them discursively as convenient labels of categorization while sustaining discourses of inclusiveness overall (see also, for example, expressions such as 'although their culture is different we can still work together for a better Europe'). On the other hand, it must be noted that some members deployed the deictics *they/them/their* to construct relations of difference among groups and to portray exclusiveness (see, for example, how the construction of Europeans was achieved via the juxtapositions with the Americans discussed in Extract 7 and Extract 8 or with the Russians in Extract 43). In addition, as illustrated in Section 5.3.4 some strategies of dismantling nationhood relied on a juxtaposition of *us/the transnational civil society* versus *them/national apparatuses/structures/governments* (see, for example, Extract 28 and Extract 29). Furthermore the analysis has shown how, for some members, the otherization of nationhood (achieved via the construction of the national community as *them*) was key in processes of identification as European, an identity which, to some extent, indexed 'what one is not' (see, for example, Extract 10 and Extract 22). It was therefore the specific discursive strategy, narrative or ideational frame that seemed to drive the inclusive/exclusive meanings of personal and collective deictics, as for most members constructing an identity involved demarcating their 'situatedness' – that is defining their *here* and *now*. In many cases, the process of situating themselves saw members engaging in reflexive awareness of their social, cultural and historical locations which could give continuity to personal and collective narratives of belonging.

In this sense, the analysis has revealed how, for most members, the process of identification with a European civic community was discursively related to a general reconceptualization of narratives of nationhood. In most cases, the nineteenth-century grand narratives of nations as 'communities of fate' or as cohesive and distinct cultural aggregates were displaced by transnational and cosmopolitan ideals of diversity, sharedness and bottom-up construction of a bigger and better society, coupled with a conceptualization of history as the progress of mankind. At the same time, it must be emphasized that, in the discourses of members, the negotiation of national identity constituted almost an inescapable element in the construction of their Europeanness, if only in the conventional use of terms such as French, German and the like as denominational characterizations of individuals, groups, cultures and so on. However, while the analysis has shown that in some cases the production of Europeanness occurred through accommodation (and reproduction) of national identities, it has also produced robust evidence of a general transformation and *volatility* of nationhood as, in many instances, identification with national communities/referents was in fact problematized and rejected.

In this respect, one of the insights emerging from the analysis is that nationhood played a key role in members' construction of their Europeanness as an *index* of culture-specific and socio-historical discourses. For some members, rejecting a national identity was thus a way of overcoming one's country's negative past actions (see, for example, the negative meaning of 'being German' in Extract 22 and that of 'being French' in Extract 22 and, in more general terms, the negative connotation of nation states in Section 5.3.4. In some other cases, Europeanness indexed a new relation between East and West and allowed members to position themselves in this changed scenario. For example, the ideological value of mobility for the Romanian cohort (discussed in Extract 17) was representative of their emancipation from the Communist past and their claims of Europeanness appeared driven by their willingness to distance themselves from such a legacy. At the same time the validation of Europeanness deriving from the formal accession of new EU countries was treated cautiously and sceptically by some members (see, for example, Extract 16).

While the analysis has deliberately resisted 'methodological nationalism' as an overarching approach, at this stage it must nevertheless recognize the role of national variables (i.e. the national specificity of certain discourses or topoi) in the articulation of one's Europeanness. However, the interplay between national and European discourses did not follow widely generalizable patterns. Instead, in members narratives, the interdiscursivity and indexicality of nationhood and Europeanness tapped into collective and, at the same time, individual repertoires of meanings and often lay in the contextuality of certain forms of belonging. In other words, nationhood and Europeanness often represented discursive resources which were functional to the realization of particular strategies or discursive purposes thus allowing for multicausal and, at times, contradictory identification processes with different communities of relevance. Overall, in members' discourses, collective identities such as national, European, transnational or cosmopolitan were thus primarily constructed around 'floating nodal points' – that is powerful social imaginaries capable of providing 'narrative stability' but also instrumentally defining antagonistic boundaries between different groups and interests (e.g. 'what is Europe' and 'who is inside or outside Europe') in relation to which members, as social actors, were able to position themselves.

6.5 A transnational conceptualization of Europeanness

An overall consideration deriving from the analysis is that, rather than representing an identity per se, transnationalism operated as an ideological lens or a general socio-cognitive reference framework providing members with critical and reflexive perspectives on the meaning of their identities – that is their (physical and social) locations in transforming spaces. In this sense, by indexing the historical transformation of relations between (national) groups, discourses of transnationalism urged most members to negotiate their *national habitus* by associating themselves with and by dissociating themselves from culture-specific conceptualizations of Europeanness. Similarly, the indexicality of transnationalism (differently conceptualized as a rejection of nationalism, mobility, world democracy and affirmation of cosmopolitan ideals of openness and equality) offered members opportunities for imagining society anew. The analysis has therefore suggested that the specific discursive framing of transnational Europe 'sutured' (Hall 1992) both collective and individual levels of identities as, on the one hand, it gave members 'ontological security' and continuity to their personal narratives while, on the other, it shaped their perspectives of the world and their social actions. Furthermore, through such a framing, members were able to negotiate global and local dimensions often (re)constructing multiple, cross-cutting, hybrid and overlapping affiliations with European referents via the metaphorical expansion and progression of an imagined community. It is thus possible to conceptualize Europeanness as represented and enacted by members from different discursive locations and linguistically realized through different deictic centres, in other words, different 'here' and 'now' of the imagined European space.

Trading from such a conceptualization (and in the light of the considerations made so far in discussing the data), it might be helpful to visualize the results of this study by means of a diagram which, in broad terms, interprets *Europeanness as the expansion of community of relevance on a continuum from nation-centric to cosmopolitan levels* as illustrated by Figure 6.1. It is important to underscore that nation-centric perspectives emerged in the data only with a minority of outliers and that members' discourses were far more frequently oriented towards the Euro-centric and cosmopolitan ends of the continuum. The different relevance

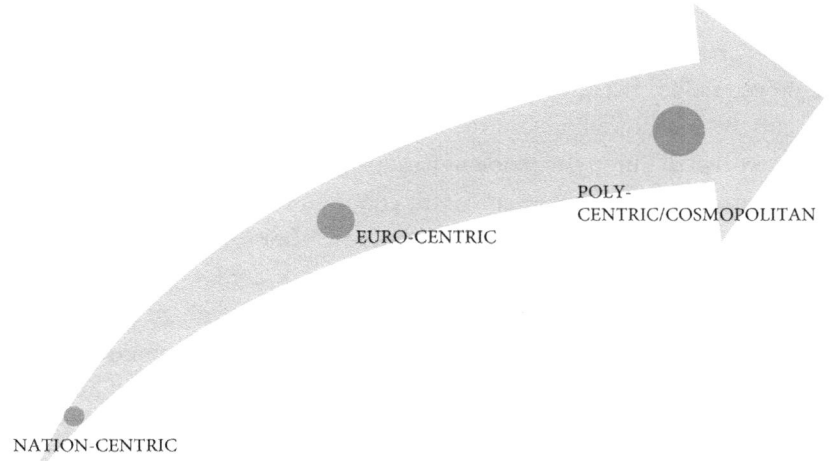

Figure 6.1 A diagram representing the expansion of 'imagined' community along a nation-centric to cosmopolitan continuum.

Table 6.3 The Two Ends of the Nation-Centric/Euro-centric/Polycentric Continuum

Nation-centric	Cosmopolitan
- Banal or 'weak' transnationalism	- Reflexive or 'strong' transnationalism
- Europeanness as a way of being	- Europeanness as a way of belonging
- 'Thick' understanding of identities	- 'Thin' understanding of identities
- Nationhood mutually compatible with Europeanness (accommodated)	- Nationhood incompatible with Europeanness (otherized, rejected)
- European project as a goal	- European project as an experiment
- Convergence EU/Europe	- Divergence EU/Europe

of these orientations has therefore been reflected in the diagram by the different sizes of the 'dots' and of the 'arrow'. In order to help contextualize the scope of this continuum, a table has also been provided with a heuristic dichotomization of different understanding of identities, transnationalism and Europe at either pole of the continuum. This will be further discussed below.

From a nation-centric perspective Europeanness represents a projection of national identities on a European trajectory. In other words, the nation-centric stance accepts/validates the world order of states and it conceives of EU-rope as the sum of its parts – that is a 'union of states'. From this perspective, transnationalism represents the individual or collective ability to connect across borders through different practices of mobility, cultural exchange and so on, therefore suggesting a 'weak' interpretation of the term. Intra-state mobility and the coming together of different cultures are valued positively; however, they mainly represent 'ways of being', while belonging remains primarily indexed to the reproduction of national identities, albeit accommodated with European referents. By and large, therefore, these views align themselves with Risse's theory on the process of Europeanization of national identities discussed on page 52.

By contrast, at the opposite end of the continuum, a cosmopolitan framing of transnationalism conceives of it as a consequence of the natural interconnectedness of the world, which is not only instantiated in everyday practices but also emphatically recognized as the universality of mankind. Through such a reflexive perspective, for example, Europeanness can be interpreted as a node capable of interconnecting individuals with a wider cosmopolitan network of individuals and experiences. Through the deterritorialization of one's cultural location, the transportability of one's civic engagement and the deconstruction of the 'container theory of society', a cosmopolitan social order is no longer reliant on the core-periphery logic and, as such, can thus be defined as polycentric as it allows for multiple social positionings. In this case, Europeanness can represent a salient way of belonging, an intermediate and not exclusive stage linking the local with the global, or, in other words, a proxy for world citizenship. In these cases identification with Europe would often represent the link between local and global dimensions of belonging, or a gateway to world citizenship that enabled some members to sidestep the process of identification with a national community. Furthermore, as illustrated in the analysis, although members' self-perception as a community of Europeans was often co-existent with an interpretation of Europe as a civic and a political project, such a project was not coterminous with or necessarily driven by the EU.

The data has suggested that most members constructed their Europeanness through frames that exist between the Euro-centric and the cosmopolitan poles described above (i.e. local and global). By and large, these views tended to recognize the European space as a geopolitical entity of its own, founded on social and democratic European interests deemed to be above the national ones. In this case, while European identity was sometimes represented by members as 'brought along' by individuals in some cultural and historical forms, it was often represented as 'brought about' by participation in a mutual project and as a tool to shape the democratic society at large. Similarly, while the transnationalization of the European space was discursively constructed through the removal of physical and ideological borders inside the European space, it was equally represented as the product of global dynamics of interconnectedness. Hence its relevance extended beyond the European space. Overall, the discursive construction of a community of Europeans from a Euro-centric perspective produced a variety of representations in which the outer borders of the European space were equally invoked to highlight the potential of expansion of its inside as well as to contain and represent Europe as a cohesive community vis-à-vis other blocs/groups (e.g. 'the Americans'). As shown by the analysis, therefore, the term 'Europe' emerged as a 'floating signifier' that members used to index Euro-centric and cosmopolitan views alike.

In broader terms, the analysis has also highlighted how the imagination of Europeanness among most members related to an overall process of 'rescaling'[3] (Keating 2013) of territory, interests, social ties and organization of community. Through such a process, along with the deterritorialization and the dissociation of certain spatial/functional features of boundaries and cultural markers of identity (e.g. languages), one could also recognize the recontextualization of political and social discourses of community at a transnational level, that is in-between the spatial determinism of nation states and more idealistic forms of world citizenship.

The different conceptualizations of 'European spaces' among members have also crucially pointed to the fact that 'rescaling' of boundaries can redefine different communities of relevance and, at the same time, can impact on the inclusion and exclusion of its members. This points to the critical question as to whether the transnational narrative of community does away with groups or whether it just replaces national discourses at a bigger or transnational level (Bauböck and Faist 2010). The data has shown that, in some respects, most constructions of Europe are still reliant on the power of 'associative relations' (*demos*) and 'shared space' (*topos*)[4] which might echo national narratives. The analysis, however, has also foregrounded members' desire to anchor their belonging to an ideal community which is typically open to diversity and generally aware of the world's interdependency and the danger of nationalism. From these perspectives the transnational narrative offers an alternative to nationhood in the process of imagining communities which crucially start from bottom-up and emerge in the public sphere through consensus, rather than being imposed from top-down. The tension, however, remains in how to implement cosmopolitan ideals in the European geopolitical context and thus reconciling unity with diversity, universalism with particularism, globalized neo-liberalism with social equality. As the data has shown, the definition of Europeanness from a transnational stance confronted members with major 'ideological dilemmas' (Billig 1988). For example, the definition of a community based on 'European' values seems at odds with a cosmopolitan perspective that downplays the cultural centrality of Europe. Similarly, the permeability of a European space vis-à-vis other spaces contradicts certain institutional and public discourses that make sense of Europe as a 'fortress' with a distinct inside and outside (Balibar 2009).

Unfortunately these questions are beyond the scope of this study and therefore must be left for future research, however, they can usefully integrate existing understanding of the tensions and ambivalences in the construction on European identities, thus expanding on existing interpretations of such antinomies (see, for example, Wodak and Weiss (2005)) and helping with the framing of further investigation. Trading on this point, the contribution of this study to the advancement of the CDS literature on Europe and transnationalism and further avenues of research are discussed in the final chapter.

Conclusions

7.1 Summary of this study

This study started out as a quest to contribute new insights to the vexed question of 'European identity' from discursive and linguistic methodologies and, at the same time, by interdisciplinarily and synergistically calling upon sociological disciplines such as Political and Transnational Studies. In line with the DHA, Europeanness was approached through an understanding of its historical and current discursive and social transformations. Carrying out a review of how the CDS literature has dealt with the formation of European identities, it was argued that transnational social action in the public sphere still lacks sufficient academic attention. The main rationale for this research was then defined as aiming to fill this gap by providing views from bottom-up and transnational perspectives.

The empirical study collected and analysed the discourses of 'Europeanness' of members of EA, a grassroots association of citizens that characterizes itself as engaged in building a transnational and democratic European society. The salience of investigating EA, therefore, lies in the very nature of the organizational cross-border set up and, above all, in its advocacy for framing the debate over European issues within the construction of a transnational civic community. Such a specific context was also influential in the choice of treating the data at transnational level rather than through 'methodological nationalism'. That meant that the analysis was not concerned with looking at variations across an *a priori* taxonomy of national variables (also due to the nature of EA membership), albeit discourses of nationhood were clearly recognized as one powerful discursive element.

Following the DHA, the study was operationalized on three levels of contextualization and analysis. Chapter 2 set the scene by embedding the object of this study into the wider social context of transnational and European civil societies initiatives emerged in recent years. Subsequently, the specific nature, scope and 'fields of action' of EA were discussed explaining how the character of this organization fits the specific transnational and bottom-up perspectives adopted in the examination of European identities.

Chapter 3 constructed the toolbox for this research by exploring the notions of identities from social constructivist and 'late modern' perspectives which recognize the pivotal role of language in the construction of meanings. Furthermore the chapter provided an overview of the discursive production of social identities (such as national identities) as evolving amid dynamic socio-historical contexts and how Critical Linguists have accounted for the constructions of identities. The multifaceted concept of transnationalism was introduced explaining how transnational flows and practices have impacted on the imagination of community and on the 'glocalization' of identities. From these premises, different, but interrelated, meanings of European identity were highlighted as relevant to this study: that of Europeanness as a political project, as a site of recontextualization of global discourses and as a historical process of transformation of nationhood.

Chapter 4 offered a detailed account of the methodology used in this study, including the nature and the range of data collected, as well as the methods of collection and a socio-demographic profile of the informants. The analytical framework used in this study (DHA integrated with some statistical data) was also discussed in detail in Chapter 4.

Findings were extensively presented in Chapter 5, organized around a taxonomy of macro/micro strategies and topoi, and followed by a critical discussion of such results. The discussion focused, inter alia, on two salient linguistic realizations: the scenario of spatial dynamics and the indexicality of the terms Europe, transnationalism and nationhood which were invested by discussants with a range of meanings including ideals of democracy, diversity and equality. It was suggested that most members often made sense of their (European) identities, their cross-border practices and their situatedness through these two sets of linguistic realizations. Findings also revealed how European identities were typically produced through the recontextualization of historical discourses of nationhood with distinct discursive patterns emerging whereby some members tended to accommodate their national identities with their Europeanness while others challenged, rejected, otherized or by-passed national referents. It was thus argued that, albeit extant, nationhood emerged also as extremely volatile. Moreover, findings also suggested the interdiscursivity of Europeanness, transnationalism and cosmopolitan perspectives which were often conceptualized as convergent discourses. In this sense, this study has suggested that one of the members' frequent narratives of Europeanness was the expansion and progression of community towards ideals of equality and world citizenship.

A model was proposed that captures this dynamic as a continuum and relates it to three frames of one's 'situatedness' in the social space: nation-centric, Euro-centric and cosmopolitan or polycentric. These three 'locations' were also related to different conceptualizations of the European project which at the nation-centric end broadly overlapped the EU's vision while at the cosmopolitan end regarded it as an experiment of transnational citizenship to be replicated worldwide. It was highlighted how, for most members, the transnational dimensions of their European identities often lay between these two poles and how Europe was often discussed as a 'nodal point' and ambivalently represented as an open and closed space with tensions in the definition of insiders and outsiders. Moreover the analysis has suggested that, for EA members, the construction and transformation of Europeanness is not a linear process but, rather, a dialectic one which is achieved via multiple and dynamic identification processes with different communities of relevance and that sutures both individual and collective narratives.

Drawing on these empirical insights, the following section will highlight the major contribution of this research, its limitations, reflecting on possible ways to further this study and reaching some final conclusions.

7.2 Contribution of this study

This study has contributed to the interdisciplinary advancement of knowledge on European identity in a number of ways.

1. First, the data has been approached from a transnational stance, treating Europeanness as a series of identification processes occurring amid transnational fields, rather than along national variables. At the same time this study has clearly recognized the salience of nationhood as a socio-historical discourse.

   While the findings of this study by and large corroborate the literature on the multiplicity, fragmentation and context dependency of identities, they have cast a light on the historical transformation of discourses of nationhood, Europe and, from the specificity of the data studied, the discursive interplay of Europeanness with 'glocalization' phenomena.

The findings have suggested that the dynamic interplay between different cosmopolitan, (trans)national and local perspectives can be key in the definition of one's community of relevance and related processes of identification.

The analysis has also suggested that transnationalism can, inter alia, represent the individual awareness of globalization that urged members to (re)construct their situatedness in a global society and thus to rethink the relation with the communities to which they imagine they belong (or do not belong). In this sense, the findings of this study support existing calls for treating the sociology of Europeanization in the wider remit of global dynamics (see, for example, Delanty and Rumford 2005).

Furthermore this study has shown the recursive and yet 'liquid' nature of national and historical discourses in the construction of Europe, suggesting that it is in the transformation and volatility of such discourses and in their recontextualization and embedding into transnational referents that often members made meaning of their locations.

2. Second, while transnational dynamics can shift the imagination of borders and generate new spaces, this study has found no evidence of a global or unified European identity. Instead, the insights have suggested that, since members treated Europe as a relational spatial concept rather than an essential one, they constructed their European locations between and around micro and global dimensions.

Consequently, the interplay of identities anchored to the 'European space' with micro, national, macro-regional or global identities, as emerged from the data, does not support the logic of contained identities – for example as suggested by the Russian Doll Model (Herrmann, Risse-Kappen and Brewer 2004) – but, rather, it points to the fact that identification processes with local and global referents can work in fluid, self-reflexive and agentive ways complementing each other.

3. Third, this study strongly supports a constructivist view of identities, highlighting in particular the mutually constitutive nature of language and social interaction. For example, the analysis has highlighted how members not only used the metaphorical scenario of *spatial dynamics* to describe patterns of mobility but also as a key cognitive and discursive tool through which they made sense of their own locations, of their connections with Europe and with the wider transnational society. This should perhaps invite us to rethink certain cognitive and metaphorical conceptualizations

of Europe (e.g. house/mosaic) in favour of more dynamic ones (e.g. network, flows).

4. Fourth this study has cast some light on the interplay of European and cosmopolitan ideals/identities. While some members identified as European through the articulation of a (negative) relationality with an 'other', a large proportion of members constructed their Europeanness through a 'thin' conceptualization of identities – that is driven by the cosmopolitan ideal that identities ought no longer to be constructed in relation to the 'other'. In this sense, although Europeanness does not necessarily equate to cosmopolitan perspectives, it can closely interplay with such perspectives by bridging the 'scaling up' of community in the reconceptualization of nationhood.

5. Finally, this study has highlighted the salience of political agency in processes of identification as European/with European referents. The imagination of Europeanness as articulated and envisaged by EA members not only offered them opportunities for making sense of their 'glocal' locations but it was also key in their identification as European actors who are contributing to a democratic project, a consideration which may be relevant to the legitimization of such projects.

7.3 Limitations of this study

This study has focused on specific bottom-up and transnational perspectives for, as it has been argued, these standpoints have only been cursorily appreciated by the CDS literature. Of course, taking these angles has constrained and shaped the analysis and, therefore, the results must be embedded in the very specific nature of the organization under examination. Clearly, the high mobility, the age range and the political commitment of the informants represented key variables in their articulation of their discourses of Europeanness.

Moreover, the results must be seen as limited by the partial number of branches analysed, the fact that informants were a self-selected sample and that my membership may have influenced the responses of some members. This study, therefore, cannot make any claim about the generalizability of the findings and cannot assume that a similar investigation replicated in the wider remit of the public opinion, with similar associations of citizens, or even within EA would produce similar results.

In this respect the interpretive nature of CDA must be stressed once more. While I personally believe the heuristic approach taken by CDA is a strength in the examination of complex social phenomena, I am aware of the challenges of such an ontological and epistemological approach to language. In this research I have therefore striven to minimize the bias of my interpretations by providing as much robust evidence from the data as possible and also by taking this study as a reflexive opportunity for my own exploration of (European) identity, in the awareness that there is an inescapability for researchers to become co-constructors of social reality by decontextualizing and recontextualizing texts in the process of doing research (Fairclough and Fairclough 2012).

7.4 Where to now?

This book has suggested that the imagination of Europe as a community of relevance was produced by EA members through the interplay of several discursive dimensions driven by the transnational narrative. As social and discursive constructs, the transformative nature of identities, however, means that any exploration of processes of identification cannot be conclusive and although this study has achieved its aims, clearly there is much scope for further work on the analysis of European identities especially in the light of shifting cultural, social, economic and political contingencies that have been dramatically shaking up European affairs of late.

In this respect, I am only too aware that presenting the potential of the transnational narrative as driving (European) society further towards cosmopolitan ideals of peaceful and egalitarian coexistence of individuals may be a rosy picture that stands in stark contrast with the dramatic changes Europe's political landscape has been going through lately. In the wake of a populist and nationalist resurgence, in fact, practices and ideals associated with transnationalism have increasingly been challenged in public discourses across and beyond Europe with the UK's decision to leave the EU (Brexit) as the most notable example of such political backlash. In many respects, Brexit has been interpreted and legitimized – both at institutional and citizens' level – as a shift away from a 'risky' supranational path inside the EU back to a 'safer' world order based on a system of multilateral relations, national independence and neoliberal intergovernmentalism (Zappettini 2019a, b) in which nationally anchored referents of identity are invoked as strongholds in the face of unsettling economic and social crises. At the same time, as the vagueness and drawbacks of a nation-centric project such as Brexit become apparent by the day, much social and political resistance has been taking shape in new discursive sites and through new discursive productions by both top-down and bottom-up actors across Europe. I suggest that it is within these shifting discursive contexts and in the dynamics of Europe's current 'critical juncture' (Zappettini and Krzyżanowski 2019) that future research on European identities ought to be situated to address the critical question of legitimation of the EU project and the relationship between EU institutions and its demos.

As highlighted in this book, civic participation and agency can be key to processes of identification with an imagined European community and they can contribute to a critical appreciation of the transformation of discourses of nationhood and the different discursive trajectories into which such process may unfold. Moreover, as I have argued earlier, the production of Europeanness is not simply an issue defined by the geography or the politics of Europe but also by the spatial dynamics and the different scales brought about by transnational practices and globalization processes. Further studies on European identities therefore would also benefit from investigations related to transnational mobility and issues of citizenship since, as suggested by this study, these are crucial in the definition of community, belonging, membership and ultimately inclusion and exclusion.

Notes

Chapter 1

1 Globalization is a multifaceted, complex and contested phenomenon that has been covered by a wealth of literature (see, for example, Featherstone 1990, Appadurai 1996, Beck 2000, Giddens 2000, Pittaway 2003b, Robertson and White 2003, Sassen 2007). In broad terms globalization can be interpreted as 'a set of processes rather than ... a single linear developmental logic' (Held 1999, p. 27). In this sense, transnationalism can be seen as one process contributing to globalization as well as one of its effects. As transnationalism is central to this monograph, it has been discussed in detail in Section 3 on p. 46.

2 Lyotard (1989) argues that, in post modernity, the human condition is better understood as the plurality of small and often competing narratives than as the all-encompassing teleologies of history such as the Enlightenment and Marxism.

3 Hall (1996) uses the term 'fractured' to refer to the multiple sources of identities available in postmodern societies and the fact that, as a result, individuals no longer have a single and unified idea of their 'self'.

4 The term 'glocalization' is commonly attributed to Robertson (1992) who uses it to refer to the impact of global processes at a local level.

5 The cosmopolitan ideology, which regards all individuals as citizens of the world, has its roots in Greek philosophy where *polis*, the city-state, was the embodiment of a civic community. Cosmopolitan ideals were also key features of the Enlightenment movement (cf. Vertovec 2003, Calhoun 2006, Held 2010). Lately, in the social sciences, there has been a resurgence of interest in the cosmopolitan ideology following the debate on globalization (see Rumford 2008).

6 There exist many different terms to refer to the evolution (or demise) of national structures especially in relation to the EU. In this study I have chosen to use, as consistently as possible, the term 'post-national' in reference to the ideological transformation of nation states and the term 'supranational' in reference to the remits of power of EU institutions.

7 The term 'demos' identifies a political community sharing a (non-imposed) common denominator. While in nation states the perception of a 'demos' has often relied on ethno-cultural elements, the lack of the above has sometimes been regarded as a major limitation for the development of a European identity. This issue, associated with low levels of civic participation, and the lack of transparency

of the EU political system have often been referred to as 'democratic deficit' (Majone 1998) and have underpinned considerable criticism at the legitimacy of the EU (cf., for example, Cederman 2001, Nicolaïdis 2004, Maas 2007).

8 In this study the terms 'bottom-up' and 'top-down' refer to the two opposing poles of the hierarchical system of decision-making whereby institutional roles (such as government organs) are represented 'at the top' and 'ordinary' citizens 'at the bottom' (often called the grassroots level). While top-down politics is typically initiated by institutional action, bottom-up initiatives reverse this process by encouraging discussions, consultations, debates campaigns and the like.

9 http://www.euroalter.com/who-we-are/our-organisation. Accessed 8/2/2012.

10 ibid.

11 Although in some literature the terms 'international' and 'transnational' are used interchangeably, this monograph treats the two terms as distinct concepts. By internationalism I refer to the organization of social, political and economic relations that recognizes nations as the major agents whereas by transnationalism I refer to the links and flows of interaction between people and/or institutions across the borders of nation states' as further discussed in Sections 2.4.2 and 3.1.

12 Introduced under the Treaty of Lisbon, the European Citizens' is a legal provision that allows EU citizens to put forward legislation proposals to the European Commission (for details and legal requirements see http://www.citizens-initiative.eu/?page_id=2. Accessed 16/7/2018).

13 In sociology grand theories aim to explain the functioning of the whole social world in general and abstract terms while middle-range theories are aimed at more commensurable and phenomena-specific insights; see, for example, Boudon (1991).

14 I use the term 'EU-rope' in line with Krzyżanowski (2010) to suggest the conceptual convergence of the EU and Europe.

15 European Alternatives website http://www.euroalter.com/about-us/. Accessed 5/3/2011.

16 Local bases are open to any EU and non-EU citizen. A typical local group like Prague can thus be made up of national citizens of the Czech Republic, France and the US Transnational meetings are held in different locations on a rotational basis.

17 In broad terms, active citizenship refers to a process whereby individuals take responsibility and initiative as members of a civic community. 'Active Citizenship' has been promoted by the EU under the Citizenship Programme 2007–13 to raise awareness on citizen's rights and to encourage 'the involvement of citizens and civil society organisations in the process of European integration' http://eacea.ec.europa.eu/citizenship/programme/about_citizenship_en.php. Accessed 25/8/2012.

18 CDA sees discourses pertaining to different 'fields of action' (Wodak and Meyer 2009) that is specific 'segments' of social activities (e.g. 'fields of action' in politics can be represented by law making procedure, advertising and propaganda,

administration, etc.). Each field of action is characterized by specific 'genres' of texts (such as speeches, regulations, press releases etc.). For Fairclough (2003) a genre is a socially ratified way of using language in connection with a particular type of social activity used by communities of practice and expected to systematically perform certain social functions.

19 European Commission website http://europa.eu/legislation_summaries/ institutional_affairs/decisionmaking_process/a30000_en.htm). Accessed 14/5/2012.

20 ibid.

21 White Paper on European Communication Policy 2006. Available from europa.eu/ documents/comm/white_papers/pdf/com2006_35_en.pdf. Accessed 12/3/2012.

22 TEN was in receipt of some EU funding through the 'Europe for Citizens' and 'Youth in Action' programmes (created by the Education and Culture DG) and a grant from the European Cultural Foundation. To date, however, the organization is mainly reliant on the members' voluntary work and, to a lesser extent, to voluntary membership fees and the support of some private sponsors.

23 See, for example, the Citizen's Pact (http://www.citizenspact.eu/about/) in which the term 'alternative' is used in the same sense as in Fairclough's (2003) critique of 'TINA' ('There Is No Alternative') discourses in relation to the use of experts in policy-making.

Chapter 2

1 It is rather problematic defining clear boundaries of social constructivist and poststructuralist schools of thought as the latter developed out of the former and, although poststructuralists have critiqued and rejected certain tenets of structuralism, they also built their work on some of them (cf. Angermuller, Maingueneau and Wodak 2014).

2 Building on De Saussure's structural linguistics (de Saussure et al. 1986) – for which words or signifiers are structured in a system of differences, that is they derive their value through their relation with other signs – Derrida and other poststructuralists assume that signifieds (or word meanings) are also defined by *difference*, a term that Derrida uses in French to mean both 'difference' and 'differing'.

3 For Laclau and Mouffe (2001) meanings can only be temporarily fixed through 'systemic closure' achieved via hegemony.

4 Giddens emphasizes the conscious and creative action of individuals in the modification of structures; however, he does not see this as a straightforward process over which individual have a direct control but rather mediated through a process of 'structuration'. For Giddens (1991), while meanings can be accepted and reproduced, they can thus also be negotiated or resisted vis-à-vis the very

social structures they have created resulting in a further interplay between social structures and individual or collective agency.

5 CDA is often characterized as a denominational umbrella under which different trends exist. See Krzyżanowski (2010, p. 69) for details of these.

6 Text means any portion of written or spoken language.

7 This constitutes part of a larger theory of hegemony. For Laclau hegemony is discursively achieved through the reduction of possible meanings (or 'closure') within a certain topic.

8 The study was originally published in 1999.

9 See pp. 67–9 for a detailed discussion of discursive strategies.

10 I here refer to the top-down vision of 'being European' rather than the EU's organizational identity (cf. Wodak (2004), Abeles (2004), and Krzyżanowski (2010) for the latter).

11 The text is available at: http://www.cvce.eu/content/publication/1999/1/1/02798dc9-9c69-4b7d-b2c9-f03a8db7da32/publishable_en.pdf. Accessed 5/9/2011.

Chapter 3

1 I here refer to language as a conventionalized communication system that exists in distinct denominational forms (e.g. English, Swahili, Algonquin, etc.).

2 As suggested by much literature, the adoption and standardization of national languages have often occurred through institutional processes of selection and reproduction of certain language varieties at the expense of others (Bourdieu 1991, Spolsky 2004, Wright 2000) which have been justified by different conceptualizations of 'nation' (see Wodak et al. (2009) for a differentiation between *Kulturnation* and *Staatnation*). In the case of *Kulturnation* – as a virtue of the ties with ethnicity and 'groupness', a common language has often provided a group the ideological basis for claiming legitimacy as a nation (Smith 1991). This is, for instance, the case of the eighteenth-century German Romantic movement which led to the constitution of the German state as the expression of a perceived German *volksgeist* (the national spirit) (Edwards 2009). By contrast, in the case of *Staatnation*, a common language was often introduced and imposed by the central administration on the grounds that it would ensure the civic participation of all citizens and the functioning of the state apparatus (Chilton 2004). This is, for example, what happened in the seventeenth century under Richelieu when French became the unifying language of France (Spolsky 2004) and, in more general terms, in the institutionalization of administrations that ensued in the creation of nation states in Europe in the last few centuries. This rough distinction between 'constituvist' and 'instrumentalist' (De Schutter 2007) views on the

nature of language is consistently found throughout political philosophy literature and has impacted on the implementation of different language policies and on interpretations of linguistic justice (Zappettini and Comănaru 2014).

3 By the same token, some of the institutional and populist responses to such scenario have resulted in a reaffirmation of essentialist interpretations of identities and national languages (see, for example, Mar-Molinero and Stevenson 2009, Ruzza 2014).

4 In relation to English as a lingua franca there has been a complex debate on issues of linguistic justice, which is not possible to discuss in detail in this publication (see, inter alia, Ammon 2001, Gubbins and Holt 2002, Maurais 2003, Phillipson 2003, Mar-Molinero and Stevenson 2009, Van Parijs 2011).

5 Traditionally, nation states have granted citizenship to either any individual born in the territory of the state (*jus soli* or right of soil) or by line of descendants (*jus sanguini* or right of blood). In recent years, however, several states have changed their policies. For example, since 1999, Germany has made it easier for individuals born in Germany to foreign parents to acquire German citizenship, thus opening up the restrictive *jus sanguini* principle that for many years did not recognize a large immigrant population of *Gastarbeiter*. Since 2006 Italy has allowed for descendants of Italian immigrants (who can prove a relation with their ancestors) to claim Italian citizenship while keeping the citizenship acquired at birth (e.g. the United States), thus extending the *jus sanguini* outside the national territory.

6 At the same time there exist many examples of how the financial crisis and the negative effect of global capitalism have fuelled populist discourses promoting a resurgence of nationalism (Wodak and Richardson 2013, Angouri and Wodak 2014, Ruzza 2014).

7 For example, from sociolinguistic perspectives, the work of Milroy (1987) has relied on the concept of network to explain language variation as a function of interpersonal relationships and the enactment of social and linguistics norms within a social group. Wenger (1998) refers to network from social, psychological and anthropological perspectives to describe the dynamic interaction occurring within communities of practice where membership is enacted through mutual engagement and shared objectives.

8 Beck (2002) interprets cosmopolitanization as 'glocalization' or 'internal globalization' (p. 17) arguing a 'positive correlation between transnationalisation and cosmopolitan attitudes' (Roudometof 2005, p. 117).

9 Fligstein (2007) uses the term 'European field' to include social actors and processes involved in the integration project.

10 See http://www.euromove.org.uk/index.php?id=20539 and http://ec.europa.eu/social/main.jsp?catId=470 for details. Accessed 10/10/17.

11 http://ec.europa.eu/social/main.jsp?catId=470. Accessed 10/10/17.

12 In line with Brubaker and Cooper (2000) and their conceptualization of 'identity', a distinction is taken into account by this framework between processes of 'identification with' and 'identification as'. The former focus on personal dimension in which 'target' identities are primarily seen as ideal models that one strives to achieve while the latter essentially involve processes of social categorization although lacking the formal recognition aspect of membership – see also Cram (2010).

13 These two terms have been used widely in sociology and political studies to refer to different social attitudes to world interaction (see, for example, Hannerz 1990, 1996, Linklater 1998, Held 1999, Dobson 2006, Held 2010).

14 As Calhoun (1997) warns, much literature on the subject tends to use the terms 'public sphere' and 'civil society' as equivalent concepts while for Calhoun the latter is a component of the former. A further distinction is raised by Triandafyllidou, Wodak and Krzyżanowski (2009) between 'soft' and 'hard' dimensions of the public sphere. For Triandafyllidou, Wodak and Krzyżanowski (2009) the 'strong' dimension is politically institutionalized whereas the 'soft' dimension applies to 'civil society communication, arenas of debate and the circulation of meaning-making representations, processes of semiosis in cultural systems, identity-based group and other arenas of communication in society' (p. 133). For clarity, in this study, I generally interpret the EPS as the political debate about democracy and 'European affairs' in which the civil society (made up of movements and various organizations of citizens) engage. I thus interpret the civil society in line with Ruzza and Sala (2007) as one intermediate and (relatively) informal level of the public sphere (along with the state, politics and the social).

15 For Habermas actors in the public sphere are expected to respect certain 'ethical' rules of discourse (e.g. openness of expression and truthfulness of their assertions) that comply with an 'ideal speech situation'. In other words, they are supposed to make rational use of arguments to achieve consensus. Habermas argues that, although an argument comes from within the self, it is the strength of individual arguments (i.e. their persuasiveness) and their intersubjective validity that allow members of a civic community to reach consensus and deliberation (the final objectives of democratic participation). The view that actors, being given equal opportunity to have a voice in the political debate, are free from external influence of power remains a rather idealized notion as Habermas himself recognized and, as many have critiqued (see, for example, Kompridis (2006)).

16 However, see also Calhoun (1997) for whom some identities are already consolidated before entering the public sphere.

17 For detailed discussions of transnational networking activities in Europe see, for example: Kaiser, Leucht and Gehler (2010) for networks of regionalist movements; Montoya (2008) and Kollman (2009) for gender-related recognition of civil rights.

Moreover, for citizens' initiatives, see http://european-citizens-network.eu; http://www.citizensforeurope.eu; http://www.ceecn.net/; http://www.activecitizenship.net; http://www.neac2.eu/. Accessed 3/7/2014.

18 See, for example, Issue 6(4) of the Journal of European Public Policy (1999) dedicated to a social constructivist approach to Europe.

Chapter 4

1   In line with Krzyżanowski (2008), I refer to 'primary' topics as the main subjects of discussion that were broadly introduced by the moderators at the focus groups. Secondary topics constitute salient themes developed by participants either embedded in or independent of the general primary themes and they also were covered by the analysis.

2   All material examined was available in English, except for the website and the Trans Europa Journal which were available in English, Italian, French and Romanian. In this case the English and Italian versions were consulted.

3   http://www.euroalter.com/2011/being-european/ and http://www.youtube.com/watch?v=_AuiLYa2Wss&feature=player_embedded. Accessed 21/5/2015.
    http://www.youtube.com/user/euroalter voices. Accessed 21/5/2015.
    Some videos feature interviews in different languages for which English subtitles are provided.

4   http://www.euroalter.com/who-we-are/our-organisation

5   The Human Library is a worldwide project where people volunteer to talk about specific subjects (such as 'being a Muslim') to other people. It is seen as a way to promote dialogue, understanding prejudices and ultimately to stop violence. Since 2003, it has been one of the activities supported by the Council of Europe. For more information see http://humanlibrary.org/index.html. Accessed 30/3/2013

6   Wodak et al. (2009) conduct an analysis of contents, strategies and means of realizations while Krzyżanowski (2010) proposes a 'thematic' analysis and an 'in-depth' analysis of argumentation and linguistic features. Although they both make use of strategies and topoi as analytical tools, Wodak et al. (2009) foreground the former while in Krzyżanowski (2010) the analysis is guided by the latter. The linguistic analysis carried out in this study has been based on a model that combines the two as further explained in this section.

7   In keeping with Wodak et al. (2009) I use the term 'realization' in the meaning of linguistically enacted.

8   For transcripts not in English, the translated English version was analysed.

9   By and large, Wodak et al. (2009) treat linguistic strategies as the realization of both social practices and social action, assuming that, in their discourses, the

speakers realize both their agency and their habitus, or to paraphrase Barthes and Sontag (1982) they are both the 'masters and the slaves' of language. The analysis of strategies, therefore, adopts a heuristic approach which takes into account a 'soft' determinism in communicative structures (i.e. the reproduction of some habitus), but also, in the light of the specific nature of the informants, it assumes a large degree of conscious intentionality in their discourses.

10 See, for example, Encyclopedia of Philosophy (1997, p. 80) for a definition of Aristotle's distinction between general arguments (*koinoi*) and special arguments (*idioi*).

11 I treat all warrants in argumentation schemes as *topoi* including those which infringe or violate rationality rules and which Wodak et al. (2009) refer to as *fallacies*.

12 This use of topoi in DHA has been criticized by Zagar (2010) for its departure from classical argumentation theory; however, it has widely been used in pragmatics (cf. Kienpointner and Kindt 1997).

13 Cf. also the shift from the metaphor of Europe as a Christian-rooted 'family' to that of a mosaic and the 'Russian Doll' and 'Marble cake' conceptual models (all discussed in Section 2.4.1).

Chapter 5

1 The noun 'European Movement' was exclusively used by LO3 to discuss her membership in the 'European Federalist Movement'.

2 LO1's use of 'we' could also refer to his identification as Italian since Italy was one of the original six founders of the EU. The context however suggests he was using the pronoun 'we' in the historical meaning of the larger European political community.

3 See, for example, Eder and Spohn (2005) for a discussion of narratives of Europe as a 'community of memories'.

4 The expression 'third country' is commonly used to refer to non-EU countries.

5 I use the word 'reflexive' both in the metaphorical meaning of mirrors through which one recognizes one's self-image and thinking about oneself in society and time (Giddens 1991).

6 I borrow these terms from sociolinguistic work, for example, Baynham (2011). In general such literature have emphasized how the enactment of identities in discourse can be accounted for by elements that are generated or 'brought about' by the narrative itself as well as more stable features that are 'brought along' in the narration. While the latter could thus constitute the more 'essentialist' dimensions of identity, the former emerge from the co-constructive process of discursive interaction. (This note has been reproduced in Zappettini 2014, p. 400.)

7 Anadiplosis is the use of a final word in a clause, which is subsequently repeated at the beginning of the following clause.

8 LO3 is also an active member of the Young European Movement.

9 Although it was not possible to ascertain each member's individual circumstances, in most cases this information was partly derived from the questionnaire or emerged in the discussion, or through personal communication.

10 The *topos of network* was invoked several times and used in different contexts by members. In this section I have illustrated examples of members implicitly or explicitly referring to a 'network' of positive experiences to construct their identities and position themselves. On the other hand, the topos of 'network' in reference to EA's the organizational structure and a transnational form of political activism will be discussed later in the analysis as it primarily relates to strategies of constructing a civic community. For a discussion on the metaphor of network in the social sciences see McEntee-Atalianis and Zappettini (2014).

11 Extract 12, Extract 13, Extract 26 and Extract 33 have been reproduced and discussed in McEntee-Atalianis and Zappettini (2014). As McEntee-Atalianis and Zappettini (2014) draws on the data of this study, part of the analysis related to these extracts builds on some of the insights presented in the paper.

12 In the last few years there have been different movements in Spain which have campaigned in support of the right to affordable housing (*Vde Vivienda*) and against the lack of certainty (*precariedad*) in employment and social welfare (*Precarios en movimiento*); See also *Juventud Sin Futuro* (Youth without a Future) which have campaigned under the slogan 'no house, no job, no pension, no fear'. In general the deregulation of the job markets in the 1990s and 2000s has resulted in more temporary jobs being available at the expense of long-term and fixed jobs and the emergence as the 'Precariat' as a new social class (Standing 2011). European Alternatives has run a number of campaigns to demand radical changes to the current job situation and VA1 has been actively involved in these activities.

13 The topic of citizenship was also discussed frequently by other members. However, as these discussions related primarily to 'active' citizenship, the analysis of this latter topos has been dealt with in detail in Section 5.1.5.3 as a stand-alone discursive feature in the construction of Europe as a civic community.

14 Under the Romanian communist regime (1947–89), visas were subject to government approval and citizens who wanted to travel abroad had their passports held by the police. Furthermore, citizens who applied to emigrate had their civic and economic rights revoked and they were systematically disparaged by authorities. The relevance of being able to travel freely therefore must be interpreted in the light of such political and historical contingencies.

15 By contrast, see also, Extract 14 for a negative representation of in-betweenness.

16 Cf. 'the myth of Anglo-Saxon exceptionalism' (Marcussen and Roscher 2010).

17 As a consequence of this action most Roma living in France (who were Romanian
    and Bulgarian citizens) were repatriated to their countries thus leaving France in
    infringement of the freedom of movement of European citizens. See http://www.
    bbc.co.uk/news/world-europe-11020429 for further details. Accessed 20/6/2014.
    In relation to this event EA ran a campaign condemning the expulsions of Roma
    from France and presented a petition to the European Commission denouncing
    the French government for violations of fundamental rights and the principle of
    non-discrimination. PR1 was actively involved in the organization of this campaign
    from the Prague office.

18 Although this would appear to contradict the proposition that Europe (and the
    world) represent a 'closer' (i.e. more relevant) community, the speaker (and other
    members) constructed these referents just as relevant as local communities through
    frames of mobility and interconnectedness as discussed in detail under the topos of
    interconnectedness (see Section 5.3.3.2).

19 The *Oxford Dictionary* defines 'obsolete' (meaning 2 Biology) as '(of a part or
    characteristic of an organism) less developed than formerly or in a related species;
    rudimentary; vestigial'.

20 Cf., inter alia, Chilton and Lakoff (1995) for discussion of public representations of
    states as 'containers', Drulak (2004) for representations of Europe as an 'equilibrium
    of containers', and Charteris-Black (2006) for representations of 'Britain as a
    container' in relation to discourses of immigration.

21 Under the Italian legislation, non-national spouses of Italian citizens acquire
    citizenship status as effect of marriage. However, as at the time of this interview the
    Italian state did not recognize same-sex unions, it had rejected all applications of
    citizenship based on same-sex unions recognized abroad. In some cases, appeals
    were brought to the European Court of Justice that recognized the Italian refusal
    as discriminatory. RO1 had been campaigning for the equalization of LGBT rights
    across European states.

22 Much literature on transnationalism has contended that, in a globalized society,
    sovereign states are increasingly unable to protect their citizens from the impact of
    decisions made by other actors leaving individuals aware of their interdependence
    in the face of global issues affecting local communities (e.g. global warming, job
    relocation, transnational crime, nuclear risk) and upon which they have no direct
    control (cf. Beck 2000).

23 I borrow the term from Schegloff (1999) who defines 'communities of relevance'
    as 'academic, disciplinary, political, aesthetic, etc., communities, whose members
    share an orientation to inquiry about the world or action in it, an orientation which
    imparts relevance to certain lines of inquiry, with associated observations, rhetorics,
    etc.' (p. 579). While Schegloff (1999) uses the term 'communities of relevance'
    primarily in relation to academic investigation, I interpret the term more loosely to
    suggest that members often made meaning of their social locations by projecting

the Andersonian imagination of community onto salient interests, values, referents, and so on as further discussed in this section.

24 'Rhizomatic' thinking was first proposed by the French philosophers Gilles Deleuze and Félix Guattari (1987) who advocated a move away from a dualist and binary understanding of knowledge, which they liken to certain plants feeding through a single stalk (thus in a linear end-to-end way). Instead, they proposed a 'rhizomatic' approach to understanding social phenomena, that is, seeing society as a root system which, sprawling in many different directions, allowed the plant to feed through a crisscrossing network of buds. For Deleuze and Guattari, 'Any point of a rhizome can be connected to anything other and must be' (1987, p. 7) through many transversal connections that run and propagate with no end or beginning.

25 A similar analytical account of BE2's realizations of network as a biological system has been given by McEntee-Atalianis and Zappettini (2014, p. 404).

26 The term 'new frontier' has historical association with American settlement in the western part of the country. Moreover, the term is also politically associated with American president John F. Kennedy and his administration's social and political programmes for change and advancement including the 'space conquest'. See also, the etimology of 'frontier' (from Latin *frons* '(at the) front').

27 Coined by T. More in 1516, the term 'Utopia' refers to an imaginary island characterized by perfect social and political systems, in other words an ideal society albeit unattainable. More invented the term 'Utopia' from the Greek ou (not) and topos (place) therefore literally meaning 'no place' or 'no here' to suggest its metaphysical dimension.

28 Aristotle defines *bios* as a life endowed with meaning and dignity derived from taking part in a political community in contrast to *zoe*, which expresses the simple fact of living a 'bare life'.

29 See http://euplus.org/ for further details. Accessed 4/2/2017.

30 The notion of solidarity has been central to most symbolic constructions of community (cf., for example, Cohen 2013) and in nation states it has typically resulted in redistribution occurring through taxation and allocation of welfare services. The EU has somewhat worked on similar principles with the annual budget and 'framework' funding although this has occurred on a much smaller scale as, unlike nation states, the EU institutions have no direct power over taxation. Cf. also Magnusson and Stråth (2007) for a focused discussion of the tensions of solidarity and inequalities in the European field.

31 With this term Habermas envisages the development of a sense of community among Europeans similar to that which forged the building of nation states however without ethnic, historical, and cultural elements of a 'community of fate' (e.g. language and common descent).

32 SO1 referred to internationalism in the sense of 'international (or world) communism', that is, the ideology that the socialist revolution envisaged by

Marxism would eventually be achieved by the coming together of people following the abolition of states (as proletarians have a common cause but no 'fatherland'). In the speaker's view, this idealized interpretation of cross-state solidarity among citizens of communist countries (such as Bulgaria) was instrumentally used by the Soviets to keep such citizens under Soviet influence.

33 Following the constructions of most members, and much literature on the subject (Rindler Schjerve and Vetter 2012, Kjaer and Adamo 2013, Unger, Krzyżanowski and Wodak 2014) multilingualism is interpreted in this context as a multifarious phenomenon comprising of individual, societal and institutional dimensions.

34 Extracts 50, 51, 52 and 53 have been partly reproduced and discussed in Zappettini and Comănaru (2014).

35 In sociolinguistics the term 'diglossia' refers to language practices in a community whereby a 'high' variety of language is used for formal or literary purposes whereas a 'low' variety is used for everyday conversation.

36 Globish refers to a simplified version of English (Grzega 2006). Euro-English is an emerging variety of English often associated with European institutions and the civil society (Jenkins, Modiano and Seidlhofer 2001).

37 The 'language of democracy' has been widely debated in political and philosophical studies. See, inter alia, Archibugi (2005) and Kymlicka and Patten (2003)

Chapter 6

1 *N*-grams are sequences of co-occurring words where N stands for the number of items that make up the string. Table 6.2 shows the frequency of the contiguous occurrence of the term 'Europe' within two to six collocates.

2 See, for example, Oberhuber et al. (2005), Galasinska and Krzyżanowski (2009) for a discussion of 'core' and 'peripheral' Europe.

3 Keating (2013) refers to the rescaling of the European space as 'the migration of economic, social, and political systems of action and of regulation to new spatial levels, above, below, and across the nation-state' (p. 6).

4 See Recchi (2013, p. 3).

Bibliography

Abeles, M. (2004). Identity and borders: an anthropological approach to EU institutions. Twenty-First Century Papers, On-Line Working Papers from the Center for 21st Century Studies University of Wisconsin – Milwaukee.

Adler, E. (2005). *Communitarian International Relations: The Epistemic Foundations of International Relations*. Abingdon; New York, Routledge.

Albert, M., D. Jacobson and Y. Lapid (2001). *Identities, Borders, Orders: Rethinking International Relations Theory*. Minneapolis, University of Minnesota Press.

Alter, P. (1994). *Nationalism*. London, Edward Arnold.

Althusser, L. and F. Matheron (2003). *The Humanist Controversy and Other Writings (1966-67)*. New York, Verso.

Ammon, U. (2001). *The Dominance of English as a Language of Science: Effects on Other Languages and Language Communities*. Berlin; New York, Mouton de Gruyter.

Anderson, B. (2006). *Imagined Communities: Reflections on the Origin and Spread of Nationalism*. New York, Verso.

Angermuller, J., D. Maingueneau and R. Wodak (2014). *The Discourse Studies Reader*. Amsterdam; Philadelphia, PA, John Benjamins Publishing.

Angouri, J. and R. Wodak (2014). 'They Became Big in the Shadow of the Crisis': The Greek Success Story and the Rise of the Far Right. *Discourse & Society* 25(4): 540–65.

Antaki, C. and S. Widdicombe (1998). *Identities in Talk*. London, Sage Publications.

Anthony, L. (2012). *AntConc (Version 3.3.2)*. Tokyo, Japan, Waseda University.

Antonsich, M. (2008). The Narration of Europe in 'National' and 'Post-national' Terms. *European Journal of Social Theory* 11(4): 505–22.

Appadurai, A. (1995). The Production of Locality. In R. Fardon (ed.) *Counterworks: Managing the Diversity of Knowledge*. London; New York, Routledge: 204–25.

Appadurai, A. (1996). *Modernity Al Large: Cultural Dimensions of Globalization*. Minnesota, University of Minnesota Press.

Archibugi, D. (2005). The Language of Democracy: Vernacular or Esperanto? A Comparison between the Multiculturalist and Cosmopolitan Perspectives. *Political Studies* 53(3): 537–55.

Auer, P. (1984). *Bilingual Conversation*. Amsterdam, John Benjamins Publishing.

Baker, P., C. Gabrielatos, M. KhosraviNik, M. Krzyżanowski, T. McEnery and R. Wodak (2008). A Useful Methodological Synergy? Combining Critical Discourse Analysis and Corpus Linguistics to Examine Discourses of Refugees and Asylum Seekers in the UK Press. *Discourse & Society* 19(3): 273–306.

Balibar, E. (2004). *We, the People of Europe?: Reflections on Transnational Citizenship.* Princeton, NJ, Princeton University Press.

Balibar, E. (2009). Europe as Borderland. *Environment and Planning D: Society and Space* 27(2): 190–215.

Barbour, S. and C. Carmichael (2002). *Language and Nationalism in Europe.* Oxford, Oxford University Press.

Barthes, R. and A. Lavers (1972). *Mythologies.* New York, Hill and Wang.

Basch, L. G., N. Glick Schiller and C. Szanton Blanc (1994). *Nations Unbound: Transnational Projects, Postcolonial Predicaments, and Deterritorialized Nation-States.* London; New York, Gordon and Breach.

Bauböck, R. and T. Faist (2010). *Diaspora and Transnationalism: Concepts, Theories and Methods.* Amsterdam, Amsterdam University Press.

Bauman, Z. (2000). *Liquid Modernity.* Cambridge, Polity Press.

Bauman, Z. (2004). *Europe: An Unfinished Adventure.* Cambridge; Malden, MA, Polity Press.

Bayley, P. and G. Williams (2012). *European Identity: What the Media Say.* Oxford; New York, Oxford University Press.

Baynham, M. (2015). Identity: Brought about or Brought along? Narrative as a Privileged Site for Researching Intercultural Identities. In F. Dervin and K. Risager (eds.). *Researching Identity and Interculturality.* New York, Routledge: 67–88.

Beck, U. (1996). The Cosmopolitanism Manifesto. In G. W. Brown and D. Held (eds.) *The Cosmopolitanism Reader.* Cambridge; Malden, MA, Polity Press: 213–28.

Beck, U. (2000). *What Is Globalization?* Cambridge; Malden, MA, Polity Press.

Beck, U. (2002). The Cosmopolitan Society and Its Enemies. *Theory, Culture & Society* 19(1–2): 17–44.

Beck, U. (2008). The Cosmopolitan Perspective: Sociology of the Second Age of Modernity. *The British Journal of Sociology* 51(1): 79–105.

Beck, U. and C. Cronin (2006). *The Cosmopolitan Vision.* Cambridge; Malden, MA, Polity Press.

Beck, U., A. Giddens and S. Lash (1994). *Reflexive Modernization: Politics, Tradition and Aesthetics in the Modern Social Order.* Stanford, CA, Stanford University Press.

Beck, U. and E. Grande (2006). *Cosmopolitan Europe.* Cambridge, Polity Press.

Benford, R. and D. Snow (2000). Framing Processes and Social Movements: An Overview and Assessment. *Annual Review of Sociology,* 26, 611–39. Retrieved from http://www.jstor.org/stable/223459

Benwell, B. and E. Stokoe (2006). *Discourse and Identity.* Edinburgh, Edinburgh University Press.

Berger, P. L. and T. Luckmann (1984). *The Social Construction of Reality: A Treatise in the Sociology of Knowledge.* Harmondsworth, Middlesex, Penguin Books.

Bhabha, H. (1990). *Nation and Narration.* Abingdon, Routledge.

Bhabha, H. (1994). *The Location of Culture.* Abingdon, Routledge.

Biebuyck, W. and C. Rumford (2011). Many Europes: Rethinking Multiplicity. *European Journal of Social Theory* 15(1): 3–20.

Billig, M. (1988). *Ideological Dilemmas: A Social Psychology of Everyday Thinking.* London; Newbury Park, Sage Publications.

Billig, M. (1995). *Banal Nationalism.* London, Sage Publications.

Blackledge, A. and A. Creese (2010). *Multilingualism: A Critical Perspective.* London, Bloomsbury Academic.

Blommaert, J. (1999). *Language Ideological Debates.* Berlin, W. De Gruyter.

Blommaert, J. (2003). Commentary: A Sociolinguistics of Globalization. *Journal of Sociolinguistics* 7(4): 607–23.

Blommaert, J. (2013). *Citizenship, Language and Superdiversity: Towards Complexity.* Tilburg Papers in Cultural Studies, University of Tilburg, February 2013(45). Available online from: https://www.tilburguniversity.edu/upload/d7cb5caf-8045-40e3-9a58-91b5f37aa8f0_TPCS_45_Blommaert.pdf. Accessed 9/5/2013

Blommaert, J. and B. Rampton (2011). Language and Superdiversities. *Diversities* 13(2): 1–22.

Bloor, M. (2001). *Focus Groups in Social Research.* London; Thousand Oaks, CA, Sage Publications.

Boudon, R. (1991). What Middle-range Theories Are. *Contemporary Sociology* (American Sociological Association) 20(4): 519–22.

Bourdieu, P. (1991). *Language and Symbolic Power.* Cambridge, MA, Harvard University Press.

Bourdieu, P., C. J. Calhoun, E. LiPuma and P. Moishe (1993). *Bourdieu: Critical Perspectives.* Chicago, University of Chicago Press.

Breeze, R. (2011). Critical Discourse Analysis and Its Critics. *Pragmatics* 21(4): 493–525.

Brewer, J. D. (2000). *Ethnography.* Buckingham; Philadelphia, PA, Open University Press.

Brubaker, R. (2003). Neither Individualism nor 'Groupism': A Reply to Craig Calhoun. *Ethnicities* 3(4): 553–7.

Brubaker, R. and F. Cooper (2000). Beyond 'Identity'. *Theory and Society* 29(1): 1–47.

Bruter, M. (2005). *Citizens of Europe?: The Emergence of a Mass European Identity.* Houndmills, Basingstoke, Hampshire; New York, Palgrave Macmillan.

Bucholtz, M. and K. Hall (2005). Identity and Interaction: A Sociocultural Linguistic Approach. *Discourse Studies* 7(4–5): 585–614.

Burr, V. (2003). *Social Constructionism.* London, Routledge.

Calhoun, C. (1997). Nationalism and the Public Sphere. In J. Weintraub and K. Kumar (eds.) *Public and Private in Thought and Practice: Perspectives on a Grand Dichotomy.* Chicago, University of Chicago Press: 75–102.

Calhoun, C. (2002). *Imagining Solidarity: Cosmopolitanism, Constitutional Patriotism, and the Public Sphere.* Durham, NC, Duke University Press.

Calhoun, C. (2006). *Cosmopolitanism and Belonging.* London, Routledge.

Calhoun, C. (2012). Cosmopolitan Liberalism and Its Limits. In A. S. Krossa and R. Robertson (eds.) *European Cosmopolitanism in Question. Europe in a Global Context.* Basingstoke, Palgrave Macmillan: 105–25.

Calhoun, C. (2017). Populism, Nationalism and Brexit. In W. Outhwaite (ed.), *Brexit: Sociological Responses.* London; New York, Anthem Press: 57–76

Castells, M. (1996a). *The Information Age: Economy, Society and Culture.* Malden, MA, Blackwell Publishing.

Castells, M. (1996b). *The Rise of the Network Society.* Malden, MA, Blackwell Publishing.

Castells, M. (1997). *The Power of Identity.* Malden, MA, Blackwell Publishing.

Castells, M. (2000). Materials for an Exploratory Theory of the Network Society. *The British Journal of Sociology* 51: 5–24.

Castells, M. (2001). *European Unification in the Era of the Network State.* Open Democracy. Available from: https://www.opendemocracy.net/democracy-europ efuture/article_347.jsp. Accessed 14/7/2014

Castells, M. and G. Cardoso (2005). *The Network Society: From Knowledge to Policy.* Washington, DC, Center for Transatlantic Relations, Johns Hopkins University Press.

Castiglione, D. (2009). Political Identity in a Community of Strangers. In J. T. Checkel and P. J. Katzenstein (eds.) *European Identity.* Cambridge, Cambridge University Press: 29–51.

Castles, S. and A. Davidson (2000). *Citizenship and Migration: Globalization and the Politics of Belonging.* Abingdon, Routledge.

Cavanagh, A. (2007). *Sociology in the Age of the Internet.* Maidenhead, McGraw Hill/ Open University Press.

Cederman, L. E. (2001). Nationalism and Bounded Integration: What It Would Take to Construct a European Demos. *European Journal of International Relations* 7(2): 139–74.

Cerutti, F. (2003). *A Political Identity of the Europeans? Thesis Eleven* 72(1): 26–45.

Cerutti, F. and S. Lucarelli (2008). *The Search for a European Identity: Values, Policies and Legitimacy of the European Union.* Abingdon; New York, Routledge.

Charteris-Black, J. (2006). Britain as a Container: Immigration Metaphors in the 2005 Election Campaign. *Discourse & Society* 17(5): 563–81.

Cheah, P. (2006). Cosmopolitanism. *Theory, Culture & Society* 23(2–3): 486–96.

Checkel, J. T. (2001). Why Comply? Social Learning and European Identity Change. *International Organization* 55(3): 553–88.

Checkel, J. T. and P. J. Katzenstein (2009). *European Identity.* Cambridge, Cambridge University Press.

Cheshire, J. (2002). Who We Are and Where We're Going: Language and Identities in the New Europe. In P. P. Gubbins and M. Holt (eds.) *Beyond Boundaries: Language and Identity in Contemporary Europe.* Clevedon, Multilingual Matters: 19–34.

Chilton, P. (2004). *Analysing Political Discourse: Theory and Practice.* London; New York, Routledge.

Chilton, P. and G. Lakoff (1995). Foreign Policy by Metaphor. In C. Schaffner and W. Anita (ed.) *Language and Peace*. Aldershot, Hants; Brookfield, VT, Dartmouth: 37–60.

Chimisso, C. (2003). *Exploring European Identities*. Milton Keynes, The Open University.

Chouliaraki, L. and N. Fairclough (1999). *Discourse in Late Modernity: Rethinking Critical Discourse Analysis*. Edinburgh, Edinburgh University Press.

Closa, C. (2001). Requirements of a European Public Sphere. Civil Society, Self, and the Institutionalization of Citizenship. In K. Eder and B. Giesen (eds.) *European Citizenship between National Legacies and Postnational Projects*. Oxford; New York, Oxford University Press: 180–201.

Cohen, A. (2013). *Symbolic Construction of Community*. London, Routledge.

Connolly, W. E. (1991). *Identity/Difference: Democratic Negotiations of Political Paradox*. Ithaca, NY, Cornell University Press.

Cowles, M. G., J. A. Caporaso and T. Risse-Kappen (2001). *Transforming Europe: Europeanization and Domestic Change*. Ithaca, NY, Cornell University Press.

Cram, L. (2010). *Does the EU Need a Navel? Banal Europeanism, Appreciated Europeanism and European Integration*. ECPR Fifth Pan-European Conference. Porto 24–26 June 2010.

Davidson, A. C. (2008). Through Thick and Thin 'European Identification' for a Justified and Legitimate European Union. *Journal of Contemporary European Research* 4(1): 32–47.

Davies, B. and R. Harre´ (2001). Positioning: The Discursive Production of Selves. In M. Wetherell, S. Taylor and S. J. Yates (eds.) *Discourse Theory and Practice: A Reader*. London; Thousand Oaks, CA, Sage Publications: 261–71.

De Fina, A., D. Schiffrin and M. G. W. Bamberg (2006). *Discourse and Identity*. Cambridge, Cambridge University Press.

De Saussure, F., C. Bally, A. Sechehaye and A. Riedlinger (1986). *Course in General Linguistics*. La Salle; Chicago, Open Court.

De Schutter, H. (2007). Language Policy and Political Philosophy: On the Emerging Linguistic Justice Debate. *Language Problems & Language Planning* 31(1): 1–23.

DeBardeleben, J. and A. Hurrelmann (2011). *Transnational Europe: Promise, Paradox, Limits*. Houndmills, Basingstoke, Hampshire; New York, Palgrave Macmillan.

Delanty, G. (1995). *Inventing Europe: Idea, Identity, Reality*. New York, St. Martin's Press.

Delanty, G. (2000). *Citizenship in a Global Age: Society, Culture, Politics*. Buckingham; Philadelphia, PA, Open University Press.

Delanty, G. (2009). *The Cosmopolitan Imagination: The Renewal of Critical Social Theory*. Cambridge, Cambridge University Press.

Delanty, G. (2013). *Formations of European Modernity: A Historical and Political Sociology of Europe*. Basingstoke, Palgrave Macmillan.

Delanty, G. (2014). Introduction: Perspectives on Crisis and Critique in Europe Today. *European Journal of Social Theory* 17(3): 207–18.

Delanty, G. and C. Rumford (2005). *Rethinking Europe: Social Theory and the Implications of Europeanization*. Abingdon, Oxford, Routledge.

Deleuze, G. and C. V. Boundas (1993). *The Deleuze Reader*. New York, Columbia University Press.

Deleuze, G. and F. Guattari (1987). *A Thousand Plateaus Capitalism and Schizophrenia*. Minneapolis, University of Minnesota Press.

Della Porta, D. and M. Diani (1999). *Social Movements: An Introduction. Oxford*. Malden, MA, Blackwell Publishing.

Della Porta, D. and S. G. Tarrow (2005). *Transnational Protest and Global Activism*. Lanham, MD, Rowman & Littlefield.

Denzin, N. K. and Y. S. Lincoln (1998). *The Landscape of Qualitative Research: Theories and Issues*. Thousand Oaks, CA, Sage Publications.

Derrida, J. (1976). *Of Grammatology*. Baltimore, MD, Johns Hopkins University Press.

Dieckhoff, A. (2004). *The Politics of Belonging: Nationalism, Liberalism, and Pluralism*. Lanham, MD, Lexington Books.

Diez, T. (1999). 'Speaking Europe': The Politics of Integration Discourse. *Journal of European Public Policy* 6(4): 598–613.

Dobson, L. (2006). *Supranational Citizenship*. Manchester, Manchester University Press.

Doerr, N. (2010). Exploring Cosmopolitan and Critical Europeanist Discourses in the ESF Process as a Transnational Public Space. In S. Teune (ed.) *The Transnational Condition: Protest Dynamics in an Entangled Europe*. Oxford, Berghahn Books: 89–110.

Drulak, P. (2004). *Metaphors Europe Lives by: Language and Institutional Change of the European Union*. Florence, European University Institute. EUI Working Papers SPS 15.

Duchêne, A., M. Moyer and C. Roberts (2013). *Language, Migration and Social Inequalities: A Critical Sociolinguistic Perspective on Institutions and Work*. Clevedon, Multilingual Matters.

Duchesne, S. (2012). National Identification, Social Belonging and Questions on European Identity. In R. Friedman and M. Thiel (eds.) *European Identity and Culture: Narratives of Transnational Belongings*. Farnham, Ashgate Publishing Company: 53–73.

Eder, K. (2009). A Theory of Collective Identity – Making Sense of the Debate on a 'European Identity'. *European Journal of Social Theory* 12(4): 427–47.

Eder, K. and W. Spohn (2005). *Collective Memory and European Identity: The Effects of Integration and Enlargement*. Aldershot, Hants; Burlington, VT,, Ashgate Publishing Company.

Edwards, J. (2009). *Language and Identity: An Introduction*. Cambridge, Cambridge University Press.

Ehlich, K. (2014). HIAT: A Transcription System for Discourse Data. In J. A. Edwards and M. D. Lampert (eds.) *Talking Data: Transcription and Coding in Discourse Research*. London, Routledge: 123–48.

Eriksen, E. O. (2005). *Making the European Polity: Reflexive Intgegration in the EU.* London, Chapman & Hall.

Eriksen, E. O. and J. E. Fossum (2004). Europe in Search of Legitimacy: Strategies of Legitimation Assessed. *International Political Science Review* 25(4): 435–59.

Eriksen, E. O. and J. E. Fossum (2002). Democracy through Strong Publics in the European Union? JCMS: *Journal of Common Market Studies* 40(3): 401–24.

Erikson, E. H. (1980). *Identity and the Life Cycle.* New York, Norton.

European Commission (2001). *White Paper on European Governance.* Brussels.

European Commission (2006). *White Paper on European Communication Policy.* Brussels. Available from: europa.eu/documents/comm/white_papers/pdf/com2006_35_en.pdf. Accessed 12/3/2018.

Ezzy, D. (2013). *Qualitative Analysis.* Abingdon; New York, Routledge.

Fairclough, N. (2001). *Language and Power.* Harlow, Longman.

Fairclough, N. (2003). *Analysing Discourse: Textual Analysis for Social Research.* London, Routledge.

Fairclough, N. and I. Fairclough (2012). *Political Discourse Analysis.* New York, Routledge.

Fairclough, N. and R. Wodak (1997). Critical Discourse Analysis. In T. A. v. Dijk (ed.) *Discourse Studies: A Multidisciplinary Introduction.* London; Thousand Oaks, CA, Sage Publications: 357–78.

Featherstone, K. (2003). Introduction: In the Name of Europe. In K. Featherstone and C. M. Radaelli (eds.) *The Politics of Europeanization.* Oxford, Oxford University Press: 3–24.

Featherstone, K. and C. M. Radaelli (2003). *The Politics of Europeanization.* Oxford, Oxford University Press.

Featherstone, M. (1990). *Global Culture: Nationalism, Globalization, and Modernity: A Theory, Culture & Society Special Issue.* London; Newbury Park, Sage Publications.

Fligstein, N. (2007). Who Are the Europeans and How Does This Matter for Politics? In J. T. Checkel and P. J. Katzenstein (eds.) *European Identity.* Cambridge, Cambridge University Press: 132–66.

Fligstein, N. (2008). *Euroclash: The EU, European Identity, and the Future of Europe.* Oxford, Oxford University Press.

Fossum, J. E., and H.-J. Trenz (2006). The EU's Fledgling Society: From Deafening Silence to Critical Voice in European Constitution-Making. *Journal of Civil Society* 2(1): 57–77.

Foucault, M. (1980). *Language, Counter-Memory, Practice: Selected Essays and Interviews.* Ithaca, NY, Cornell University Press.

Foucault, M. (1984). The Order of Discourse. In M. Shapiro (ed.) *The Politics of Language.* Oxford, Blackwell Publishing: 108–38.

Fraser, N. (2007). Transnationalizing the Public Sphere: On the Legitimacy and Efficacy of Public Opinion in a Post-Westphalian World. *Theory, Culture & Society* 24(4): 7–30.

Fraser, N. and K. Nash (2014). *Transnationalizing the Public Sphere*. Cambridge, Polity Press.

Friedman, R. and M. Thiel (2012). *European Identity and Culture: Narratives of Transnational Belongings*. Farnham, Ashgate Publishing Company.

Gabrielatos, C. and P. Baker (2008). Fleeing, Sneaking, Flooding: A Corpus Analysis of Discursive Constructions of Refugees and Asylum Seekers in the UK Press, 1996-2005. *Journal of English Linguistics* 36(1): 5–38.

Gal, S. (2010a). Language and Political Space. In P. Auer and J. E. Schmidt (eds.) *Language and Space an International Handbook of Linguistic Variation*. vol. 1. Berlin; New York, De Gruyter Mouton: 33–50.

Gal, S. (2010b). *Linguistic Regimes and European Diversity*. In Keynote Lecture delivered at the Conference 'New Challenges for Multilingualism in Europe', Dubrovnik, 12 April 2010.

Galasinska, A. and M. Krzyżanowski (2009). *Discourse and Transformation in Central and Eastern Europe*. New York, Palgrave Macmillan.

Gee, J. P. (1990). *Social Linguistics and Literacies: Ideology in Discourses*. London; New York, Falmer Press.

Gellner, E. (2006). *Nations and Nationalism*. Ithaca, NY, Cornell University Press.

Gergen, K. J. (2001). *Social Construction in Context*. London; Thousand Oaks, CA, Sage Publications.

Giddens, A. (1991). *Modernity and Self-Identity: Self and Society in the Late Modern Age*. Stanford, CA, Stanford University Press.

Giddens, A. (2000). *Runaway World: How Globalization Is Reshaping Our Lives*. New York, Routledge.

Giles, H. and P. Johnson (1987). Ethnolinguistic Identity Theory: A Social Psychological Approach to Language Maintenance. *International Journal of the Sociology of Language* 68: 69–100.

Gobo, G. (2008). *Doing Ethnography*. London, Sage Publications.

Grad, H. and L. M. Rojo (2008). *Analysing Identities in Discourse*. Amsterdam; Philadelphia, PA, John Benjamins Publishing.

Grzega, J. (2006) Globish and Basic Global English (BGE): Two Alternatives for a Rapid Acquisition of Communicative Competence in a Globalized World? *Internet: Journal for EuroLinguistiX* 3: 1–13.

Gubbins, P. P. and M. Holt (2002). *Beyond Boundaries: Language and Identity in Contemporary Europe*. Clevedon, Multilingual Matters.

Guibernau, M. (2007). *The Identity of Nations*. Cambridge, Polity Press.

Gumperz, J. J. (1971). *Language in Social Groups*. Stanford, CA, Stanford University Press.

Gumperz, J. J. (1982). *Language and Social Identity*. Cambridge; New York, Cambridge University Press.

Gumperz, J. J. and S. C. Levinson (1996). *Rethinking Linguistic Relativity*. Cambridge; New York, Cambridge University Press.

Habermas, J. (1987). *The Philosophical Discourse of Modernity: Twelve Lectures.* Cambridge, MA, MIT Press.

Habermas, J. (1989). *The Structural Transformation of the Public Sphere: An Inquiry into a Category of Bourgeois Society.* Cambridge, MA, MIT Press.

Habermas, J. (1997). Reply to Grimm. In P. Gowan and P. Anderson (eds.) *The Question of Europe.* London, Verso: 259–64.

Habermas, J. (2001). The Postnational Constellation Political Essays. Cambridge, MA; London, MIT Press.

Habermas, J. (2003). Toward a Cosmopolitan Europe. *Journal of Democracy* 14(4): 86–100.

Habermas, J. (2009). *Europe: The Faltering Project.* Cambridge, Polity Press.

Habermas, J. and W. Rehg (1998). *Between Facts and Norms: Contributions to a Discourse Theory of Law and Democracy.* Cambridge, MA, MIT Press.

Hall, S. (1992). The Question of Cultural Identity. In S. Hall, D. Held and T. MacGrew (eds.) *Modernity and Its Futures.* Cambridge, Polity Press in association with the Open University: 273–326.

Hall, S. (1996). Who Needs Identity? In S. Hall and P. Du Gay (eds.) *Questions of Cultural Identity.* London; Thousand Oaks, CA, Sage Publications: 1–17.

Hall, S. (1997). *Representation: Cultural Representations and Signifying Practices.* London; Thousand Oaks, CA, Sage in association with the Open University.

Hanks, W. F. (1999). Indexicality. *Journal of Linguistic Anthropology* 9(1–2): 124–6.

Hannerz, U. (1990). Cosmopolitans and Locals in World Culture. *Theory, Culture & Society* 7(2): 237–51.

Hannerz, U. (1996). *Transnational Connections: Culture, People, Places.* London; New York, Taylor & Francis Group.

Hanquinet, L. and M. Savage (2013). *The Europeanisation of Everyday Life: Cross-Border Practices and Transnational Identifications among EU and Third-Country Citizens.* Eucross working papers series 6 (Eucross research project funded by the EC 7th Framework programme). Available online from: http://www.eucross.eu/cms/inde x.php?option=com_docman&task=cat_view&gid=7&Itemid=157. Accessed 14/1/2014

Harré, R. and L. van Lagenhove (1999). *Positioning Theory: Moral Contexts of Intentional Action.* Oxford; Malden, MA, Blackwell Publishing.

Heater, D. B. (2004). *World Citizenship Cosmopolitan Thinking and Its Opponents.* New York; London, Continuum.

Heidbreder, E. G. (2012). Civil Society Participation in EU Governance. *Living Reviews in European Governance* 7(2): 1–42.

Held, D. (1999). *Global Transformations: Politics, Economics and Culture.* Stanford, CA, Stanford University Press.

Held, D. (2010). *Cosmopolitanism: Ideals and Realities.* Cambridge; Malden, MA, Polity Press.

Heller, M. (1995). Language Choice, Social Institutions, and Symbolic Domination. *Language in Society* 24(3): 373–405.

Heller, M. (2003). Globalization, the New Economy, and the Commodification of Language and Identity. *Journal of Sociolinguistics* 7(4): 473–92.

Heller, M. (2012). *Linguistic Commodification: Multilingualism in the Globalized New Economy*-Key note speech. Multilingualism in the Public Sphere – 2nd Linee Conference. Dubrovnik. 4–6 May 2012.

Herrmann, R. K., T. Risse-Kappen and M. B. Brewer (2004). *Transnational Identities: Becoming European in the EU*. Oxford, Rowman & Littlefield.

Hobsbawm, E. (1997). *Nations and Nationalism since 1780: Programme, Myth, Reality*. Cambridge, Cambridge University Press.

Hobsbawm, E. (2010). *The Invention of Tradition*. Cambridge, Cambridge University Press.

Hobsbawm, E. J. (2007). *Globalisation, Democracy and Terrorism*. London, Abacus.

Hodge, R. and G. Kress (1988). *Social Semiotics*. Cambridge, Polity Press.

Hooghe, L. and G. Marks (2009). A Postfunctionalist Theory of European Integration: From Permissive Consensus to Constraining Dissensus. *British Journal of Political Science* 39(1): 1–23.

House, J. (2003). English as a Lingua Franca: A Threat to Multilingualism? *Journal of Sociolinguistics* 7(4): 556–78.

Ifversen, J. (2002). Europe and European Culture: A Conceptual Analysis. *European Societies* 4(1): 1–26.

Ilie, C. (2010). *European Parliaments under Scrutiny: Discourse Strategies and Interaction Practices*. Amsterdam, John Benjamins Publishing.

Jansen, T. (1999). *European Identity and/or the Identity of the European Union. Reflections on European Identity*. Brussels, European Commission Forward Studies Unit Working Paper: 27–36.

Jenkins, R. (2014). *Social Identity*. London, Routledge.

Jenkins, J., M. Modiano and B. Seidlhofer (2001). Euro-English. *English Today* 17(4): 13–19.

Jessop, B. (2010). From Hegemony to Crisis?: The Continuing Ecological Dominance of Neo-Liberalism. In K. Birch and M. Vlad (eds.) *The Rise and Fall of Neoliberalism the Collapse of an Economic Order?* London; New York, Zed Books: 177–87.

Johnstone, B. (2013). *Speaking Pittsburghese: The Story of a Dialect*. New York, Oxford University Press.

Jones, P. and M. Krzyżanowski (2008). Identity, Belonging and Migration: Beyond Describing 'Others'. In G. Delanty, R. Wodak and P. Jones (eds.) *Identity, Belonging and Migration*. Liverpool, Liverpool University Press: 38–53.

Jones, P. E. (2007). Why There Is No Such Thing as 'Critical Discourse Analysis'. *Language & Communication* 27(4): 337–68.

Joseph, J. E. (2004). *Language and Identity: National, Ethnic, Religious*. Houndmills, Basingstoke, Hampshire; New York, Palgrave Macmillan.

Kaiser, W., B. Leucht and M. Gehler (2010). *Transnational Networks in Regional Integration: Governing Europe 1945-83*. New York, Palgrave Macmillan.

Kaplan, D. (1979). On the Logic of Demonstratives. *Journal of Philosophical Logic* 8(1): 81–98.

Kastoryano, R. (2003). *Transnational Participation and Citizenship Immigrants in the European Union*. Paper presented to conference entitled The Challenges of Immigration and Integration in the European Union and Australia. 18–20 February 2003, University of Sydney.

Kaye, J. (2009). Out of Maelstroms: Crises and Parlous Developments of Europe since World War Two. In A. Triandafyllidou, R. Wodak and M. Krzyżanowski (eds.) *The European Public Sphere and the Media: Europe in Crisis*. Basingstoke; New York, Palgrave MacMillian: 53–82.

Keating, M. (2013). *Rescaling the European State: The Making of Territory and the Rise of the Meso*. Oxford, Oxford University Press.

Kendall, G. (2007). *What Is Critical Discourse Analysis*? Forum Qualitative Sozialforschung/Forum: Qualitative Social Research. Available from: http://www.qualitative-research.net/index.php/fqs/article/view/255/561. Accessed 24/3/2013.

Kienpointner, M. and W. Kindt (1997). On the Problem of Bias in Political Argumentation: An Investigation into Discussions about Political Asylum in Germany and Austria. *Journal of Pragmatics* 27(5): 555–85.

Kitzinger, J. and R. S. Barbour (1999). *Developing Focus Group Research: Politics, Theory, and Practice*. London; Thousand Oaks, CA, Sage Publications.

Kjaer, A. L. and A. P. S. Adamo (2013). *Linguistic Diversity and European Democracy*. Farnham, Ashgate Publishing Company.

Kohli, M. (2000). The Battlegrounds of European Identity. *European Societies* 2(2): 113–37.

Koller, V. (2012). How to Analyse Collective Identity in Discourse – Textual and Contextual Parameters. *Critical Approaches to Discourse Analysis across Disciplines* 5(2): 19–38.

Kollman, K. (2009). European Institutions, Transnational Networks and National Same-Sex Unions Policy: When Soft Law Hits Harder. *Contemporary Politics* 15(1): 37–53.

Kompridis, N. (2006). *Critique and Disclosure Critical Theory between Past and Future*. Cambridge, MA, MIT Press.

Koopmans, R. and P. Statham (2010). *The Making of a European Public Sphere: Media Discourse and Political Contention*. Cambridge, Cambridge University Press.

Kraus, P. A. (2008). *A Union of Diversity: Language, Identity and Polity-Building in Europe*. Cambridge, Cambridge University Press.

Kraus, P. A. (2011). Neither United Nor Diverse? The Language Issue and Political Legitimation in the European Union. In A. L. Kjaer and S. Adamo (eds). *Linguistic Diversity and European Democracy*. Aldershot; Farnham, Ashgate Publishing Company: 17–34.

Kriesi, H., A. Tresch and M. Jochum (2007). Going Public in the European Union: Action Repertoires of Western European Collective Political Actors. *Comparative Political Studies* 40(1): 48–73.

Kristeva, J. and Moi, T. (1986). *The Kristeva Reader.* New York, Columbia University Press.

Kroskrity, P. (2000). *Regimes of Language: Ideologies, Polities, and Identities.* Santa Fe, NM, School of American Research Press.

Kroskrity, P. V. (1993). *Language, History, and Identity: Ethnolinguistic Studies of the Arizona Tewa.* Tucson, AZ, University of Arizona Press.

Krueger, R. A. (1994). *Focus Groups: A Practical Guide for Applied Research.* Thousand Oaks, CA, Sage Publications.

Krzyzanowski, M. (2003). 'My European Feelings Are Not Only Based on the Fact That I Live in Europe': On the New Mechanisms in European and National Identification Patterns Emerging under the Influence of EU Enlargement. *Journal of Language and Politics* 2(1): 175–204.

Krzyzanowski, M. (2008). Analyzing Focus Groups. In R. Wodak and M. Krzyzanowski (eds.) *Qualitative Discourse Analysis in the Social Sciences.* Houndmills, Basingstoke, Hampshire; New York, Palgrave Macmillan: 162–81.

Krzyżanowski, M. (2010). *The Discursive Construction of European Identities: A Multilevel Approach to Discourse and Identity in the Transforming European Union.* Frankfurt am Main, Peter Lang.

Krzyżanowski, M. (2011). Ethnography and Critical Discourse Analysis: Towards a Problem-Oriented Research Dialogue. *Critical Discourse Studies* 8(4): 231–8.

Krzyżanowski, M. and F. Oberhuber (2007). *(Un)Doing Europe: Discourses and Practices of Negotiating the EU Constitution.* Bruxelles; New York, Peter Lang.

Kymlicka, W. (1990). *Contemporary Political Philosophy: An Introduction.* Oxford; New York, Clarendon Press; Oxford University Press.

Kymlicka, W. and A. Patten (2003). *Language Rights and Political Theory.* Oxford, Oxford University Press.

Labov, W. (1966). *The Social Stratification of English in New York City.* New York, Cambridge University Press.

Lacan, J. and J. A. Miller (1988). *The Seminar of Jacques Lacan.* New York, Norton.

Laclau, E. (1994). *The Making of Political Identities.* London; New York, Verso.

Laclau, E. and C. Mouffe (2001). *Hegemony and Socialist Strategy: Towards a Radical Democratic Politics.* London; New York, Verso.

Lacroix, J. (2002). For a European Constitutional Patriotism. *Political Studies* 50(5): 944–58.

Laffan, B. (2004) The European Union and Its Institutions as 'Identity Builders' In R. K. Herrmann, T. Risse-Kappen and M. B. Brewer (eds.). *Transnational Identities: Becoming European in the EU.* Oxford, Rowman & Littlefield: 75–94.

Lang, S. (2013). *NGOs, Civil Society, and the Public Sphere.* Cambridge, Cambridge University Press.

Lash, S. (1990). *Sociology of Postmodernism.* London; New York, Routledge.

Latour, B. (2005). *Reassembling the Social an Introduction to Actor-Network-Theory.* Oxford; New York, Oxford University Press.

Le Page, R. B. and A. Tabouret-Keller (1985). *Acts of Identity: Creole-Based Approaches to Language and Ethnicity*. Cambridge, Cambridge University Press.

Levi-Strauss, C. (1979). *Myth and Meaning*. New York, Schocken Books.

Levitt, P. and N. G. Schiller (2004). Conceptualizing Simultaneity: A Transnational Social Field Perspective on Society. *International Migration Review* 38(3): 1002–39.

Levitt, P. and Nadya B. Jaworsky (2007). Transnational Migration Studies: Past Developments and Future Trends. *Annual Review of Sociology* 33: 129.

Linklater, A. (1998). Cosmopolitan Citizenship. *Citizenship Studies* 2(1): 23–41.

Litosseliti, L. (2003). *Using Focus Groups in Research*. London, Continuum.

Lyotard, J. F. and A. E. Benjamin (1989). *The Lyotard Reader*. Oxford; Cambridge, MA, Blackwell Publishing.

Maas, W. (2007). *Creating European Citizens*. Lanham, MD, Rowman & Littlefield.

MacDonald, K. (2006). *Global Movements: Action and Culture*. Malden, MA, Blackwell Publishing.

MacLuhan, M., T. W. Gordon and B. Nevitt (2005). *The Humanities in the Electronic Age*. Berkeley, CA, Gingko Press.

Mackert, J. and Turner, B. (2017) *The Transformation of Citizenship, Volume 2: Boundaries of Inclusion and Exclusion*. London, Taylor & Francis,

Magnusson, L. and B. Stråth (2007). *European Solidarities: Tensions and Contentions of a Concept*. Frankfurt am Main, Peter Lang.

Majone, G. (1998). Europe's 'Democratic Deficit': The Question of Standards. *European Law Journal* 4(1): 5–28.

Malesevic, S. (2013). *Nation-states and Nationalisms: Organization, Ideology and Solidarity*. Cambridge; Malden, MA, Polity Press.

Malmborg, M. and B. Strath (2002). *The Meaning of Europe: Variety and Contention within and among Nations*. Oxford; New York, Berg.

Mar-Molinero, C. and P. Stevenson (2009). *Language Ideologies, Policies and Practices: Language and the Future of Europe*. Basingstoke, Palgrave Macmillan.

Marcussen, M. and K. Roscher (2010). The Social Construction of 'Europe': Life-cycles of Nation-State Identities in France, Germany and Great Britain. In B. Stråth (ed.) *Europe and the Other and Europe as the Other*. Brussels, Peter Lang: 325–58.

Marsili, L. and Milanese, N. (2018). *Citizens of Nowhere: How Europe Can Be Saved from Itself*. London, Zed Books.

Maurais, J. and Michael A. Morris (2003). *Languages in a Globalising World*. Cambridge; New York, Cambridge University Press.

Mautner, G. (2007). Mining Large Corpora for Social Information: The Case of Elderly. *Language in Society* 36(1): 51–72.

McEntee-Atalianis, L. and F. Zappettini (2014). Networked Identities. *Critical Discourse Studies* 11(4): 397–415.

Mead, G., M. Herbert and L. David (1982). *The Individual and the Social Self: Unpublished Work of George Herbert Mead*. Chicago, University of Chicago Press.

Meinhof, U. H. (2001). Imagining Multiple Identities on Europe's Eastern Borders: Between the 'Russian doll' and the 'volcano'. In *Socio-economic Research – 'European Citizenship: Beyond Borders, across Identities' project funded by EU's 5th framework Programme Brussels*, 23–24 April 2001.

Meinhof, U. H. and D. Galasinski (2007). *The Language of Belonging*. Basingstoke, Palgrave Macmillan.

Meinhof, U. H. and Triandafyllidou, A. (2006) Transcultural Europe: An Introduction to Cultural Policy in a Changing Europe. In U. H. Meinhof and A. Triandafyllidou (eds.) *Transcultural Europe: Cultural Policy in a Changing Europe*. Basingstoke; New York, Palgrave Macmillan, 3–23.

Mercer, C. (2002). NGOs, Civil Society and Democratization: A Critical Review of the Literature. *Progress in Development Studies* 2(1): 5–22.

Meyerhoff, M. (2006). *Introducing Sociolinguistics*. London; New York, Routledge.

Millar, S. and J. Wilson (2007). *The Discourse of Europe: Talk and Text in Everyday Life*. Amsterdam, John Benjamins Publishing.

Milroy, L. (1987). *Language and Social Networks*. Oxford; New York, NY, Blackwell Publishing.

Milward, A. S., G. Brennan and F. Romero (2000). *The European Rescue of the Nation-State*. London, Chapman and Hall.

Mole, R. C. M. (2007). *Discursive Constructions of Identity in European Politics*. Basingstoke, Palgrave Macmillan.

Montoya, C. (2008). The European Union, Capacity Building, and Transnational Networks: Combating Violence against Women through the Daphne Program. *International Organization* 62(2): 359–72.

Morin, J. F. and C. Carta (2014). *EU Foreign Policy through the Lens of Discourse Analysis: Making Sense of Diversity*. Aldershot; Farnham, Ashgate Publishing Company.

Munch, R. (2001). *Nations and Citizenship in the Global Age: From National to Transnational Ties and Identities*. Basingstoke, Palgrave Macmillan.

Musolff, A. (2006). Metaphor Scenarios in Public Discourse. *Metaphor and Symbol* 1(21): 23–38.

Myers-Scotton, C. (1998). *Codes and Consequences: Choosing Linguistic Varieties*. Oxford, Oxford University Press.

Nicolaïdis, K. (2004). 'We, the Peoples of Europe ...'. *Foreign Affairs* 83(6): 97–110.

Niedermüller, P. and B. Stoklund (2001). *Europe: Cultural Construction and Reality*. Copenhagen, Museum Tusculanum Press, University of Copenhagen.

Oberhuber, F. (2007) *Legitimating the European Union: The Contested Meanings of an EU Constitution*. Florence, European University Institute. EUI Working Papers RCAS 2007 25.

Oberhuber, F., C. Bärenreuter, M. Krzyzanowski, H. Schönbauer and R. Wodak (2005). Debating the European Constitution: On Representations of Europe/the EU in the Press. *Journal of Language and Politics* 4(2): 227–71.

Ong, A. (1999). *Flexible Citizenship: The Cultural Logics of Transnationality.* Durham, NC, Duke University Press.

Orwell, G. (1949). *Nineteen Eighty-Four.* London, Penguin.

Paasi, A. (2001). Europe as a Social Process and Discourse: Considerations of Place, Boundaries and Identity. *European Urban and Regional Studies* 8(1): 7–28.

Pagden, A. (2002). *The Idea of Europe from Antiquity to the European Union.* Washington, DC; Cambridge; New York, Cambridge University Press.

Parekh, B. C. (2000). *Rethinking Multiculturalism: Cultural Diversity and Political Theory.* Cambridge, MA, Harvard University Press.

Pavlenko, A. and A. Blackledge (2004). *Negotiation of Identities in Multilingual Contexts.* Clevendon; Bristol, Multilingual Matters.

Phillipson, R. (2003). *English-Only Europe?: Challenging Language Policy.* London; New York, Routledge.

Piaget, J. (1970). *Science of Education and the Psychology of the Child.* New York, Orion Press.

Pittaway, M. (2003a). *The Fluid Borders of Europe.* Milton Keynes, Open University.

Pittaway, M. (2003b). *Globalization and Europe.* Milton Keynes, Open University.

Pleines, H. (2006). *Participation of Civil Society in New Modes of Governance.* The Case of the New EU Member States Working Papers of the Research Centre for East European Studies, Bremen: NO. 74.

Portes, A. (1997). *Globalization from Below: The Rise of Transnational Communities.* Oxford, University of Oxford Transnational Communities Programme.

Portes, A., L. E. Guarnizo and P. Landolt (1999). Transnational Communities. *Ethnic and Racial Studies* 22(2): 290–315.

Potter, J., M. Wetherell and P. M. Wetherell (1987). *Discourse and Social Psychology: Beyond Attitudes and Behaviour.* London; Newbury Park, Calif., Sage Publications.

Priban, J. (2007). *Legal Symbolism on Law, Time and European Identity.* Aldershot, Hampshire; Burlington, VT, Ashgate Publishing Company.

Pries, L. (2013). Ambiguities of Global and Transnational Collective Identities. *Global Networks* 13(1): 22–40.

Rampton, B. (1995). *Crossing: Language and Ethnicity among Adolescents.* London; New York, Longman.

Recchi, E. and A. Favell (2009). *Pioneers of European Integration: Citizenship and Mobility in the EU.* Cheltenham; Northampton, MA, Edward Elgar.

Recchi, E. (2014). Pathways to European Identity Formation: A Tale of Two Models. *Innovation: The European Journal of Social Science Research* 27(2), 119–33.

Rembold, R. and P. Carrier (2011) Space and Identity: Constructions of National Identities in an Age of Globalisation. *National Identities* 13(4): 361–77

Renkema, J. (2004). *Introduction to Discourse Studies.* Amsterdam; Philadelphia, PA, John Benjamins Publishing.

Ricento, T. (2006). *An Introduction to Language Policy: Theory and Method.* Malden, MA, Blackwell Publishing.

Rindler Schjerve, R. and E. Vetter (2012). *European Multilingualism: Current Perspectives and Challenges*. Bristol; Buffalo, Multilingual Matters.

Risse, T. (2010). *A Community of Europeans?: Transnational Identities and Public Spheres*. Ithaca, NY, Cornell University Press.

Risse-Kappen, T. (1995). *Bringing Transnational Relations Back In: Non-state Actors, Domestic Structures, and International Institutions*. Cambridge; New York, Cambridge University Press.

Robertson, R. (1992). *Globalization: Social Theory and Global Culture*. London, Sage Publications.

Robertson, R. and K. E. White (2003). *Globalization: Analytical perspectives*. London; New York, Taylor and Francis.

Robinson, W. I. (2004). *A Theory of Global Capitalism: Production, Class, and State in a Transnational World*. Baltimore, MD, Johns Hopkins University Press.

Robyn, R. (2005). *The Changing Face of European Identity*. London; New York, Routledge.

Rosamond, B. (1999). Discourses of Globalization and the Social Construction of European Identities. *Journal of European Public Policy* 6(4): 652–68.

Roudometof, V. (2005). Transnationalism, Cosmopolitanism and Glocalization. *Current Sociology* 53(1): 113–35.

Ruggie, J. (1993). Territoriality and Beyond: Problematizing Modernity in International Relations. *International Organization* 47(1): 139–74.

Rumford, C. (2003). European Civil Society or Transnational Social Space?: Conceptions of Society in Discourses of EU Citizenship, Governance and the Democratic Deficit: An Emerging Agenda. *European Journal of Social Theory* 6(1): 25–43.

Rumford, C. (2006). *Borders and Rebordering*. In G. Delanty (ed.) *Europe and Asia beyond East and West: Towards a New Cosmopolitanism*. London Routledge: 181–92.

Rumford, C. (2008). *Cosmopolitan Spaces: Europe, Globalization, Theory*. New York, Routledge.

Rumford, C. (2011). Editorial: New Perspectives on Turkey–EU Relations. *Journal of Contemporary European Studies* 19(4): 459–62.

Ruzza, C. (2009). Populism and Euroscepticism: Towards Uncivil Society? *Policy and Society* 28(1): 87–98.

Ruzza, C. (2011). Social Movements and the European Interest Intermediation of Public Interest Groups. *Journal of European Integration* 33(4): 453–69.

Ruzza, C. (2014). Keynote Presentation 'Language and Nationalism in Italian Politics'. Political Linguistics: (Re)construing Nationhood in '(Un)doing Europe Today. Warsaw, 8–10 May 2014.

Ruzza, C. and V. D. Sala (2007). *Governance and Civil Society in the European Union, Vol. 2: Normative Perspectives*. Manchester, Manchester University Press.

Said, E. W. (1979). *Orientalism*. New York, Vintage Books.

Salvatore, A., O. Schmidtke and H. J. Trenz (2013). *Struggling with the Concept of a Public Sphere.* Basingstoke, Palgrave Macmillan.

Šarić, L., A. Musolff, S. Manz and I. Hudabiunigg (2010). *Contesting Europe's Eastern Rim: Cultural Identities in Public Discourse.* Bristol, Multilingual Matters.

Sassen, S. (2002). *Towards Post-National and Denationalized Citizenship.* In E. F. Isin and B. S. Turner (eds.) *Handbook of Citizenship Studies.* London; Thousand Oaks, CA, Sage Publications: 277–91.

Sassen, S. (2007). *A Sociology of Globalization.* New York, W. Norton & Co.

Scharpf, F. W. (1999). *Governing in Europe: Effective and Democratic?* Oxford, Oxford University Press.

Schegloff, E. (1999). Naivete vs Sophistication or Discipline vs Self-Indulgence: A Rejoinder to Billig. *Discourse & Society* 10(4): 577–82.

Searle, J. (1997). *The Construction of Social Reality.* New York, Free Press.

Shohamy, E. G. (2006). *Language Policy.* London; New York, Routledge.

Shore, C. (2000). *Building Europe: The Cultural Politics of European Integration.* London; New York, Routledge.

Sigona, N. (2013). Campzenship: Rethinking the Camp as a Political Space. In *Keynote Speech International Symposium – Within and beyond Citizenship: Lived Experiences of Contemporary Membership, Oxford,* 11–12 April 2013.

Silverman, D. (1993). *Interpreting Qualitative Data: Methods for Analysing Talk, Text, and Interaction.* London; Thousand Oaks, CA, Sage Publications.

Silverstein, M. (2003). Indexical Order and the Dialectics of Sociolinguistic Life. *Language and Communication* 23(3/4): 193–229.

Sinclair, J. (1991). *Corpus, Concordance, Collocation.* Oxford, Oxford University Press.

Smismans, S. (2009). European Civil Society and Citizenship: Complementary or Exclusionary Concepts? *Policy and Society* 28(1): 59–70.

Smith, A. D. (1991). *National Identity.* Reno, NV, University of Nevada Press.

Smith, A. D. (1997). National Identity and the Idea of European Unity. In P. Gowan and P. Anderson (eds.) *The Question of Europe.* London, Verso: 318–44.

Smith, J., C. Chatfield and P. Ron (1997). *Transnational Social Movements and Global Politics: Solidarity beyond the State.* Syracuse, NY, Syracuse University Press.

Smith, M. P. and L. Guarnizo (1998). *Transnationalism from Below.* Piscataway, NJ, Transaction Publishers.

Soja, E. W. (1989). *Postmodern Geographies: The Reassertion of Space in Critical Social Theory.* London; New York, Verso.

Sowinska, A. (2009). A European Identity on the Periphery: A Comparative Study of the Representations of Europe in the Awkward Squad's Press. *Critical Approaches to Discourse Analysis across Disciplines* 3(1): 21–35.

Soysal, Y. (1997). Changing Parameters of Citizenship and Claims-Making: Organized Islam in European Public Spheres. *Theory and Society* 26(4): 509–27.

Sparke, M. (2013). *Introducing Globalization: Ties, Tension, and Uneven Integration.* Malden, MA; Oxford, Wiley.

Splichal, S. (2006). In Search of a Strong European Public Sphere: Some Critical Observations on Conceptualizations of Publicness and the (European) Public Sphere. *Media, Culture & Society* 28(5): 695–714.

Spolsky, B. (2004). *Language Policy*. Cambridge, Cambridge University Press.

Spotti, M. (2007). What Lies Beneath? Immigrant Minority Pupils' Identity Construction in a Multicultural Flemish Primary Classroom. *Journal of Language, Identity & Education* 6(1): 31–51.

Standing, G. (2011). *The Precariat: The New Dangerous Class*. London; New York, NY, Bloomsbury Academic.

Steffek, J., C. Kissling and P. Nanz (2008). *Civil Society Participation in European and Global Governance: A Cure for the Democratic Deficit?*. Palgrave Macmillan.

Stevenson, N. (2003). *Cultural Citizenship: Cosmopolitan Questions*. Maidenhead, Open University Press.

Stråth, B. (2010). *Europe and the Other and Europe as the Other*. Frankfurt am Mein, Peter Lang.

Stubbs, M. (1996). *Text and Corpus Analysis: Computer-Assisted Studies of Language and Culture*. Oxford; Cambridge, MA, Blackwell Publishing.

Tajfel, H. and J. Turner (1979). An Integrative Theory of Intergroup Conflict. In W. G. Austin and S. Worchel (eds.) *The Social Psychology of Intergroup Relations*. Ann Arbor, The University of Michigan, Brooks/Cole Pub. Co.; 33–48.

Tarrow, S. (2001). Transnational Politics: Contention and Institutions in International Politics. *Annual Review of Political Science* 4(1): 1–20.

Tarrow, S. G. (2005). *The New Transnational Activism*. New York, Cambridge University Press.

Teets, J. (2008). *Governance in Non-democracies: The Role of Civil Society in Increasing Pluralism and Accountability in Local Public Policy*. Boulder, University of Colorado.

Toolan, M. (2002). *Critical Discourse Analysis: Critical Concepts in Linguistics Vol. III*. London, Routledge.

Triandafyllidou, A. (2008). Popular Perceptions of Europe and the Nation: The Case of Italy. *Nations and Nationalism* 14(2): 261–82.

Triandafyllidou, A. and R. Wodak (2003). Conceptual and Methodological Questions in the Study of Collective Identities: An Introduction. *Journal of Language and Politics* 2(2): 202–25.

Triandafyllidou, A., R. Wodak and M. Krzyżanowski (2009). *The European Public Sphere and the Media: Europe in Crisis*. Basingstoke, Palgrave Macmillan.

Unger, J., M. Krzyżanowski and R. Wodak (2014). *Multilingual Encounters in Europe's Institutional Spaces*. London, Bloomsbury Publishing.

Urry, J. (2003). *Global Complexity*. Malden, MA; Oxford, Polity Press in association with Wiley.

van Dijk, T. (1985). *Discourse and Communication: New Approaches to the Analysis of Mass Media Discourse and Communication*. Berlin; New York, W. de Gruyter.

van Dijk, T. (1995). Discourse Semantics and Ideology. *Discourse & Society* 6(2): 243–89.

van Dijk, T. (1997). *Discourse as Social Interaction*. London, Sage Publications.

van Dijk, T. (2000). *The Reality of Racism*. In G. Zurstiege (ed.) *Festschrift für die Wirklichkeit*. Wiesbaden, VS Verlag für Sozialwissenschaften: 211–25.

van Dijk, J. (2006). *The Network Society Social Aspects of New Media*. Thousand Oaks, CA, Sage Publications.

Van Parijs, P. (2011). *Linguistic Justice for Europe and for the World*. Oxford; New York, Oxford University Press.

Vertovec, S. (1999). Conceiving and Researching Transnationalism. *Ethnic and Racial Studies* 22(2): 447–62.

Vertovec, S. (2001). Transnationalism and Identity. *Journal of Ethnic and Migration Studies* 27(4): 573–82.

Vertovec, S. (2007). Super-Diversity and Its Implications. *Ethnic and Racial Studies* 30(6): 1024–54.

Vertovec, S. (2009). *Transnationalism*. Oxford; New York, Taylor & Francis.

Vertovec, S. and R. Cohen (2003). *Conceiving Cosmopolitanism: Theory, Context and Practice*. New York, Oxford University Press.

Vygotskii, L. S. (1962). *Thought and Language*. Cambridge, MA, MIT Press.

Walsh, T., G. Wilson and E. O'Connor (2010). Local, European and Global: An Exploration of Migration Patterns of Social Workers into Ireland. *British Journal of Social Work* 40(6): 1978–95.

Warf, B. and A. Santa (2009). *The Spatial Turn: Interdisciplinary Perspectives*. London; New York, Routledge.

Weiner, E. S. C., Simpson, J. A. and Oxford University Press. (2004). *Oxford English Dictionary*. Oxford: Oxford University Press.

Wenger, E. (1998). *Communities of Practice: Learning, Meaning, and Identity*. Cambridge; New York, NY, Cambridge University Press.

Westwod, S. and A. Phizacklea (2000). *Trans-Nationalism and the Politics of Belonging*. London; New York, NY, Routledge.

Widdowson, H. G. (1995). Discourse Analysis: A Critical View. *Language and Literature* 4(3): 157–72.

Wimmer, A. and N. Schiller Glick (2002). Methodological Nationalism and Beyond: Nation-State Building, Migration and the Social Sciences. *Global Networks* 2(4): 301–34.

Wittgenstein, L. (1953). *Philosophical Investigations*. New York, Macmillan.

Wodak, R. (1996). 'Others in Discourse' – Racism and Antisemitism in Present Day Austria. *Research on Democracy and Society* 3: 275–96.

Wodak, R. (1997). Das Ausland and Anti-semitic Discourse: The Discursive Construction of the Other. In S. Riggins (ed.) *The Language and Politics of Exclusion*. London, Sage Publications: 65–87.

Wodak, R. (2001). The Discourse-Historical Approach. In R. Wodak and M. Meyer (eds.) *Methods of Critical Discourse Analysis*. London, Sage Publications: 63–95.

Wodak, R. (2003). Multiple Identities: The Roles of Female Parliamentarians in the EU Parliament. In J. Holmes and M. Meyerhoff (eds.) *The Handbook of Language and Gender*. Malden, MA, Blackwell Publishing: 671–98.

Wodak, R. (2004). National and Transnational identities: European and Other Identities Constructed in Interviews with EU Officials. In R. K. Herrmann, T. Risse-Kappen and M. B. Brewer (eds.). *Transnational Identities: Becoming European in the EU*. London, Rowman & Littlefield: 97–128.

Wodak, R. (2007). 'Doing Europe': The Discursive Construction of European Identities. In R. C. M. Mole (ed.) *Discursive Constructions of Identity in European Politics*. Basingstoke, Palgrave Macmillan: 70–94.

Wodak, R. (2008). *Semiotic Approaches to Racism – European Perpsectives* – Keynote speak. CADAAD 11/07/2008. Hertfordshire.

Wodak, R. (2009). The Discourse-Historical Approach. In R. Wodak and M. Meyer (eds.) *Methods of Critical Discourse Analysis* (2nd Edition). London, Sage Publications: 63–94.

Wodak, R. (2010). 'Communicating Europe': Analyzing, Interpreting, and Understanding Multilingualism and the Discursive Construction of Transnational Identities. In R. Wodak (ed.) *Globalization, Discourse, Media: In a Critical Perspective*. Warsaw, Warsaw University Press: 17–60.

Wodak, R., R. de Cillia, M. Reisigl and K. Liebhart (2009). *The Discursive Construction of National Identity*. Edinburgh, Edinburgh University Press.

Wodak, R. and V. Koller (2008). *Handbook of Communication in the Public Sphere*. Berlin; New York, Mouton De Gruyter.

Wodak, R. and M. Meyer (2009). Critical Discourse Analysis: History, Agenda, Theory, and Methodology. In R. Wodak and M. Meyer (eds.). *Methods of Critical Discourse Analysis*. London, Sage Publications: 1–32.

Wodak, R. and J. E. Richardson (2013). *Analysing Fascist Discourse: European Fascism in Talk and Text*. New York, Routledge.

Wodak, R. and G. Weiss (2005). Analyzing European Union Discourses: Theories and Applications. In R. Wodak and P. Chilton (eds.) *A New Agenda in (Critical) Discourse Analysis: Theory, Methodology and Interdisciplinarity*. Amsterdam, John Benjamins Publishing: 121–33.

Wright, S. (2000). *Community and Communication: The Role of Language in Nation State Building and European Integration*. Clevedon, Multilingual Matters.

Wright, S. (2009). The Elephant in the Room: Language Issues in the European Union. *European Journal of Language Policy* 1(2): 93–119.

Yuval-Davis, N. (2006). Belonging and the Politics of Belonging. *Patterns of Prejudice* 40(3): 197–214.

Yuval-Davis, N. (2011). *The Politics of Belonging: Intersectional Contestations*. Los Angeles; London, Sage Publications.

Zagar, I. Z. (2010). Topoi in Critical Discourse Analysis. *Lodz Papers in Pragmatics* 6: 3–27.

Zalta, E. (ed.). (1997). *The Stanford Encyclopedia of Philosophy* (Winter 2012 Edition). Stanford Press, USA.

Zappettini, F. (2014). 'A Badge of Europeanness': Shaping Identity through the Eu's Institutional Discourse on Multilingualism. *Journal of Language and Politics* 13(3): 375–403.

Zappettini, F. and R. Comănaru (2014). Bottom-Up Perspectives on Multilingual Ideologies in the EU: The Case of a Transnational NGO. *Journal of Contemporary European Research* 10(4): 402–22.

Zappettini, F. (2016). The Construction of Transnational Identities in the Narratives of a European Civic Organisation. *Critical Approaches to Discourse Analysis across Disciplines* 8(1): 84–107.

Zappettini, F. (2017). Transnationalism as an Index to Construct European Identities: An Analysis of 'Transeuropean' Discourses. In C. Karner, & M. Kopytowska (eds.), *National Identity and Europe in Times of Crisis Doing and Undoing Europe*. Bingley: Emerald Group Publishing: 13–35.

Zappettini, F. (2019a). The Official Vision for 'Global Britain': Free Trade between Liberal Internationalism and Economic Nationalism. In V. Koller, S. Kopf and M. Milgbauer (eds.) *Discourses of Brexit*. Abingdon: Routledge.

Zappettini, F. (2019b) The Brexit Referendum: How Trade and Immigration in the Discourses of the Official Campaigns Have Legitimised a Toxic (Inter)national Logic. *Critical Discourse Studies* 16 (4).

Zappettini, F. and Krzyżanowski, M. (2019) The Critical juncture of Brexit in Media & Political Discourses: from National Populist Imaginary to Cross-National Social and Political Crisis. *Critical Discourse Studies*, 16(4).

Zimmerman, D. H. (1998). Identity, Context and Interaction. In C. Antaki and S. Widdicombe (eds.) *Identities in Talk*. London, Sage Publications: 87–107.

Appendix

1.1 Transcription conventions used in this study[1]

FZ = Moderator; Interviewer; (RC in the Cluj focus group)

CL5, PR1, BO4,…= Coded respondents

(.) Short pause – up to 3 seconds

(..) Medium pause – up to 5 seconds

(…) Long pause – up to 10 seconds

Remarks in square brackets [ ] indicate tone, or non-verbal behaviour. For example: [*high tone*], [*softly spoken*], [*clears throat*], [*laughs*].

Para-verbal features were transcribed by approximating the sound. For example: *mmh, erm, aah.*

When unable to interpret a sound clearly, the nearest approximate interpretation was provided with a question mark. For example: 'and then (..) and (.) then it is this [new?] idea that we have to go with'

[*sic*] was used to mark an ungrammatical form. For example: 'but this don't [*sic*] work in practice'

Capitalized words indicate stressed elements of speech. For example: 'I do NOT believe this is the case.'

When dialogues are reproduced in examples, three dots … indicate that part of the transcript has been omitted

---

[1] Adapted from the HIAT conventions (Ehlich 2014). See http://www.exmaralda.org/hiat/en_index.html for further details.

Index